More Advance Praise for *Good Soil*

"This book is pure grace for anyone who has wrestled with questions of faith and belonging, offering hard-won insights on who we are and who we might yet become."

—KATE BOWLER,
New York Times bestselling author of
Have a Beautiful, Terrible Day!

"Part memoir, part meditation, *Good Soil* is an extraordinary work of grace and courage that announces Jeff Chu as a major figure in an emerging field of modern and rigorous Christian thinkers. And he's funny: Baby chickens with eyeliner! Progressive fundamentalists! Passive-aggressive bok choy! If Wendell Berry and David Sedaris had a love child, they could only hope he might be as fine a thinker and as funny a writer as Jeff Chu."

—ELIZA GRISWOLD,
Pulitzer Prize–winning author of
Amity and Prosperity and *Circle of Hope*

GOOD SOIL

GOOD SOIL

THE EDUCATION OF AN
ACCIDENTAL FARMHAND

JEFF CHU

CONVERGENT
NEW YORK

Penguin Random House values and supports copyright. Copyright fuels creativity, encourages diverse voices, promotes free speech, and creates a vibrant culture. Thank you for buying an authorized edition of this book and for complying with copyright laws by not reproducing, scanning, or distributing any part of it in any form without permission. You are supporting writers and allowing Penguin Random House to continue to publish books for every reader. Please note that no part of this book may be used or reproduced in any manner for the purpose of training artificial intelligence technologies or systems.

Published in the United States by Convergent Books, an imprint of Random House, a division of Penguin Random House LLC, New York.

CONVERGENT with colophon is a trademark of Penguin Random House LLC.

Hardback ISBN 978-0-593-72736-2
Ebook ISBN 978-0-593-72737-9

Printed in the United States of America on acid-free paper

convergentbooks.com

9 8 7 6 5 4 3 2 1

First Edition

Book design by Diane Hobbing

Interior art from stock.adobe.com: berdsigns (honey bee), dariastiugova (pumpkins), zzayko (winter branch), Belenova_art (botanical plant)

In memory of Ashie, my mother-in-law,
who saw me and blessed me and loved me

CONTENTS

spring

summer

autumn

winter

spring

In high school, my English teacher taught me that the proper way to write an essay is to present your thesis statement, then offer the proofs. When I became a journalist, I was told that a story requires a captivating lede and a billboard paragraph that outlines what you plan to do in the rest of the piece, followed by your evidence. Both structures reflect a tendency in the West toward linear storytelling.

Our stories, though, are not that tidy. As I began working on this book, I thought about the reality of how we live, how we learn, how we grow.

One venerable form of Chinese storytelling orbits its subject. The story unfolds in a series of observations. Sometimes it might feel as if the details are sketchy, even scant. Digressions are common, particularly as fragments of memory emerge in the light of new information, and thus the storyteller can seem to be going in circles or meandering around their subject. Slowly, though, a body of data accumulates. You never get a thesis statement and then an array of proofs, because you're imagining and discovering and putting the pieces together alongside the storyteller. Your conclusions will rarely be identical to theirs. But (one hopes) coherence builds.

In traditional Chinese philosophy, life is seen as cyclical. We move again and again through the moon-marked seasons, again and again through the twelve animals of the zodiac, all the while recognizing that change is inevitable, perspectives differ, and only through community and conversation do we get a fuller picture.

In honor of my ancestors, this book moves through the seasons, both metaphorical and literal. It circles around the three years I spent on a farm in New Jersey, like an osprey seeking its prey. (Except that we don't intend to kill that prey—metaphors have their limits.) My desire is to find some hope, some evidence of grace, and some insight into the precarious yet beautiful reality of being human.

orchid

The magazine where I worked occupied half of the twenty-ninth floor of a Manhattan skyscraper. There was nothing organic about the space. It was all sleek steel and polished glass, shouting of progress, technology, and human ingenuity.

My husband used to send me flowers from time to time: elegant lilies, cheery sunflowers, delicate tea roses.

Tristan knew never to send anything with carnations, which reminded me of cheap grocery store bouquets and perfunctory Mother's Day church giveaways. He also learned not to order predominantly white arrangements; among my people, white flowers show up at funerals.

Occasionally the arrangement included something more unusual. Ranunculus, each orange bloom like a miniature labyrinth. Long stems of delphinium, which I loved because pale blue flowers aren't common; also, they're named for dolphins, and who doesn't like dolphins? If I was especially lucky, lisianthus, whose slightly ruffled petals were showy, but never to the point of garish.

I loved the gentleness the flowers brought to my office. When anxiety flooded in, when one of my stories came back rewritten (read: mangled), when yet another idea was rejected by the higher-ups, I could pause, take in the bouquet's beauty, and summon a deep breath.

One day, a courier brought a potted orchid. It was a phalae-
nopsis, the kind that costs maybe fifteen dollars at Walmart but
multiple times that if you get some Midtown Manhattan florist
to wrap it in cellophane and send it downtown. This one had
purple speckles on white petals. Its wide, droopy, deep green
leaves shone with health.

I took very good care of that orchid. I watered it, but never
too much. My mother had kept orchids when I was a child—
dendrobiums and cattleyas and oncidiums—and I could hear
her voice in my head, warning me against overwatering: "The
roots will rot!"

My goodness, this orchid flourished. Even though there was
little natural light in the office, this plant burst with life and
color—a beacon of serenity amid the mess of papers scattered
across my desk. It had arrived in full and vigorous bloom,
branches heavy with flowers, and it just kept on blooming. I felt
like a good son who had absorbed his parent's wisdom about
caring for another living thing. I imagined myself a faithful partner, nurturing this apt and enduring symbol of Tristan's and my
love.

A couple of months later, I was sitting at my desk and—
I don't even know why—I reached out to touch a blossom. So
purple. So pretty!

As soon as my fingers brushed a petal, they drew back in horror and my whole body felt hot. I wanted the thing to die. Except it couldn't. The orchid was fake.

autumn

fried rice

When I don't know what else to make for dinner, I poke around the kitchen to see if I have the ingredients for fried rice.

First, do we have leftover rice? If I think of it early enough in the day, I can make a batch, and then let the rice dry out for three or four hours. To make fried rice with freshly cooked rice is to risk disaster in the form of a mushy, sodden mess.

Next, what do we have in the fridge? I've made fried rice from the leftovers of a roast chicken, bits picked off the carcass of a Thanksgiving turkey, even half of an uneaten hamburger patty. It doesn't much matter if your mushrooms have been languishing too long, as long as they're not moldy. A slightly shriveled bell pepper will do. Half an onion? Lovely. Droopy green onions? Fine.

It's a magical dish, and a hopeful one. In the warmth of a well-oiled wok, old rice, yesterday's meat, and last week's sad vegetables can be transformed. Reinvigorated by sesame and soy, all happily married with an egg or two cracked over the top, they sing a song of resurrection.

———

When I was young, my grandmother made me fried rice in her battered old flat-bottomed wok.

I don't remember ever asking for fried rice. A good Chinese child eats whatever he's served, and a Chinese grandmother's primary love language is food. At my grandparents' apartment, I'd hear the sizzle of vegetables hitting hot oil and then the *clack-clack-clack* of metal on metal as the wok turner met the wok, and I just knew what was coming.

There are multiple ways to make fried rice. When my mom makes it, she often scrambles the egg first and then chops it up. When my grandmother made it, she'd crack the egg right over the rice, so that each grain was coated. As the egg cooked, the rice would fluff up. I love my mom, and she has always been the best cook in the family, but I preferred my grandmother's version of fried rice.

Grandma's fried rice developed a crispy crust on the bottom of the wok. Once these near-burnt bits—called 飯焦 ("fan jiu")—were mixed in, the best bites had just a little crunch. 飯 ("fan") is the Cantonese word for cooked rice. 焦 ("jiu") can mean "scorched" or "burnt," but it can also mean "focus." The heat concentrates all the rice's goodness into that crispy layer. 飯焦 is the Chinese cousin of Persian tahdig as well as the socarrat you find at the bottom of the best paella. Deeply savory and rich with umami, it tasted to me like comfort and love.

I cook fried rice the way I learned from my grandmother, but I've never quite been able to replicate her 飯焦. Maybe I don't give it enough time. "*Shhhh,*" my grandmother would probably say. "You need to wait. Just wait."

———

Long before she became my grandmother, Yim Mo Lan taught Bible at a Baptist primary school in Hong Kong. The eldest of nine children, she was the only daughter, and her father doted on her, sending her away to boarding school to be educated—an unusual thing for a working-class girl.

Nobody ever told me the full story of how she met my grandfather, a pastor and Bible college professor seven years her elder. I suspect some minor scandal: He had been married before and had two daughters, who lived in his home village in southern China. I heard something once about her being his student, but nobody ever wanted to flesh out that story.

They married in 1934 and began building a life together in Hong Kong. At the time, the border between the British-ruled territory and nationalist-governed China was porous, and my grandfather would go back and forth between Hong Kong and Canton, preaching and teaching.

Canton fell to the Japanese in 1938, Hong Kong three years later. My grandparents, their three young children, and an entourage of my grandfather's students fled westward to Guangxi Province, where the jagged peaks that tower over deep river valleys had inspired countless painters and sheltered innumerable refugees.

I wonder sometimes if that's when Psalm 121 became my grandmother's favorite Bible passage. By repetition throughout my childhood, she taught it to me in Cantonese. As she recited the words, which she knew by heart, she held her worn Bible open for my benefit, her wrinkly fingers slowly chasing the characters down each column of text. Later I learned the words in English: "I lift my eyes to the hills; where does my help come from?"

On the refugee road, the students' help came from my grandparents. I imagine them huddled together in prayer, my grandfather's preacherly baritone rising in their midst. Maybe my grandmother made fried rice for them, too.

After the war ended, my grandparents returned to Hong Kong with their growing family. Somehow they'd managed to produce two more children while in exile, and while my grandfather shuttled back and forth between Hong Kong and Canton, my grandmother taught and mothered.

She developed a formidable reputation as a strict taskmaster. Her classroom manner was famously brusque, her tolerance for misbehavior nonexistent. Every third grader at Pui Ching Primary School took Bible from her, and they never forgot the experience. Whenever we went back to Hong Kong, I'd hear the same story: Remember that time when Teacher Yim called on _____ in class? The custom then was that, if called on to answer a question, you'd stand up next to your desk to give your reply. This girl was so petrified that she stood and peed on the spot.

The story seemed so wild to me—and confusing, too. I thought of my grandmother as gentle, her spirit as soft as her hands.

"You didn't know your grandmother then," relatives would say to me.

No, I didn't. Obviously. I was born eight years after they immigrated to the United States.

"You didn't know your grandmother then," they would reiterate. "She dotes on you," they'd say, as if surprised that she had softened.

I wanted to tell them how embarrassing she could be. Before leaving for Chinatown to go grocery shopping, she'd tuck a thick stack of religious tracts into her tote bag. As she chose her oranges and surveyed the greens, she'd proffer one of the pamphlets and say to whatever unsuspecting old lady was standing nearby, "Do you believe in Jesus?" She relished these encounters most when the target of her proselytizing said they believed in Buddha or in the old Chinese gods. As she unspooled a mini-sermon about their need to be saved, I'd wish for some salvation myself, mainly from this mortification.

She could be annoying, too. When I would have preferred to watch TV, she'd pull out stacks of graph paper, write a series of Chinese characters across the top row, and hand me a pen. I knew that my job was to copy and copy and copy. She hovered over my right shoulder, correcting the order in which I made the strokes, unsatisfied until it was clear to her that I was no longer copying but writing, the characters all my own.

Sometimes, I wanted to tell them, she'd take my sister and me to the McDonald's down the street from her apartment. She'd muster the tiniest bit of English to order a "filet fishuuuu" for me and McNuggets for my sister. Then she'd show her senior card to get herself a free cup of hot coffee. Generosity and thriftiness, all wrapped up in one moment.

Sometimes, I wanted to tell them, she made me fried rice—the best fried rice I'd ever tasted. Nobody else made me fried rice like she did, always with lots of green onions, because she knew I loved them, and on an especially lucky day, morsels of Chinese sausage instead of leftover meat.

I wanted to tell them all that, but I didn't, because a good Chinese child only speaks when asked a question. They hadn't asked me any questions.

When I was nine, we left California, for my dad's job, but my sister and I returned to stay with my grandparents every summer. We were like migratory birds. We flew west, spent a couple of months fattening up on excellent Chinese food, and then returned to Miami, where, in my view, there was none beyond my mother's kitchen.

One of the things I remember most about those summers was bedtime. Every night after we watched the news on the Chinese TV channel, we'd fold out the creaky old sofa bed in the living room, and my grandmother would lead my sister and me in bedtime prayers. This took a while. These were Baptist prayers, after all.

She prayed for the Chinese Communists and the American Democrats and Republicans.

She prayed for our relatives in Hong Kong and China, Britain and Australia, Canada and New Zealand, especially the ones who didn't go to church anymore—and here, her voice softened nearly to a whisper as she begged God to turn their hearts.

"Amen," she said. Except that the "amen" didn't mean she was done.

She prayed for the victims of whatever tragedy had been on the news that evening.

"Hallelujah," she said, as if she were mounting her own prayer chorus to rebuke my sister's silence and mine.

She prayed for our family's church in Hong Kong and our family's church in San Francisco and for the church universal.

"Hallelujah," she said again, still not done.

She prayed for protection from the devil and his minions.

"Praise Jesus!" she said.

She prayed for us, for our studies, for our spirits. But she didn't limit her prayers just to present-day us; she also sent up some intercessions for future us—and even for my future wife and for my sister's future husband.

I always did think that was a bit presumptuous, but what did I know?

I never knew my grandmother to be a yeller; she could hush my sister and me with a stern glance. She wasn't a crier, either, except on one occasion that I can remember.

When I was a senior in high school, we went back to California for the Christmas break. It was the usual flurry of family gatherings and meals—dim sum; roast duck noodle soup; beef and Chinese greens stir-fried with wide rice noodles; lazy Susans spinning with Peking-style spareribs; clay pots filled with tofu, plump scallops, and fat prawns; steamed whole fish; fried rice.

A few days after Christmas, as we said goodbye to my grandparents, I gave her a hug and told her that I was looking forward to seeing her at my high school graduation. She had never visited us in Miami, and we already had her plane ticket.

She held me in her embrace for an unusually long time, and I could smell the Aqua Net in her hair. She had never been much of a hugger, so this seemed strange. When she finally let go, I looked down at her—she was just five feet tall—and I saw tears in her eyes. I grabbed her hand, and she rubbed her thumb across the back of mine, as if to soothe me. I started crying because she was crying, and then I went back in for another hug. But why was she crying?

"*Shhh*. Be obedient," she said to me in Cantonese. "Be obedient, and Grandma will be happy."

A couple of weeks later, a call came: She'd had a massive stroke. We flew back to California on the first flight the next morning and went straight to the hospital, where I held her hand and begged her not to leave me.

Two days later, she died.

belonging

Fried rice is what I most often cook for myself when I'm feeling unsettled, when I need to be reminded of where—and whom—I come from, when I crave a little taste of belonging.

Is there any human sentiment more primal or universal?

You hear it in babies' cries for their parents' embrace.

You glimpse it on a first date or at a job interview, in the nervous fumbling for connection.

You witness it even in the worst, most violent tribalism, one group seeking strength in the diminution of another.

You find it in every family, natural-born or chosen, healthy or dysfunctional.

Fried rice returns me to myself and to my people. All I have to do is close my eyes and breathe in the fragrance of sesame and soy, and I remember: my grandmother's love, my parents' sacrifices, the long journeys across an ocean and to a new country, renewal and possibility.

In that way, fried rice is my ultimate comfort food. Still, even as I eat, I often wonder what my grandmother would have made of my life now, and whether she would still cook me fried rice if she could.

When my grandmother said, "Be obedient," it wasn't some vague suggestion. I understood it as a multifaceted command-ment that applied well beyond childhood. It meant working hard at whatever I did, watching over my sister, never missing a Sunday of church, telling people about Jesus, not watching movies (she was of the firm conviction that the cinema was one of the devil's prime playgrounds), honoring my elders, and being thrifty.

There were some significant long-term expectations packed into her tidy little phrase. The main one: When I came of age, I would find a nice, polite Chinese girl to marry—definitely Chris-tian and preferably Baptist—the girl for whom my grandmother had prayed. We would produce nice, polite Chinese children who carried the family name—a particularly crucial responsibil-ity for me, as the only son of a son. And then, like my parents and my aunts and uncles and my grandparents and my great-aunts and great-uncles (except for the few who had stopped going to church, for whom we had interceded ardently), I would become a pillar of our family's church.

These expectations were rarely expressed directly. Instead, they crept out of the crevices of everyday interactions. When-ever I ate rice in my grandmother's presence, I knew there would come a moment when she'd inspect my bowl to see if I'd left any uneaten. Then she'd trot out an old warning of hers: However many grains of rice I wasted would show up as pock-marks on my wife's face.

The math behind this warning always puzzled me. Were the pockmarks to be calculated from a random sampling on any given day? Was it the average over a particular period of time? Was it the aggregate of all the rice I wasted over the entirety of my childhood?

I found a way around the threat, though. There would be no wife. I married a man.

Probably the hardest moment of my coming-out was when my mother turned to me, in the midst of yet another argument, and asked, "What would your grandmother think?"

It was undoubtedly a rhetorical device of last resort. Where gentle persuasion and Bible verses and maternal tears had failed, she still had this one blunt instrument. My mom knew its power. She was willing to wield it because, to her, this was about the fate of my eternal soul.

What she didn't know was that I'd thought about that question plenty already, over the course of thousands of tear-filled nights.

What would my grandmother think about my marriage? I'm almost certain she'd disapprove.

Every Sunday morning during Pride, we'd drive past queer folks on their way to the festivities. That night, she'd include the 同性人—"tung sing yan," literally, "same-gender people"—in her prayers. She'd urge God to free them from their bondage (to demons) and to turn them toward repentance. I can't imagine that she knew she was praying for me; at the time I was pretending even to myself that I was straight.

If I could, I would tell her that my Texas-born Tristan is as polite and diligent as the Chinese girl of her prayers, not to mention compassionate and kind, too. I'd add that he's kind of a geek—if I could figure out how to say "geek" in Cantonese.

What would my grandmother think about my faith?

She wouldn't have been happy about me brunching on Sundays at eleven A.M., as I did for four or five years instead of sitting in the pews of a church. But then there was something in me that didn't feel great about it either; guilt and mimosas are not a natural pairing. She would have felt some relief that eventually I did find my way back into the pews, even if it wasn't a Baptist congregation.

But I also remember how eagerly she received relatives into her home who had lost their faith or whose lives had gone in directions that she had not mapped in her prayers. Once, when one of my dad's apostate cousins visited from overseas, I watched as my grandmother embraced her with tear-filled eyes and held her hand for hours as they talked. I eavesdropped as this auntie transmitted news of her parents, of her siblings, and eventually, of her own faltering faith. I didn't hear a word of judgment from my grandmother, though of course there was the quiet pleading that my auntie should absolutely read her Bible, pray more, and go back to church.

If I could, I would tell her that it was my husband—my Catholic husband!—who most stubbornly encouraged me to go back to church. If nothing else, he argued, that hour of contemplative quiet offered a brief respite from New York's hustle and din.

What would my grandmother think about my work?

My Cantonese isn't as good as it used to be, and I'm embarrassed that I probably couldn't summon the vocabulary to explain a journalism career that has taken me to six continents. But she always had some Chinese newspapers around the apartment, she'd undertaken some tremendous journeys herself, and she did like to travel when she could. I bet she'd understand.

What would my grandmother think about the life I'd built?

I told myself that she would pray for me as she always did. I told myself that she would still cook fried rice for me if she could.

I found myself cooking fried rice a little more often a few years into our marriage, as I felt a growing sense of restlessness.

There's a kind of discontent you can work through: Dig deeper. Push harder. Deploy [insert some platitude about productivity here that wouldn't have become a cliché if it hadn't worked for someone]. I was reared by two extraordinarily diligent parents who never complained, at least within my earshot, about a bad boss or heavy workloads or jobs that didn't align perfectly with their passions. They taught me that there wasn't any worldly trouble that couldn't be overcome by a combination of effort and prayer.

Things at the office had not been going well. Where my story pitches had once glided through the editorial pipeline, now they were constantly stuck. At one point, I reviewed my archive of published articles and realized I hadn't managed to get a single one of my own ideas into the magazine in over a year. I kept pitching, kept writing whatever my bosses wanted me to write (a feature about a fashion designer, a profile of a celebrity architect, a piece about a lifestyle brand), kept trying to be the obedient employee, kept working myself to exhaustion, kept trying to prove my worth.

Don't forget to pray. You need to pray more!

Sometimes I could hear the faint echoes of my grandmother's voice, nagging me from beyond.

Don't forget to pray. You need to pray more!

I guess she was right. Usually, she was right.

On a soul-deep level, I knew my disquiet couldn't be addressed by ordinary labor. Problem was, the gods of work were the ones I knew how to serve, and at least they always gave me that biweekly paycheck. It had been so long since I'd offered anything to that other God beyond a perfunctory premeal blessing, and even longer since I'd received anything in return. Plus, my concerns seemed petty and impertinent; so much else in the world deserved divine attention more than my quotidian misery.

Rage is misery that does not know where else to go. Sometimes I think rage gets mischaracterized as necessarily loud or shouty. If the rage-burdened person tends not to be loud or shouty, though, it can also manifest in other ways, as it did with me: as brittleness, or constant irritability, or extreme irascibility, or tetchy irrationality, or a total failure of self-control, or even all these things. Just ask Tristan.

Some evenings, we'd both come home from a difficult day's work, and he wanted nothing more than a quiet, relaxed evening with a little bit of space. He'd even give me advance warning that his plan was to put on the radio so that he could sit with a glass of wine in one hand and a book in the other. Still, I'd crowd him with my angst, pouring out a litany of complaints— about the noise from the neighbors, about my job, about my stress.

Then there was the time I lashed out at him for sitting in the same spot on the living room sofa every night. This was a profoundly absurd critique on my part, particularly given that we lived in a small Brooklyn apartment. It deserved instant and complete dismissal—but that's not how Tristan responded: For days, he instead sat in all different places, all over our apartment.

Tristan and I rarely fight. When we do, it's usually because we have feelings that haven't yet resolved themselves into words. I knew he could sense my unease. I also knew that it made both of us nervous. Was this about us?

It was absolutely not about *us*, as any amateur relationship analyst could have discerned from our squabbles—and as Tristan soon realized. "You need to figure out what you want," he said to me one night, ending yet another ridiculous argument that I'd instigated. His voice was soft, almost pleading, but his aim was true. "You don't even know what you want."

When Tristan and I first moved into our Brooklyn home, a towering Blue Atlas cedar was growing in the tiny backyard. It was a regal tree; the crown was nearly as tall as our building—at least thirty, thirty-five feet. You had to stand all the way against our back fence to regard its full glory, but if the sun hit just so, its silver-tinged needles almost shimmered. Its branches formed a canopy that covered nearly the whole yard, which was only twelve feet wide.

The cedar was the backyard umbrella we'd never wanted or needed. The north-facing yard didn't get much sun anyway, except briefly in the morning, and as the cedar grew, it stole more and more of the light. It created its own mini-ecosystem, too: No matter if it hadn't rained in days. Sit out in the yard, and you'd get a dripping reminder of how the cedar's needles and ample limbs doubled as cisterns, nourishing generations of mosquitoes above and slowly irrigating the hostas and mosses below.

It had to go.

We didn't make this decision easily or quickly. We love trees, especially in cities, where the asphalt and concrete hold so much heat. But an aspiring giant native to a North African mountain range doesn't fit into a nook-sized New York City backyard. Its roots were already undermining the brick-paved patio, and I worried about how shallow they might be. I could just imagine a disastrous thunderstorm—a lightning strike, perhaps, then a crack, then a crash. The trunk, a foot and a half thick, was no more than ten feet from our back door. And those mosquitoes!

One day, the arborists came. One of them, who was apparently a giant squirrel costumed as a human, shimmied up the trunk of the cedar and started chopping off branches. The others gathered them down below and carried them by the armload through our apartment and out to the street. Needles scattered everywhere, falling as if in protest. Then came the trunk, piece by two-foot piece. Soon, all that was left was an eighteen-inch stump.

I'd read that, occasionally, an especially robust and stubborn cedar can resprout from a stump. I wondered if anything would grow from what remained.

How do you know when something no longer belongs? What signs tell you that what was once good, what used to feel right, isn't anymore? How do you understand when one season is ending and another beginning? Is there any way to be sure of what's to come?

One day, I got to work before anyone else had arrived at the office, and I stood at the window, watching the streets twenty-nine stories below. They had their own steady pulse: Every minute or two, the subway exits would disgorge a wave of commuters, who then dispersed to their offices throughout the area.

I turned from the window and scanned the empty office: the table where we perused photos, the wall where we pinned layouts, the meeting room where a few people talked and everyone else sat in silence.

What did our work matter? I thought. The magazine could disappear tomorrow—I could decide never to write another article—and it wouldn't make any difference. This was a luxury product, utterly unnecessary and superfluous.

I wanted to do work that mattered. But in the rare moments when I felt brave enough to follow that desire to its underlying roots, I knew it wasn't about the work itself so much as what the work represented: *Did I really matter? What makes a person matter? Where do I belong?*

These questions frightened me—or perhaps it would be more accurate to say that I feared I wouldn't like the answers. I wish I could tell you that I went on a silent retreat or sought the wisdom of monks, that I meditated my way to resolution or that a life coach gave me a ten-step plan for a new beginning. Truth is, I just started googling. And one day, in the safe sanctuary of a browser tab, my fingers typed something that my conscious brain didn't expect: *seminary.*

About six months later, Tristan and I went out to dinner at a tapas bar.

"I think I finally know what I want," I told him.

He sat there waiting for me to elaborate—not an unreasonable expectation. When I didn't, he prodded me gently: "Are you going to tell me?"

"I'm not ready yet," I said, picking at my potatoes.

He looked down for a moment, then back up at me, right in the eyes.

"Okay," he said. "The only thing I'll say is that I'm not going to be a very good pastor's wife."

My heart started thumping: Wait, nobody said anything about being a pastor! I'd just been googling "seminary." But how did he know anything about any of this? I'd never discussed it with him—or with anyone. We didn't share a laptop. Had I said something in my sleep?

A likelier, more gratifying possibility: He knew me. Also, he adores mystery novels and *Murder, She Wrote*, so he's learned a thing or two about gathering clues. Nearly a decade into our relationship, he understood that love sometimes knows things that are never said aloud.

A few days later, I emailed him a memo, because we're weird like that. I told him I wanted to figure out how to write better, more meaningful stories. I also expressed my desire to explore my own spirituality. I broached the possibility of attending seminary, but I quickly clarified that I had zero desire to be a pastor. A better religious education, I argued, would make me a better writer on ethics and religion. I also craved space to learn, to think, and to ask the hard questions I'd avoided.

If this all seems kind of vague, that's because it was. I didn't really know what I was doing. Tristan (mostly) didn't shame me for that. In his own patient and quiet way, in his expectant silence and in his thoughtful knowing, he was making room for me to flail and to figure things out.

He wrote back a few minutes later: "I'm so proud of you."

A year later, at the age of thirty-nine, I started seminary.

compost

The Brooklyn apartment that we moved into a few months after we married had the stoop of my dreams, with those classic reddish-brown sandstone steps. I imagined a series of clay pots ascending the steps, each one overflowing with herbs and flowers.

It took me a few years, but eventually I set about bringing this picture to life. I had never grown much of anything, except for green onions. My grandmother had taught me that the nubby root ends of green onions shouldn't be thrown away. All you had to do was pop them back into the soil and they would grow again.

Most Saturday mornings, Tristan and I walked four blocks to our local farmers market. In the spring, several of the farmstands sold seedlings. After we got the clay pots, I bought basil and sage, rosemary and thyme, lemon verbena and mint, and I planted them on our front steps, along with the nubby root ends of a few green onions that I hadn't thrown away.

The basil died first, collapsing into a little brown heap one hot and sunny weekend while we were away.

The rosemary and green onions died next, and the lemon verbena after that—though I did manage to make one batch of lemon verbena panna cotta before that plant failed.

The sage and thyme hung on for a while until they, too, withered. As I conducted a quick rescue operation, salvaging a few desiccated stems of each, I told myself a story about the utility of dried herbs.

Eventually, I uprooted all the shriveled remnants and deposited them into the small compost tumbler that we kept in the backyard. But I remained confident in my mint. I'd read of mint's resilience—how hardy it was, how it refused to die even when a gardener wished that it would, how resolutely it spread, how its strong roots kept it going beneath the soil's surface even after the leaves had browned and wilted.

We came back from another trip, and as I looked up the steps at my pots, I searched for green. There was none. It took me weeks and weeks to accept the brutal reality: I am not only the person who waters a fabric-and-plastic orchid for months but also the gardener who manages to kill mint.

This was the gardening résumé I brought to Ecologies of Faith Formation, an unusual class that I had spotted in the pages of the seminary course catalog. The seminary had something called the Farminary (farm + seminary = Farminary), a twenty-one-acre working farm that doubled as a classroom. That semester, the seminary was offering this one class at the farm. It was a by-application-only course taught by Kenda Dean, a youth-ministry professor, and Nate Stucky, the Farminary's director, involving hands-on work in the garden.

The rest of my schedule was packed with requirements— biblical Greek, systematic theology, intro to Old Testament, speech. I didn't know what "ecologies of faith formation" meant, I had zero interest in youth ministry, and the course catalog offered scant detail. But I was pretty nervous about being back in school after all these years, and this class would allow me some time beyond the four walls of a conventional classroom, which, I bargained, could only be a good thing. My horticultural record wasn't a strong selling point, so I tried a different tactic in my application: I offered the professors a bribe, in the form of a home-cooked Chinese dinner.

Whether Kenda and Nate overlooked that detail or saw in it an opportunity to redeem a lost soul who would try to bribe his way into a seminary class, I couldn't tell you. But I got into the class.

Our first gathering was not at the farm. Kenda invited us to a dinner at her house, a gracious Victorian that sits at the center of the seminary campus. I arrived a couple of minutes late—the well-rehearsed strategy of a shy introvert who is allergic to small talk. But the food wasn't quite ready, so I fell into my usual habit of eavesdropping on others' conversations while simultaneously trying to avoid any myself. What I heard was mostly your standard introductory chitchat, except with the enthusiasm ramped up to pastor-in-training levels.

"Where are you from?"

"Pennsylvania."

"Oh, that's *great!*"

(Is it great? Is it really?)

While everyone else made small talk, I lingered awkwardly in doorways for a few minutes, then escaped to the bathroom to hide and flick mindlessly through my phone. Then I did it again.

During one of the awkward doorway moments, Kenda approached and introduced herself. She knew I was a journalist in New York City, and she went straight to the question that had been vexing her: "So why are you really here? Are you writing an exposé?"

I did not expect this question.

"An exposé?" I said, trying to buy time as I thought about how to respond. Then, before I could self-edit: "The reader has to care about the subject before you can write an exposé."

"Touché," she said with a smile.

I wanted to believe that I'd parried Kenda's question because I didn't trust her yet, but the truth was, I hadn't even answered that question for myself. Why *was* I really here? I didn't have any other words, because I didn't actually know. But I was certain of this: I didn't want her to know I didn't know. After all, this was the first day of class.

Kenda and Nate ushered us all into her living room. They had one question they wanted every one of us to answer: What soils do you come from?

It was an icebreaker and, shy introvert that I am, I detest icebreakers. There is nothing wrong with a little ice. Ice can be useful; ask the penguins. Why the violent need to break it, when it could more naturally and gently thaw?

I had found my customary spot: hovering against a doorway, in case I needed to make a quick exit. Near me, standing by another doorway, was a woman named Pearl, who kept shifting in place and who looked almost as uncomfortable as I was.

"Give us five words or phrases," Nate said, "to describe the soils you come from."

The prompt seemed to confuse most of my new classmates, and Nate didn't clarify whether he was talking about literal or metaphorical soils. The answers were generic and mostly didn't follow the instructions. Perhaps this reflected less the challenge of the task than the intimidation of telling twenty strangers about oneself. Almost everyone struggled to name anything related to soil:

"Christian."

"Midwestern."

"Presbyterian."

"I'm from East Texas."

"I grew up in a really close family."

In uncomfortable situations, I revert to what I've always done as a reporter: I gather data, and I try to analyze it. As anodyne as some of the answers were, I quickly noted that Nate and Kenda had assembled a group that was unusually diverse, at least in the context of a seminary where nearly every student was Protestant and under the age of thirty. Megan and Lexi weren't even seminarians; they were undergraduates at Princeton. Mirjam was from Germany, Hyun from Korea. Werner was a Guatemalan immigrant. Danny's parents hailed from Egypt. A student named Wes had one of the more intriguing, unusual stories; in short form, we learned he'd spent part of his childhood in Uganda and that he was half Chinese.

Then we got to Pearl. She suddenly stood up straighter, took one step into the room, and announced, in a clear and steady voice: "I am a child of many soils."

To name the soils that you come from is to acknowledge that you were not self-made, because there is no such thing as a self-made human. It places you in the context of an ecosystem. It confesses that you are a creature—simply, someone created by forces beyond you—which is to say reared and scarred and sanded and formed. It admits that you are not some nebula floating in the ether but that you have roots and are inescapably interdependent with the world around you.

It's laughable to me that the verb form of the word "soil" somehow came to be associated with filth, given how necessary it is for life. The Jewish and Christian creation myths describe humankind as having originally been made from soil. The Ojibwe say the same, as does one Chinese origin story—yellow clay, of course, shaped by the nimble hands of the goddess 女娲 (Nuwa).

Soil can be denuded and degraded, and it can be nourished and amended. This, Nate told us, was our work to do at the Farminary—both literally, with the help of the compost pile, and figuratively, as we tended to our own spiritual lives. Together, we'd study the soils we came from, and we'd examine the growing conditions we were creating for others, and ourselves.

Soil teems with so many lifeforms that help feed us. Scientists estimate that just one teaspoon of healthy topsoil can contain ten thousand different species of microbe—bacteria and protozoa, fungi and viruses. Without soil, we wouldn't have so many of the things of modern life, including glass (sand), pottery (clay), and Scotch (peat).

In this seminary class, we'd carefully examine the soils of our lives, identifying where we had flourished and where we had struggled. What characteristics had fostered our growth? How could we recognize poor spiritual soil?

We weren't required to buy any textbooks. Our primary "texts" would be our own stories, which we were expected to parse thoughtfully and courageously. That inner work would be complemented by our tasks at the farm: We'd sow and weed, harvest and compost. We would tend the soil.

But this was seminary, not therapy. The course's goal wasn't merely deeper self-awareness, or self-acceptance, or self-anything. "Whether you become a pastor or a teacher after this, you're going to have to help other people understand their own stories," Kenda said. "How can you do that if you haven't at least tried to understand your own?"

As a nod toward that outward purpose—and as another reminder that this would be no ordinary grad school class—Nate and Kenda also told us that we'd be feeding one another. Every class session would include a potluck meal.

After dinner, Kenda had one last thing to say, and it startled me: "We expect love to grow here." She paused, and her eyes did a slow turn around the room. "We love you, and we're going to be honest with you." Then she repeated herself: "We expect love to grow here."

Who tells a whole class, on the first day, that she loves them? In all my overeducated life, I'd never heard a professor say such a thing. I'd only just met most of these folks a few minutes before, and here was this lady throwing around words like "love."

I've always believed in high hopes and low expectations. But she'd said "expect," not "hope." What mess had I gotten myself into?

Three days later, the twenty of us went out to the Farminary for the first time.

It was easy to miss the farm's entrance if you didn't know what to look for: a small break in the trees and a narrow gravel driveway. Some days, Nate remembered to put up the Farminary's sign—two small pieces of posterboard sandwiching a metal stake. Some days, he didn't.

"Barn" seems too pastoral a word for the cinder-block building that housed most of the farm's indoor activities. Occupying the western third of the building, behind a garage-style door, was the classroom—which, again, should be understood in the most basic sense of the word. It had some folding tables, a couple dozen stackable chairs, and a single dry-erase board on the wall. There was a refrigerator, but no Wi-Fi, no air-conditioning, no heating, no indoor plumbing.

Nate welcomed the twenty of us to the farm. He described its twenty-one acres as "wounded land," marked by decades of agricultural overuse. He offered us options should nature call in its particular way: the trees or the porta potty.

Then he showed us where the tools were stored and invited each of us to grab a shovel or a spade. "We're going to the compost pile," he said.

We straggled over to a small hill, about twelve feet around and maybe three feet high at its peak. Nate invited us to start digging. "Look for signs of life and death and resurrection," he said.

Some of my classmates launched right in; I hung back and did the looking. It was easy to spot all the death—blackened banana peels and spent coffee grounds, a previous season's fallen leaves and wood chips, moldy zucchini and melon rinds, disintegrating eggshells and leaves of spinach liquefying in the heat. I could smell that top layer, a faint sweetness in the thick air that could make you sick if you inhaled too deeply. I felt the rot, too—sludgy in places, squishy underfoot.

I gave silent thanks for my choice of tool—a shovel, not a spade, all the better to keep my distance from the mess. I half-heartedly tossed some rotting vegetables aside. I had spent an embarrassing amount of time choosing my outfit for a hot, humid, late-summer New Jersey afternoon on the farm: a button-down shirt, khakis, and a pristine pair of Hunter boots. At first, I'd wondered whether I looked ridiculous. But now I saw my classmates' bare legs, which were splattered with com-post goo and flecked with rotting vegetables—why did they wear shorts?! I gave silent thanks for the cotton that had offered up its fibers for my pants and the rubber tree that had given its sap for my boots.

As we kept digging and our eyes adjusted, we started to see squirming, skittering, and slithering. The pile writhed with life: worms and grubs, millipedes and mites. As we went deeper, the colors and textures began to change, and the mixture began to resemble fresh soil.

I knelt and grabbed a handful. The soil felt unexpectedly light and soft, almost fluffy. I took a sniff. It smelled surprisingly clean, even fresh, like the woods on a crisp morning, if I pause mid-hike to draw in a deep breath. I sniffed again, and then I stopped: What was I even doing, standing ankle-deep in rotting vegetables and huffing dirt?

soils

Nate grew up in the soils of central Kansas, where his family raised wheat and cattle outside the town of Kingman (population: 2,900) and worshipped at the First Mennonite Church of Pretty Prairie. He was blessed with a slightly goofy smile and big, expressive eyes that often seemed to brim with tears. After college, he'd done a stint as a farm manager and another as a youth pastor before enrolling at Princeton Seminary in 2007. He intended to stay in New Jersey for just two years. After that, he planned to move back to Kansas, "for work," he told me, though he wasn't exactly sure what that work would be. But then he switched degree programs, extending the two years to three. Then he stayed a little longer, to pursue a PhD.

Partway through seminary, a friend planted a seed: What if you combined theological education with sustainable agriculture? It made sense. There were so many agrarian tales in the Bible, and so many of Jesus's stories assumed an intimate relationship with farming. Perhaps a farm could double as a classroom. Perhaps growing peppers and tomatoes and the flowers of the field could be a way to deepen students' understandings of all the biblical narratives about agrarian life, all the parables that Jesus told about land and seeds and soil.

Mennonite that he was, Nate didn't talk much about his dream, for fear of immodesty. (Anyone who has spent any time in higher education knows the ivory tower is where so many innovative ideas go to die.) But eventually, he fashioned a plan and began talking about the idea all over campus.

One day in 2014, Nate was called to the seminary president's office. He felt the dread of a schoolboy summoned by the principal. When he walked in, the president, Craig Barnes, had a map rolled out on his desk. He had heard about Nate's idea. "So it turns out we already own a farm," Barnes said. The seminary's endowment had been diversifying its billion-dollar investment portfolio a few years prior and had bought some acreage in neighboring Lawrence Township. Part of the land was still being rented to a local nursery and landscaping business, but plenty of the space wasn't being used. "Will this work?"

The following spring, before he had even defended his dissertation, Nate taught the first pilot course at the farm. The Farminary was born.

Nate planted the first Farminary garden, forty feet by sixty feet, on the back corner of the property. He erected fencing to protect the space from the abundant white-tailed deer, then worked with a few students to start a mix of crops that he described as "typical fare for a white, Mennonite, Kansas farmer": radishes and lettuces, onions and beans, tomatoes and squash. About twenty feet away, he established the Farminary's first compost pile.

Starting in the late nineteenth century, the U.S. Department of Agriculture dispatched surveyors across the country to test the soil. Over the subsequent decades, they managed to cover nearly every county in the United States. According to that survey, the best soil on the farm should have been where Nate planted the garden—a silty loam in which most vegetables would flourish.

It wasn't.

When Nate had the soil tested again, he learned that he'd established the garden on some of the poorest soil on the entire farm. "It's crap back there," he told me.

Actually, it would probably have been richer if there were crap—deer crap, fox crap, chicken crap. Manure adds nitrogen, potassium, and phosphorus that plants need to thrive. Instead, the Farminary plot was just denuded, degraded soil, the consequence of years of exploitation.

For decades, this land served as a sod farm, growing grass to feed the insatiable American appetite for green lawns. With each harvest, a thin layer of topsoil had been removed and transplanted to someone else's land. Eventually, most of the good topsoil was gone.

In 1998, the land was sold, and the new owners began planting a couple of its acres with fast-growing eastern white pine and slower-growing Norway spruce—in other words, Christmas trees, which can thrive even in suboptimal conditions. By the time the seminary acquired the land twelve years later, there were more than six hundred conifers on the farm.

The yield in the Farminary's first garden was adequate. But Nate had his eyes on a larger planting space closer to the barn, in an expansive field within view of the pond. In the fall, he planted one hundred cloves of garlic in the old garden. Then he began planning the new garden.

The following summer, he and his students filled the fifty-by-fifty-foot fenced square with seven compost-enriched rows that were soon bursting with a progressive summer menu: basil and tomatoes and watermelons, onions and eggplant, cabbages and kohlrabi, with zinnias and sunflowers to grace the table. Nate also found four families who were willing to pay a couple hundred dollars in exchange for weekly baskets of produce during the growing season. This tiny venture into community-supported agriculture (CSA) would provide a small income stream for the Farminary, and it would also serve as marketing.

Not everything was Instagrammable bliss: Flea beetles plagued the greens, their feasts leaving polka dots on the leaves. The tomatoes drew dozens of hornworms. The voracious, fat caterpillars cannily stayed in the safe shelter of the stems by day. Only around dawn and dusk would they wander toward the outer leaves, chomping away until the branches were bare and gouging half-moon-shaped chunks from unripe fruit. A groundhog that nobody ever saw tunneled under the fence, leaving trails of evidence of late-night snacks.

Nate accepted these interspecies attacks, reminding students that the land didn't belong only to humans. Occasionally we discovered unexpected allies. The tomatoes were still in season when I began coming to the farm, and not long afterward, I noticed a chubby green creature that the internet quickly helped me identify as one of those dastardly hornworms.

This hornworm looked different from the others. Instead of smooth skin, this one appeared to have fallen into a bin of white rice and emerged with grains stuck all over its body. These, I learned, were the cocoons of dozens of tiny braconid wasps—

a little pest-control army. The mother wasp targets a hornworm, laying eggs just under its skin. After hatching, the parasitic larvae eat the hornworm alive, gradually chewing their way out before spinning the cocoons in which they grow to adulthood. The hornworm survives just long enough to nourish its unwanted passengers until they can take flight.

Anyway, while there were flowers and vegetables being cultivated on the farm, Nate insisted the primary crop would be good soil. "Life ultimately gets the last word," he said. "But the only way you move along the path to the fertile soil is if you go through the cycle of life and death, life and death."

The compost pile was not merely a teaching tool or a prop. It was the point.

scars

Almost as soon as we arrived at the farm, Kenda and Nate took us away again. Our third class session was a three-day field trip to North Carolina.

Early one Friday morning, we met outside the campus center, where a small bus was waiting. Some of my classmates were still in their pajamas, hugging the pillows they'd brought with them. Kenda had asked a student named Annalise to chronicle our journey on video, and she was standing by the door of the bus asking each person to say something or make a silly face. "Nope," I said as I boarded. I hadn't been on a field trip in nearly two decades. This was the first moment of seminary when I thought, *I am too old for this shit.*

Our destination was a church-run farm in a town called Conetoe, about seven hours to the south if you're going approximately the speed limit. Kenda and Nate wanted us to witness how other people had taken a painful relationship with the land and written something new, life-giving, and beautiful with it.

———————

We'd been instructed to bring our first assignments on the bus with us: maps that showed our spiritual development. The exercise was based on the work of the psychologist Urie Bronfenbrenner, the architect of a social-development model sometimes called ecological systems theory. Bronfenbrenner hypothesized that multiple key systems, including one's family, one's peer groups, and the wider world in which we all live, work together to shape humans in their early years. All these layers of relationship and environment combine to form a person's worldview and outlook.

Our task was to map our own stories using his model, singling out a few key events that had particular import. Kenda and Nate had warned us that we would be asked to share these maps with others, in case that affected what we decided to include. Honesty, they said, did not require full disclosure.

Pearl sat next to me on the bus. Behind us were two white women: Andrea, a cherubic Wesleyan from Pennsylvania who was planning to become a pastor, and Ashley, a Methodist from Texas who had already done three years as a youth pastor and was in seminary to prepare for a career in youth ministry.

Andrea shared her map first. She'd had a pretty happy childhood as a pastor's kid and described a spiritual journey that seemed straightforward and problem-free. She'd gone to her denomination's college, taught at a Christian school, then moved to Princeton so that her husband could attend seminary. She enrolled a year after him—probably the most rebellious thing on her record, since Princeton was Presbyterian and seen by some as liberal. On weekends she worked as a worship coordinator at a local church.

Pearl went next. She told us about her peripatetic childhood.

She elaborated on those "many soils" in which she'd grown up: first, the projects in New York City; then, because her dad was in the military, North Carolina, where her parents bought a farm; as well as Germany and Egypt. She talked about not having been brought up with any particular faith. The most memorable lesson her mother taught her and her sisters: "A mouse should never have just one hole."

I gave her a questioning look. "Wait, Pearl, was she talking about what I think she was talking about?"

Pearl burst out laughing. "*Yes*, Jeff," she said. "She was talking about *men*. She was talking about *sex*."

Pearl told us that she had been shaped profoundly by her father's death, the toll of mental illness in her family, and being sexually assaulted. "What other pivotal moments would I talk about?" she said. "This wasn't hard." Even though she didn't add much detail, I was struck by how freely she offered these facts.

I glanced at Andrea, whose eyes were as wide as could be.

I had dithered about what to share and what not to; these were strangers, after all. Slightly emboldened by Pearl's candor, I gave a heavily censored version of my reality: Chinese Baptist childhood, the trauma of being sexually abused as a teenager (no details), coming out, leaving religion, then unexpectedly finding it again.

Finally, Ashley. I had already decided Ashley was your basic twentysomething white girl—ombre dye job trying to dress up her mousy brown hair, a T-shirt from her high school, floral Vera Bradley bag, Nalgene water bottle covered in stickers.

She told us she was from East Texas. Her parents divorced when she was five, and her dad remarried when she was in second grade. Her stepmom was Baptist and her dad Catholic, so they compromised and Ashley grew up Methodist. But everyone still lived in the same small town. "It was awkward," she said, "because my mom was a drug addict and my dad was a police officer."

In that moment, my face felt hot with guilt about my superficial judgment. "You weren't wrong, Jeff," Ashley said when I confessed and apologized later. "I *am* a basic white girl!"

Except that I *was* wrong. In prejudging Ashley, I'd written her off as "not useful" for my education. To dismiss anyone based on appearance or ethnicity or any other classification—including seeming "basic," whatever that means—was to reduce, dishonor, disrespect, even dehumanize. I'd always hated it when it had been done to me, yet here I was, doing it to someone else.

I turned toward the window. While the bus trundled through the Virginia exurbs somewhere south of Washington, D.C., I was stuck in my shame. A week into the class, I'd already forgotten the objective Kenda had laid out that first night: "We expect love to grow here."

On my first day of seminary, as I drove from Brooklyn to Princeton, a thought had formed in my mind: *I am not going to make new friends. I have good friends. I don't need new friends.*

I could make up various semi-plausible explanations for these statements—sensible allocation of emotional resources, say, or the need to tend the relationships I already have rather than chasing more—but here's the underlying truth: I was putting on protective armor. I told myself it didn't matter if I was liked, because I wasn't going back to graduate school for likes.

Yet there was no way to keep that armor on while also accepting Kenda and Nate's assignment. They were insistent: Our time together in graduate school, our sojourn at the Farminary, everything we studied and learned—it all had to point us beyond ourselves. And if it was to mean anything beyond self-soothing, if it was to bring about anything resembling healing, it all had to expand our understanding of love.

This North Carolina field trip seemed perfectly designed to rebuke my selfishness. Kenda and Nate wanted us to understand the simultaneous intimacy and enormity of the call to love God and love one's neighbor and the implications that had not just for ourselves but also for all kinds of neighbors, for the soil, for the ecosystem, and indeed for the world.

In 2005, the Reverend Richard Joyner, the pastor of Conetoe Chapel Missionary Baptist Church and a hospital chaplain, was struck by a horrifying statistic: He was performing funerals at least twice a month in a community of just a few hundred people. A startling number of those funerals were for people who hadn't even reached middle age. He knew from his rounds at the hospital that they were dying from diabetes, heart disease, and other ailments that stemmed from poverty and terrible diets.

"As a pastor, I didn't want to yell at another young person and tell them everything was going to be all right. That's a damn lie," he told me. "How do you tell a child who just lost a parent who is thirty years old that this was God's plan when it was totally preventable? Who would hang out with that God?"

One night he was driving home, exhausted after yet another hospital shift, when he heard the echo of his mother's voice in his mind: "My mama told me, *Richard, pray*," he said. He immediately pulled onto the shoulder and closed his eyes. Then, he told me, God spoke to him. "I literally heard a voice saying, *Open your eyes and look around.* I opened my eyes and I looked around, and there was farmland all around."

Joyner's great-grandparents had been enslaved, his grand-parents and parents sharecroppers who worked the same land for others' benefit. In his youth, he had watched, season after season, as his father brought the harvest in, delivered it to buyers, and returned home with barely enough money to subsist. He and his twelve siblings worked the land alongside their parents, too, straining and sweating to grow enough food to feed the family. His father died at sixty-four, of a heart attack suffered on a farm—though the real cause of death, Joyner said, was "anger unexpressed." Determined not to suffer the same fate, Joyner left, joining the army and then studying theology at Shaw University in Raleigh.

He returned home eventually, but always kept his distance from the fields. So this felt like some divine prank. What kind of mischief-making God would point him back to the land? "I said, 'Is there anyone else up there? This isn't a time to be joking around!'"

Joyner received the message, even as he wanted wholeheartedly to reject it: The balm for his people's broken bodies would be found in the fertile soils that stretched for miles in every direction, the very fields that held generational trauma and deep sorrow. "I hate farming," he told me. "I hate farming."

Within months, a project rooted in his greatest fears and most devastating family memories had taken root: a garden that grew into a farm. The fresh produce cultivated there would feed the people of Conetoe.

Joyner took us to visit the farm, but we weren't to be mere sightseers. We spent the morning working the fields alongside members of his congregation, planting collard greens and weeding the rows and hearing their stories.

In 1885, twenty years after emancipation, Princeville, just up the road from Conetoe, became the first African American community in the entire United States to receive an official charter. Much of the surrounding land had been granted to formerly enslaved people. But the white landowners had kept all the high ground for themselves, assigning deceptively fertile but remarkably flood-prone soils to the freedmen. Ever since, every heavy rain has threatened to drown what they grow, every storm system bringing echoes of that long-ago injustice.

From the start, the church's young people were the most enthusiastic about Joyner's project. The least? The old folks. This didn't surprise Joyner. "Some of the elders in the church, they felt they didn't want to go back to that. It was too painful memories. They were the children and grandchildren of sharecroppers." He couldn't blame them, remembering in his bones how his parents had struggled and how he and his siblings had tilled and sowed, weeded and reaped throughout their childhoods. "The children didn't have the same sense of remembrance."

It was the children who took to the fields, the children who lovingly tended the crops, the children who harvested the produce, the children who made the deliveries in the community. And the proof of the project's worth—the thing that ultimately won over the elders—was in the eating. "It was the hen-pecked salad," Joyner told me. Tucked in the baskets that the young people brought, the elders found an heirloom variety of mustard green, called "hen-pecked" because its jagged leaves look almost as if they've been nibbled by chickens. The greens' robustly savory, peppery flavor shot through the parishioners' venerable defenses. "They remembered how good they tasted," Joyner said. "It was the hen-pecked salad that tasted like love."

Joyner's garden hadn't changed everything. A few days prior to our conversation, he had presided at the funeral of a woman who had died at twenty-seven from renal failure. Her uncle had died several years before, at thirty-four, from the same kidney condition. In both cases, doctors attributed the disease to lifestyle and diet.

But the youngsters in the family were all eager participants in the church's farmwork. One young woman—the daughter of that thirty-four-year-old man—had become the head beekeeper. "I'm totally hopeful about these children," Joyner said. "These children are rising up."

On our last morning in North Carolina, we went to Sunday worship at Conetoe Chapel. Pastor Joyner was preaching on the famous verse in the Gospel of John where Jesus says, "Greater love has no one than this, than to lay down one's life for his friends."

"Just be a friend," he said. In his thick Carolina accent, "friend" stretched out to two syllables—*FREN-uh.*

"Just be a friend," he went on. "What we need to learn to do is to walk with each other. If we are willing to take the journey, knowing God will transform us on the journey, just be a friend and walk by their side. Just be a friend. That's one of the things we are losing. Our children are losing it, too. Because we are prostituting ourselves for stuff.

"Have I got a witness?" he asked the congregation.

I wasn't sure whether Joyner's question was rhetorical or a real call that demanded a response. Maybe it was both, but nobody in the church replied.

He turned up the dial on his deep baritone, which filled the space and threatened to burst through the windows and doors. Maybe he did want an answer.

"Have I got a WITNESS?"

He put a little thunder in the last word on the second go.

"HAVE I GOT A WITNESS?"

Finally, you could hear a few "amens," a few "hallelujahs," and even a "praise Jesus" around the sanctuary.

He was preaching a barn burner of a sermon, an apt message for a group of progressive seminarians who typically believed that they knew the right thing to do. Most of us had been well trained in the rich litany of performative social justice: land acknowledgments, disclosure of pronouns, the self-absolving naming of privilege. A week into the class, one student had reprimanded another for perpetuating patriarchy by using the word "father" to address God in a premeal prayer. But did we know how to be human? Did we know how to be friends?

I heard in Joyner's words a convicting call to attend to the small things—not the grand gestures that might draw attention but the tiny details that telegraph attentive grace and let someone know they are truly loved. It wasn't a fancy selection of organic microgreens or a doctor's high-handed advice about healthy diets that had helped his people begin eating better; it was the flash of gustatory recognition when an old lady tasted the hen-pecked greens of her childhood.

"Friendship is deeper than what you do. Friendship is deeper than actions," Joyner said. "If Jesus can be honest, how about you and I be honest? If Jesus can be transparent, how about you and I be transparent? That's how we are going to transform these communities: Not by being churches. Not by being preachers. We are going to transform them by being friends.

"*Have I got a witness?*"

I could try.

hermeneutic

From our first meeting, Pearl had struck me as an uncommon force. Her warmth—a full-body emotional embrace—was both wonderful and fearsome. Her face seemed incapable of a half smile. If her lips weren't pursed in quiet concentration, they were stretched wide in a grin. She never giggled; she screamed in delight. She was a lot: a lot of laughter, a lot of noise, a lot of curiosity, a lot of wit.

From the start, it was apparent how different the two of us were. She was the raging extrovert to my intense introvert, bold where I was shy, a middle-of-the-room dancer to my wallflower, ebullience personified, contrasted with my deep reserve. I'd been reared in urban and suburban settings and knew nothing about farming; she grew up all over the place, but even when she wasn't in a rural environment, she was always cultivating things. "There were always gardening spaces in the projects, and my mom was from the South—a full-on gardener. No matter where we lived, we were always going to grow food," she told me. "So my gardening started in the projects."

Somehow we always found each other in the Farminary's garden, and those early conversations were rich. I told her about my childhood—growing up in just about the churchiest family you could imagine—and she told me about hers. Born in Harlem, she spent her earliest years in public housing in Manhattan. Unusually for a seminarian, she had not grown up in church. Though she remembered her mother owning a Bible, neither of her parents had shared much with Pearl about religion or spirituality. But her mother had taught her to grow things.

When she was eight, the army posted her father to Fort Bragg, so they moved to North Carolina, where her parents bought some land. "That's when I really got into it. We had seven acres, and we grew everything," she said. "We were hog farmers, and my dad taught me how to slaughter and also how to hunt deer."

After her parents split up, she spent her junior high and high school years globetrotting with her dad from post to post, their relationship deepening with every move. Wherever they went, "in our little base homes, my dad always made sure I had a little planter box," she said. "It felt good to me. No matter where we were, I wanted to keep growing. Herbs. Lettuces. Tomatoes. I wanted to keep growing things."

Pearl's father died a year after she graduated from high school. She had already known she wasn't ready for college. She'd always been a daddy's girl, and her devastation in the wake of her father's passing delayed her education even more. She heard about WWOOF (World Wide Opportunities on Organic Farms), an organization that connects volunteers with farms in need of extra hands. "I signed myself up, and I looked all over the world, and I found this place in upstate New York called Golden Eagle Farms, run by this insane woman whom I loved. I stayed for two and a half years when it was supposed to be four months," she said. Pearl learned how to tend goats and horses. "It was so beautiful and so awkward. [The owner] would say, 'I can't have you farming in front of the house, because people are going to drive by and think, *Why does this white lady have this Black girl farming her land?*' "

Eventually, Pearl ended up at Sarah Lawrence College. During the week she studied biology, and on weekends she took the train down to the Bronx, where she helped turn empty lots into pocket vegetable gardens.

Pearl was as surprised as anyone that she'd ended up in seminary. She had only been a Christian for about a year when a friend, who knew of her budding faith as well as her longtime love of farming, mentioned a conference on faith and food justice at Princeton Seminary. She signed up immediately.

The Farminary had just started, and as soon as she saw the land, she was entranced by its possibilities. The following year, she attended the conference again and met Nate. He and a couple of other people suggested that she interview for admission: "I said, 'I don't want to come to seminary. I just became a Christian!' But I did the interview just because I was there. And then they said, 'Just finish the damn application!' So I did, even though I didn't know anything."

She got a full scholarship and arrived on campus ready for a full slate of classes at the Farminary. "I had it all in my head: I'm going to take all these beautiful classes at the farm, and I'm going to study the Bible in the garden. It was all so angelic. It was all going to be so nice," she told me.

Then she met with her academic adviser, who told her that there were prerequisites and requirements.

"Can I not just go to the farm?" she asked.

"No, Pearl," he said.

"This is some bullshit!" she remembers replying. "It was absolutely heartbreaking."

Those first days of seminary shocked Pearl: the stultifying hours in orientation sessions, the countless icebreakers in which she tried to share vulnerably, only to be met by superficial responses and theological jargon. She realized she'd had no idea what she had signed up for. She felt out of place, not just among the predominantly white student body but even with the Black students, nearly all of whom had been reared in the rich traditions of the Black church. "As a Black, queer woman who was not brought up in church or religion, all of a sudden I was in seminary," she said. "It felt all wrong."

After the first session of our Introduction to the Old Testament class, she loudly asked some classmates who "Herman Ootic" was, because the professor kept mentioning him. Their explanations escaped her.

"Jeff, I still don't understand," she said as we tucked our laptops and notebooks into our backpacks.

"A hermeneutic is just the lens through which you read Scripture, or anything else," I said. "We all read from a particular perspective. What's the frame? What's the context?"

She took a deep breath. "Thank you."

Then she went back to her room and called her godmother in New York City.

"I want to come home," she said.

"We will start packing up your things," her godmother replied.

That Pearl didn't immediately pack her things had much to do with the farm. She had arrived on campus weeks before the semester started, and Nate welcomed the extra help. Over those hot summer weeks, she had come to know the land well, and she loved all of it, even trudging through the marshy sections and exploring the thick woods that everyone else avoided. Our Farminary class, which promised more time on the land she'd quickly come to adore, was perhaps the main reason she stayed.

The early days of a friendship can be heady. With Pearl, I felt the glory in my body. She was gifted with exquisite comic timing and a powerful side-eye that, more than once, left me laughing and crying in the middle of class. I found it so alluring, so gorgeous beyond words, to be with a soul who had endured tremendous trauma yet hadn't lost the ability to revel in dumb jokes.

Despite my lifelong reserve, I began to open up in Pearl's presence. It felt safe to be more fully human with her, and I appreciated how she could create powerful emotional weather systems. If I walked around the garden with rain clouds over my head, she could radiate sunshine, her raucous laughter often driving my melancholy away. But what sometimes happens when a warm front collides with a cold one is that conditions grow unsettled, even occasionally stormy.

dog

Our Farminary class had one unregistered auditor who attended almost every week. His name was Lincoln. He was an eleven-year-old Jack Russell terrier and my first real friend at the farm.

Lincoln's human was Wes, the half Chinese pastor's kid in my Farminary class. Wes had spent much of his childhood in Kampala, Uganda, where his dad led a largely expatriate congregation. His family had always had dogs, and they got Lincoln when he was just a puppy. (The name was a compromise; Wes's dad had suggested "Abraham," which Wes and his siblings vetoed because they did not want a biblical name.)

Wes's family had always intended for Lincoln to be an outdoor dog. "But Lincoln was small enough that he could fit through the gate, so he kept coming inside at night to sleep indoors," Wes told me later. During the daytime, he'd roam the streets of Kampala and pick fights with other dogs. "He had a reputation for being wild," Wes said. "He was feral, even deranged."

Wes's next-door neighbors were a surgeon and an anesthesiologist who worked for a medical nonprofit, and they had a German shepherd and a golden Lab. Lincoln would slip through the fences and hide in the neighbors' bushes until it was feeding time. Then he'd sprint out of his hiding place and start eating the other dogs' food. When Lincoln was three or four, the bigger dogs finally had enough of Lincoln's thievery. They mauled him. "The neighbors picked Lincoln up and tore him out of their dog's mouth," Wes said. "His lower body was flapping open, and they stitched him back up. He got in a fight that he couldn't finish. He almost died that night."

This trauma didn't deter Lincoln from running away. Usually he'd come home after a day or two at most, but one time he disappeared for months. Finally, Wes's parents heard that he had been kidnapped, and the abductors wanted a ransom.

Wes's dad got in contact and said, "We're not giving you anything until we see the dog." The kidnappers brought Lincoln over, and as soon as Wes's sisters saw the dog, they shrieked with joy. "We were supposed to play it cool. We did not play it cool," Wes said. With his sisters' squeals, his dad's leverage disappeared.

Anyway, the kidnappers were done with Lincoln: "They said, 'Please take him back. We're sick of him. He's getting in fights constantly.'"

A few months before Wes started seminary, his parents moved from Uganda to China. They couldn't take Lincoln with them, so they asked Wes and his wife, Hana, whether they wanted him. That's how Lincoln immigrated to the United States in May 2016.

By the time I met Lincoln, age had softened his rough edges, revealing an emotional intelligence and a surprisingly perceptive spirit. He hadn't lost his fierce independence, and he was still prone to wander. But more and more, he also displayed a pastoral instinct. The dog could sniff out grief anywhere.

Hana was then working at Swarthmore College, where she and Wes had done their undergraduate studies. Sometimes she'd take Lincoln into the office. As students came and went throughout the day, Hana noticed that Lincoln could somehow identify when someone carried heavy emotional baggage into the room. He'd jump onto their lap or sit close to them.

They lived in inner-city Philadelphia, where Lincoln never had the chance to run free. So Wes asked Nate for permission to bring Lincoln along whenever he came to the farm. Nate isn't a pet person, but he also doesn't like to disappoint people. He reluctantly assented.

On one of Lincoln's first visits to the Farminary, Wes thought he'd made a grave error. Lincoln sprinted away immediately upon arrival. A few hours later, when it was time to leave, Wes walked all over the farm, calling for Lincoln, but he couldn't find him anywhere. After ten, fifteen, twenty minutes, Wes was worried, almost angry. Where had Lincoln gone? Had a fox gotten hold of him? The Farminary had no fence; what if he'd left the property and run onto a busy road? Was this a repeat of his Ugandan shenanigans?

Finally, Wes gave up and walked back to his car. There was Lincoln, sitting right next to it.

I suspect Lincoln came to know that land intimately much more quickly than the rest of us did. While we were harvesting or turning the compost, Lincoln would roam. Sometimes he'd hang out in the garden with us. On hot days, he'd tuck himself under the broad leaves of the soybeans, his panting tongue a flash of pink amid the greenery. Occasionally, we'd spot him sprinting toward the woods, but we were never sure where exactly he went or what he did. All we knew was that, eventually, he'd reappear, often covered in dirt—evidence of his love of digging and burrowing.

I'm not ashamed to admit that I bought my way into a friendship with Lincoln. I snuck him morsels of meat under the table throughout our class's potluck dinners. If I sensed Lincoln hovering near my ankles, I would tear off a piece of beef or chicken or pork—he wasn't picky, as long as it was meat—send my hand downward, and feel him licking it right up.

Soon, whenever I arrived at the farm, Lincoln would greet me in a way that Wes and Hana insisted he never did with anyone else. I'd crouch down to say hello and give him a couple of ear scratches, and he would bury his head between my legs, as if it were a readymade, Lincoln-sized burrow.

Wes and Hana were leaving the country for a trip just after Christmas, and they asked if Lincoln could stay with Tristan and me in Brooklyn. Of course we said yes.

We quickly noticed Lincoln's quirks. If we were sitting on the sofa, he'd jump up right in between us, forcing us apart so that he could snuggle in between, a position we came to call the Lincoln sandwich. When we went out for walks, he wouldn't poop on a patch of grass; he had to back up against a wall or a fence, looking outward as if to protect himself from potential attack.

We became Lincoln's go-to caretakers whenever Wes and Hana traveled, and Tristan grew to love him as much as I did. When Tristan got home from work, he'd open the door and say, "Hi. I'm home." Then Lincoln would come hurtling down the stairs or sprint over from wherever he happened to be in the house, and suddenly I'd hear a gush: "Lincoln! I'm so happy to see you! How's my Lincoln? How was your day? I'm so glad to see you!"

I remembered the counsel of an older pastor whose wisdom I'd sought before starting seminary. She, too, had gone back to graduate school well into her adulthood, after she and her partner had built a life together. I'd told her that our plan was to maintain our home in Brooklyn—I'd commute back and forth to Princeton, and Tristan would keep his corporate real estate job—and she'd had some doubts. For all my learning, she warned, seminary would be a risky thing if the experience was just mine alone and especially if Tristan came to see graduate school as something that was drawing me away from him. "How could this also bless Tristan?" she asked. "Where might he find joy in it? How might it be a good experience for him?"

In Lincoln, I'd found one answer. Grace showed up in a little Jack Russell body, and it wasn't just for me. It was for us.

winter

land

Every Farminary class included a farm labor component. Nate and Kenda had squeezed our course into the first six weeks of the semester, when the garden demanded the most attention: plenty of tomatoes and peppers to harvest, floral bouquets to be arranged, abundant weeds to be addressed.

Everyone always wanted to harvest tomatoes, because you got to eat as you worked. The most popular thing in the garden was undoubtedly the Sun Sugar, a hybrid cherry tomato whose name tells you what you need to know—bright, orange, and bursting with sweetness. Pluck a leaf off a nearby basil plant, wrap the tomato, and you had a nearly perfect bite; if only you'd had a morsel of fresh mozzarella, too.

Even after the class concluded in late October, I kept going to the farm anyway. Sometimes I'd ask Nate ahead of time whether there was any work that needed to be done. But often, I'd just head to the garden and start weeding. I relished the quiet.

Though there was rarely any other human at the farm, I

never felt lonely. Even as the weather grew colder, there were almost always Canada geese in the pond and some robins hopping through the grass. I talked to the plants as I weeded. "Who are you?" I'd say to a cluster of leaves I didn't recognize. Weeding calmed me. As my fingers navigated the greenery, plucking out what wasn't wanted and sparing what was, I felt myself breathe in a way I rarely could on the main campus.

Maybe I'd been naïve: I hadn't expected to feel like a misfit at seminary, but within a few weeks of starting school, I'd sensed that I didn't belong. Most of my classmates were in their twenties; those in the small cohort of second-career students tended to be in their fifties and sixties. The Asian students were mostly theologically conservative, my marriage a barrier for them, while other queer students didn't seem to trust me. (One friend eventually told me that he'd heard someone say I "wasn't queer enough.") Often, when I did sense some connection, it quickly became clear why: A professor wanted advice about getting published in a nonacademic magazine. A classmate asked if I might proofread a paper. A seminary staffer suggested I help with PR.

Nate was closer to me in age than anyone else I met—just three months older. Though he was officially my professor, he treated me more like a peer than anyone else. If he was at the farm when I was, we'd talk—about his kids, about Tristan, about his hopes for the Farminary, about what I was learning and what it was changing in me. I confided in Nate that I was struggling to figure out where I belonged.

One day, as I was unpacking some farm metaphor and trying desperately to apply it to my circumstances, he stopped me. He'd heard me do this again and again and again, and there was nothing inherently wrong with it, he said. But he also wondered whether I could try something else: Could I view the land in the same way I so deeply wished others would view me? "What if," he asked, "you just tried to see this place for what it is, not what it could do for you?"

A regular joke among the seminarians who frequented the Farminary was that our chief crop wasn't soil, as Nate liked to say; it was sermon illustrations. It was so tempting to look all over this land and glean metaphor after metaphor, gathering the flowers of the field for spiritual bouquets and harvesting herbs for theological garnish.

But whether we were focusing on the literal produce or the metaphorical, we were still defining the land by what it did for us rather than by what it actually was. To call these acres a farm was, in a sense, a reductive act. It centered human activity on the land rather than the land itself, a move that minimized other aspects of its existence.

I thought about Nate's question more and more as winter fell. There were no more bouquets to make, no more tomatoes to eat. The cold had halted the growth even of the weeds. With less to do, fewer people showed up.

The morning after the first snowfall, I drove out to the farm, just to see what there was to see. The sun hadn't yet warmed the air, so the snow still laced the tree branches, and the flat, grassy parts of the farm looked as if a smooth sheet of crisp cotton had been spread over them. Except in one area: There, I could see dozens of triangular footprints going in all different directions, like the Canada geese had had a dance party.

To know what a place is, one has to learn what it has been—and what it has been through. So I started to read.

Most of what's now New Jersey was once part of Lenape-hoking, the traditional homeland of the Lenape people. The Farminary sits about a mile south of an ancient Native American trail that the Lenape used to travel between the Raritan River to the north and the Delaware River to the south. There were no known permanent settlements in the immediate area; mostly, this region was oak and hickory forest that hosted seasonal hunters and foragers.

In 1664, the British Crown granted the land to two British aristocrats, John Berkeley and George Carteret, who quickly set about mapping and selling it. Neither man ever visited, instead dispatching underlings to do the work. Daniel Coxe, who in the 1680s was appointed governor of West Jersey by Berkeley, sent an agent to negotiate with the Native American chiefs. One deed records the "purchase" of a huge tract of land for strange and sundry goods, including some thirty-six thousand wampum beads, twenty shirts, forty pairs of stockings, ten gallons of rum, two barrels of beer, and twenty kettles.

I wonder how the Lenape would have understood the exchange. In their culture, land was stewarded communally. While a clan or a family might hold the right to hunt or farm an area, land couldn't be bought, sold, or permanently owned. It wasn't a commodity, but it was a resource that could be shared, even with strangers. I wonder, too, whether the colonists grasped—and exploited—that gap in understanding or whether they just assumed that every culture viewed land as they did.

In the 1690s, a man named Ralph Hunt moved to New Jersey from New York. He was the fourth child of a London-born father, also named Ralph, who had fought the Dutch; after New Netherland came under English rule, the elder Hunt was one of the first colonial magistrates appointed by the Crown. Before Ralph, Sr., died in 1677, he instructed his eldest son, Edward, to pay each of the three younger sons for their equal shares in his estate; his daughter, Mary, got six sheep, two cows, and, according to the will he wrote not long before he passed away, "the feather bed on which I now ly [sic]."

With his inheritance, the younger Ralph gradually accumulated more than one thousand acres in central New Jersey, land that was quickly deforested to make way for fields of barley, rye, and wheat. Over the subsequent centuries, the acreage was divvied up, mostly into ever-smaller farms, including what's now the Farminary.

This plot sat on the east side of Princeton Pike. In the early 1800s, the Princeton and Kingston Turnpike was constructed as a (relatively) high-speed corridor between Philadelphia and New York. For six dollars (about $180 in today's dollars), one could board a stagecoach in Philadelphia at four A.M., eat breakfast in Trenton, then lunch in New Brunswick, transfer to a steam-powered ferry in Hoboken, and be in New York City by evening.

Gradually, farmland surrendered to suburbia's growth. Today, homes surround the Farminary's twenty-one acres on three sides; the fourth fronts an expanse of preserved land owned by the state of New Jersey.

After the compost pile, my favorite place on the farm was a tongue of land framed by the pond and the brook feeding it. I'd often go and just sit, greeting the two tall sugar maples and the lone oak that stood guard in that spot. "Hello, trees," I'd say. I wished they could tell me what they had witnessed. What had these waters seen?

I knew the parts of the farm near the buildings—the barn, the small cinder-block pumphouse, a ramshackle home nobody was allowed to enter—had long ago been cleared of the original forest. Near the pumphouse, someone had planted Japanese cherry trees, which in the springtime unfurled veils of pink flowers, and of course there were the Christmas trees. But tall trees grew in abundance behind the barn and all along the edge of the biggest field. I told myself those woods must be ancient— a remnant of how things used to be.

I confess I'm among those who fetishize things like "wilderness" and "old-growth forests" and "how things used to be." We imagine nature to be purer, better, less sullied by humanity. Even among those who have come to acknowledge the long, precolonial history of Indigenous people, there can be a tendency to combine false ideas of unspoiled ecosystems with hoary clichés about noble savages.

There has never been an unchanging ecosystem; even in Lenape times, this landscape bore human fingerprints. Only recently have we come to understand the intensity and sophistication of their land-management techniques. The oak, chestnut, and hickory forests here were maintained by regular, strategic burnings that benefited not only those nut-bearing trees but also blackberry canes and blueberry bushes. The flourishing of those trees and shrubs provided more food for humans, as well as for prey the Lenape liked to hunt, including bear and elk, deer and raccoon. The thinned understory afforded hunters better light and sight lines. In the soil fed by the nutrient-rich ash, ritually important plants—including goldenrod, which was used for sweat baths—thrived.

Without the editing effects of fire, sugar maples, elms, and poplars would have risen up, eventually crowding out the slower-growing but more fire-resilient oak and hickory. That would have been more "natural." Would it have been "better"?

I kept turning Nate's question over in my mind: "What if," he had said, "you just tried to see this place for what it is, not what it could do for you?"

As someone who has never known how to be content with what is and who is constantly striving for what could be, the question was almost impossible to answer. I have always sought to exert control—to work a little harder, to make myself a little more presentable, to be seen as more useful and more put together than I felt on the inside.

Even my tendency to overdress on the farm betrayed me, at least to those who knew me best. One day, I posted a picture on social media of myself working in the garden in my usual khakis and a button-down, and my friend Rachel texted to tease me lovingly about the outfit. "Only you," she said.

I didn't respond, but not because I was irritated. Her text actually felt like a grace—she had seen me as I was. It was also a helpful reminder: Love pays attention.

After a heavy rainstorm that winter, I saw undulations in the land that my eye didn't perceive in the dry. Water rushed to the low places, and small pools formed in depressions where I'd thought the ground was just flat. Near the stream, much of the grass was underwater.

I crouched on the bridge over the stream, regarding the sodden landscape. There wasn't anything else I could do.

plum blossom

The Chinese plum tree (*Prunus mume*) buds in midsummer, but it doesn't fully flower until January, when the late-winter cold stirs the buds awake. Then the plum's bare branches unfurl clouds of white blossoms, some blushing slightly pink, others tinged with green.

In the fifth and sixth centuries, Chinese poets and philosophers regularly maligned the flower. How rude that it should make such an ostentatious appearance when the season clearly called for austerity. How unseemly that it should show off when most other plants lay dormant. How obnoxious that it should want this spotlight for itself.

Within a few centuries, though, the plum blossom experienced reputational rehab. Perhaps, some writers speculated, this bloom could be understood not as a show-off but as a sign. Perhaps it came as a messenger of resilience, flowering when nothing else could. Perhaps it was not late, but early. "Amid all that has fallen, the fragrant plum alone flourishes / only it possesses the little garden," the Song dynasty poet Lin Bu writes in his poem "Little Plum Blossom in a Mountain Garden."

The plum blossom became a sign of hope, a herald of the coming of spring, and one of the most beloved flowers in Chinese culture.

Even after all these years, I'm not sure I've fully processed all that happened after I came out. I've told my closest friends snippets of stories. But I've tucked much more away among my memories—reluctant to say anything that might be construed as insulting my parents, courting sympathy, or letting the pain define me.

The vault of memory is a funny place, less like a neat filing system than a cluttered closet into which a teenager has thrown all their belongings when told to clean their room. There, the easiest things to find are the ones that reek.

I remember the long, handwritten letter from one of my dearest relatives, warning me of eternal damnation. It quoted Leviticus 18:22: "You shall not lie with a male as with a woman; it is an abomination."

I remember being shouted at in the midst of a family argument: "We don't even know who you are anymore."

I remember only anger about who I was supposed to be. If they had any interest in who I was or who I was becoming, my parents didn't betray it—especially striking, given that Chinese families can be incredibly nosy: No inquisitiveness about my shifting faith. No curiosity about the handsome Texan with whom I was building a life. Really, no questions at all—only statements and judgments, calls to prayer as well as prayers for repentance.

I remember my parents' boycott of my wedding. My father never acknowledged that it happened. My mother wrote to express regret that I had not changed my mind. "Regardless, I still love you," she said. "I shall continue praying for you and Tristan, that the Holy Spirit be your guide."

But—

Two of my aunts did witness Tristan and me making our vows. Auntie Maisy came from South Carolina. And Auntie Kitty flew all the way from her home in Switzerland. She brought a well-worn family Bible and read Psalm 121 in Cantonese during the ceremony.

Two of my cousins also showed up. One took the custom-made cloth napkins from our wedding dinner and transformed them into a quilt, which arrived in the mail months later.

Then there was Auntie Dorothy, who wasn't my aunt at all. In a sense, she had shown up for me even earlier than the rest of them.

In 1971, my mother left Hong Kong to attend the University of Oregon. She ended up renting a room from Dorothy and her husband, Jack, who ran a small boardinghouse. They became her surrogate parents, and eventually—after she married and had my sister and me—our surrogate grandparents, whom we called Auntie Dorothy and Uncle Jack. Dorothy and Jack were the ones who taught me about rural American life.

The summer I turned ten, my sister and I went to stay with them in the southern Washington countryside. Dorothy was born in rural Missouri. What brought her and her family to Washington, I don't know, but she never lost the accent of her childhood. "Missouri" was always "Missour-ah," and "Washington" was pronounced "War-shington." When we went shopping, she would look at the prices and inevitably say, "Well, that's spendy!"

Jack was a retired lumberjack. Each summer, the two of them

would search their dozens of acres and log whatever trees had fallen during the winter. He taught me how to set a choker, let me try my hand at driving the small Caterpillar tractor, and took me to the mill to see how wood becomes lumber.

On the walk back to the house from the logging site, we'd pick wild blackberries along the roadside—some to make pie for dessert, some to turn into jam. Before dinner, Auntie Dorothy would send me to the garden to fetch some lettuce or scallions. Then, most nights after we ate, we hiked up the hill to the high meadows, in search of elk.

Uncle Jack died my senior year of college. He had always been the more faithful correspondent of the two; Auntie Dorothy said she wasn't much of a writer. But not long after I came out, I got a card in the mail from her, asking me to call her when I had some time.

Auntie Dorothy was a woman of quiet but steady faith. Most Sundays, you could find her in the pews of a little clapboard country church where the congregants believed in the healing comfort of a handmade quilt, the restorative powers of a pot-luck supper, and the utter perfection of the Holy Bible.

I put the call off for days—picking up my phone, then setting it down, dialing the first few digits of the number I'd known since childhood, then stopping. I'd had so many hard conversations over the years, so many difficult talks with devout loved ones in which my hopes of warmth and understanding had been met with ice and judgment.

Finally, I made it through all ten digits and heard a familiar, singsong "Hellooooo" after the second ring.

"Hi, Auntie Dorothy," I said.

"Jeffrey!" she said, warmth swelling in her voice. The only people who call me Jeffrey are those who have known me since before I could speak. "Well, I am just so glad you called."

She swept me up in a rush of chatter and updates: The deer had been getting into her garden, eating the lettuce as they did every year. The blackberries had been okay that summer. She had done some canning, putting up some green beans and some fruit for the winter.

Then a pause.

"Now, your mom called," she finally said.

I didn't respond, because I didn't know how.

"You know I don't understand all these things, Jeffrey," she said. "But I want you to know that I love you very much, no matter what. I just needed you to know that."

Like so many other plants, the Chinese plum tree prefers full sunshine and fertile, well-drained soil. But over the millennia, it has proved itself to be adaptable to all kinds of growing conditions.

"Amid all that has fallen, the fragrant plum alone flourishes."

Classical Chinese poetry defies easy translation, but that's my best attempt. That first line from Lin Bu can be read literally as "great fragrance astounds fall alone beautiful genial." For the original audience, each word, each phrase, evoked worlds. Between each character, one can imagine white space, which the reader is invited to fill with their own knowledge, their own experience, much like an impressionist painting in written form.

The poet Edward C. Chang renders it this way: "The plum tree is the only one in blossom after all other flowers have fallen." The translator Red Pine took a different approach: "When everything has faded they alone shine forth."

Which translation is right? It might seem odd, but it isn't inaccurate to say all of them. The classical Chinese poet's goal was an austerity of language that, paradoxically, created a wide-open hospitality. He—and it was almost always a "he"—tacitly acknowledged that every encounter with a poem would be unique, every reading an interaction between the same words and a different spirit. There is no key to unlocking the precise meaning, because a poem is not a puzzle to be solved. Each reader encounters a poem as nobody else ever has.

Memory feels much the same way to me: snippets, fragments, a word here or there. Scientists might tell us what they know about how it works, hypothesizing about why some wisps become vivid, even concrete, while others vanish. Yet none of us can access an unedited chronicle of what happened—and this seems as true of yesterday as it is of yesteryear.

But this, too, was true: If I were in a mountain garden in winter, my focus would be on the lifeless leaves and the forbidding crunch of the ice on the ground, not the plum blossom stirring brilliantly awake. My body reflexively feels the wind as a rude bite, not an invigorating breeze.

The third line of Lin Bu's poem reads: "A faint fragrance floats amid the hazy glow of a golden moon." There are other things to notice, he suggests, if only one tries—and it's possible, even in dim light. It often takes effort to perceive what matters. It sometimes requires perspective to glimpse beauty.

sabbath

The final days of the Chinese lunar year are a whirl of activity: deep-cleaning the house to sweep away any remnants of bad luck, paying off debts so that the new year will come with a clean financial slate, preparing to feast.

The celebration technically stretches across two gluttonous weeks, but the main event happens on New Year's Eve, when families gather for the reunion dinner. In China, it sparks the world's biggest annual human migration. More than four hundred million people crowd planes and trains and buses to return to their native villages and hometowns.

Even though the celebration takes place in the meteorological winter, it is formally known in mainland China as the Spring Festival, because it marks the traditional beginning of the growing season. Though there might not be much to see beyond the plum blossoms, anticipation builds for what's to come: Offerings are made to the gods of spring. Farmers will soon begin preparations for planting. But the not-to-do list seems just as long as the to-do list: Starting on New Year's Day, we aren't supposed to do any cleaning for two weeks—no sweeping, no washing, no housework of any kind. Nor are we to wash our hair. The underlying belief is that one should not sweep or rinse away the good luck that arrives with every new year.

Yes, we are a superstitious people.

My parents and grandparents have always maintained a complicated relationship with Chinese superstitions. The Baptist missionaries who converted my family insisted that they were heathen. When I was a kid, I sensed a tension in my deeply devout clan: Which traditions were we to keep, and which would we dispense with? What old practices were acceptable in a family that had chosen a new, foreign religion, and what might be seen by others as signs that we weren't sufficiently faithful to our Christianity?

So we flailed. Some years I got the red envelopes of money that elders traditionally give children; other years I didn't. Some years my mom would wear the lucky red on New Year's Day, which is said to usher in luck and ward off evil; other years she didn't. I never heard my parents offer the typical Cantonese New Year's greeting—"恭喜發財" ("gong hei fat choy")—which means, "Congratulations! I hope you prosper," because the emphasis on material wealth wasn't Christian. We did not leave our hair unwashed. We definitely cleaned the house when we weren't supposed to.

As I got older, I began to reclaim some of the old practices, though not the superstitious rationales behind them. Sometimes I put my own spin on the traditions. The settling of debts, for instance, was historically accompanied by sacrifices of thanksgiving to the deities and to one's ancestors. So, one year, I decided to write notes of gratitude to people who had mattered to me: an elementary school teacher, a particularly kind magazine editor, a friend who had said or done something encouraging. I also tried to cook a big meal on New Year's Eve, packing the room with friends, because I didn't live near family.

Why was I doing any of it, though?

It didn't occur to me until I took a class at the farm called Soil and Sabbath that there's a parallel between biblical time and Chinese time.

I'd always thought of Sabbath as the well-earned reward at the end of a hard week—rest for the weary. But then Nate encouraged us to have another look at the biblical creation story.

You know how the story goes, according to the Book of Genesis: On the first day, God turns the cosmic lights on. On the second, God forms sky and sea. On the third, land, then plants of all kinds. Day four brings the sun, moon, and stars. Day five, animals fill the skies and the seas. And day six, land animals as well as humans.

"Thus the heavens and the earth, and all the host of them, were finished," the story continues. Then God rests and invites everything and everyone else to do the same.

"What has humankind done to earn rest at this point?" Nate asked. "Nothing."

In other words, according to the creation myth that has defined so much of how we live, humanity's first full day of existence was rest—pure, unadulterated, unearned rest, much like the Lunar New Year begins with an extended break from work. God might have earned a paid vacation day, but Adam and Eve hadn't done any of that work. Sabbath was, for us, not an end. It was our beginning.

In mid-February, on the last day of the lunar year, I went for a walk at the farm. My house wasn't as clean as it should have been, but I told myself I was doing some mental housekeeping.

The previous semester had been a doozy: I'd chosen Princeton in part because it was within driving distance of Brooklyn,
but the New Jersey Turnpike does not inspire holy thoughts
even at the best of times. I did some of my worst work in all my
years of education. I tuned out in class. My papers showed little
original thought, even less heart, and plenty of parroted theological jargon—precisely the combination that had so irritated
me in some of my classmates when I first started seminary. I
scored some of the lowest grades I've ever gotten, including a
35 percent on a Hebrew quiz (and that was after the professor
had spotted us five points).

In the main garden, everything was some shade of beige or
brown—the dead stalks of last summer's sunflowers, the damp
soil, the fallen maple and oak leaves that had surfed the winds
and then settled on the ground. In the soil at my feet, I spotted
something lacy. It looked like a locket, heart-shaped and made
of some sort of filigree. I picked it up. It felt feather-light, almost
weightless.

I studied the lacework and suddenly realized what it was: the
decayed husk of a dead tomatillo. The flesh had rotted away, as
had the papery portions of the husk. All that remained was the
frail tracery and, tucked within, a cluster of tiny seeds.

It was a remarkably beautiful thing—an epitaph in gossamer.
Of course I couldn't just let it be pretty. Here, I thought, was a
reminder of life after death. Even the tiniest seeds, like the ones
in this deceased tomatillo, have so much potential, such pent-
up possibility. With these in my hand, I had some choices. I
could plant them in a tray in the hopes of a harvest (or not).
Assuming the seeds germinated, I could transplant the seedlings
to the ground and then faithfully weed to give them the best
possible chance of absorbing all the nutrients they needed to
thrive (or not). And I could surrender everything else, all that

was beyond my control—from the weather to the movements of the subterranean microbes—and bless the plants, trusting them to do what they were designed to do (or not, and just worry, which has always been my go-to strategy).

As I held the remnants of the tomatillo, I also thought, *Maybe this is a sign!* Then I laughed at myself, because I was taught not to believe in signs. In the churches of my childhood, we never even said "Good luck!" But when you're down, you'll take an auspicious sign wherever you can get one. The tomatillo didn't have to represent luck; I could just call it a messenger of hope.

That the Chinese New Year begins with a feast is not accidental. The meal is seen as both celebration and fortification for whatever is to come, shared with those who are supposed to be there for you no matter what.

Each dish on the table has a purpose (okay, a superstition): There's fish, because the word 魚 ("yu," said with a rising tone) is roughly homophonous with words that mean "abundance" and "more than." It's preferably served whole, because who would want their abundance, their "more than," dismembered or cut down? An entire chicken is also often prepared, to represent unity and wholeness. There might be oysters, because the Cantonese word for "oyster" ("ho") sounds like the word for "good." Noodles traditionally symbolize long life. Spring rolls and daikon cakes resemble gold bars.

You will never find pumpkin or squash on a traditional New Year's menu; the word 瓜 ("gua") sounds just like one for "death." Crab typically isn't served either. Someone once told me it's because crabs typically scuttle sideways, so you're just asking for a year without progress. (That always seemed like a stretch to me.) The more common explanation is much more basic: In Cantonese, 蟹, pronounced "hai," sounds too much like one of our typical sighs of exasperation, "haaaai."

Yes, we are a superstitious people.

That year, for the first time in a while, I didn't make a big Chinese New Year's Eve dinner. It seemed too much. So it was Tristan and me, sharing a simple meal together—fish; fried tofu, which also resembled gold bars, not that I was trying; vegetables; rice. That felt auspicious enough to me: A deep breath. Resting in each other's good company. A fresh beginning.

A couple of weeks before, I'd gone to a talk by the Duke historian Kate Bowler. She studies American religion and has developed something of a specialty in prosperity theology. This kind of thinking has knit itself into the modern psyche in various ways. There are churchier versions, which declare, sometimes more brazenly but often more subtly, that God wants us to be rich. Then there are secularized forms, which take the shape of practices like manifesting or simply believing that the universe is conspiring for your personal benefit, if only you'd open yourself up to receive.

In her book *Everything Happens for a Reason (and Other Lies I've Loved)*, Bowler writes, "What gives the prosperity movement breadth and depth for many is its thorough accounting for the pain of life, and for the longing we have for restoration. Those Americans trapped in failing bodies or broken relationships or the painful possibility that their lives might never be made whole can turn to this message of hope. If it is a game—with rules for success that anyone can use—then maybe they can win."

I'd encountered prosperity theology before. As a reporter at *Time*, I'd traveled to Houston to interview the preacher Joel

Osteen, author of bestsellers including *Your Best Life Now* and
*It's Your Time: Activate Your Faith, Achieve Your Dreams, and In-
crease in God's Favor.* After hearing Osteen preach, I spent some
time talking to worshippers. "God doesn't want me to be a run-
of-the-mill person," one man told me. After losing his factory
job in Ohio, he'd moved his family to Texas, to attend Osteen's
church and find his fortune. "It's a new day God has given me!"
he said. "I'm on my way to a six-figure income!" That six-figure
income would buy the twenty-five acres he had been dreaming
of, as well as a schoolhouse for his home-schooled kids, horses
and ponies, a barn, a pond, "and maybe some cattle. I'm dreaming big—because all of heaven is dreaming big."

I encountered prosperity theology again in a seminary class
about poverty. One day, we were wrestling with prosperity theology's enduring appeal when one student loudly dismissed this
kind of thinking as shallow and selfish. "I don't agree with prosperity theology either," another classmate said. "But I can understand why people believe it. What if it's their hope for
survival? Wouldn't you want to believe that God was on your
side?"

It was tempting for me to mock the man I'd met in Houston,
but I also recognized that I'd internalized some version of the
underlying belief: that if I were faithful enough, God would see
me and act on my behalf. For years, I prayed that if I were holy
enough, God might turn me straight and give me a wife—the
heteronormative jackpot. Other times, I prayed that if I worked
hard enough, God would bless me. I was (usually) careful not to
specify what form those blessings would take—twenty-five acres
seemed audacious. But still, I had to admit that I believed that
if I were conscientious, good things would come, if not in this
life, then surely in the next.

At age thirty-five, Bowler was diagnosed with incurable

stage 4 colon cancer. Before then, she'd achieved much of what she thought she wanted: a tenured professorship at a prestigious university, a good marriage, a cute kid. She'd been a good Mennonite and a diligent worker. And now this. "When I found myself facing death in a country that believes everything happens for a reason," she said, "I felt like a loser."

In her book, she recalls meeting with a cancer researcher who unabashedly says to her, "We're all terminal." He meant that, from birth, we're all dying. We might not know when or how, but Bowler's diagnosis didn't make her all that special and her circumstances weren't that unusual. Anyway, she still had choices to make. The researcher's blunt comment "answers my unspoken question: How do you stop?" Bowler writes. "You just stop. You come to the end of yourself. And then you take a deep breath. And say a prayer. And get back to work."

We get back to work not because we're trying to earn anything but because the calling is to live a good and loving life, to be a part of something that's not individual but collective, to be in communion with other humans and beauty and the dead tomatillo and the whole fish on the table and the sky and the sea.

"Don't skip to the end," the cancer researcher said to Bowler. "Don't skip to the end."

Maybe that deep breath was akin to rest—and perhaps it reminded her to remember the beginning: We began in grace. And if we began in grace, and keep returning to grace, perhaps everything else unfolds in gratitude. Or at least it should.

brisket

I was juggling my full-time seminary studies with my freelance work, which often required me to travel. Almost always, I made time on my business trips to eat well. In Dallas, I ate some of the best brisket I'd ever tasted, the meat slowly softened over an oak-and-hickory fire, its exterior crusty with pepper. (Cattleack Barbeque, if you're ever in the area.) I wasn't able to eat even half of what I ordered, so I got a to-go box, wrapped it well in plastic, and tucked it carefully into my backpack for the trip home to Brooklyn.

At the Dallas airport security checkpoint, the guy manning the X-ray machine stopped the conveyor belt for a long moment as he narrowed his eyes and stared at the image on his screen. I knew he was looking at my backpack. He glanced over to those of us who were waiting for our bags, as if trying to decipher what weirdo had done this odd thing.

"It's mine," I said. "It's brisket."

His face immediately brightened. He gave me a thumbs-up and sent my backpack on its way.

A couple of nights later, I opened the fridge to see what I might be able to make for dinner. I saw the box containing the leftover brisket, and my stomach rumbled its gladness. I also had some leftover rice in the fridge. I thought, *Why not?*

I took the brisket out and chopped it up, along with some onion, mushroom, green onion, and green pepper. All of that went into the wok, along with the rice. I added an egg, soy sauce, and sesame oil, and then I stirred it all together and waited for the egg to cook. (Always, always wait for the egg to cook, even though it might be tempting not to. Turn the heat off too early, and the rice will be wet, even leaden.)

My first-ever bite of brisket fried rice told me that this wok was full of something special. The brisket's fat had melted beautifully into the rice, the onion and the green pepper cut that fat, and the combination just worked. Why hadn't I ever thought to do this before?

What's more, here was a dish worthy of our home and our marriage. It took a Cantonese classic and a Texan one, and it melded them into something even better, something harmonious, something that told the story of us.

A funny thing: Tristan was still away on his own travels that night. I ate that whole pan of brisket fried rice by myself.

If my need for comfort food was growing, that was because I was halfway through seminary and still struggling to make sense of it.

I didn't like most of my classes. I'd naïvely expected deep, thoughtful conversations about the meaning of life and the mysteries of the universe. Instead, there were dry lectures read by jaded instructors and seminars full of students who treated theology as if it were accounting—clear rules and right principles to be mastered and deployed.

While the administration liked to publish glossy pamphlets full of phrases like "covenant community" and "preparing leaders to serve," I experienced a toxic combination of deep cynicism, theological polarization, and bureaucracy-minded hierarchy. Conservative and progressive students quietly loathed one another. Often the most difficult were the formerly conservative Christians who had turned progressive. In the early days of their conversion, they had both the zeal of new believers and the fundamentalist instincts of their upbringings.

So many of the professors and administrators liked to proclaim their open-mindedness, but in practice, they were profoundly conservative, mainly in the sense of preserving their own power. Every new idea was treated as a potential liability. Wes had the idea to install a fire pit at the farm, a way of creating a new space for gathering. Word came down from on high that students couldn't be trusted with fire.

The more discouraged I felt, the more I became my own worst enemy. After one professor took points off on every single one of my papers for "style and grammar"—she even circled a rhetorical question and scrawled "inappropriate for academic writing" in the margin of one essay—I began to question my skills in the medium in which I'd built a career. Tristan saw me in my academic struggles and was unfailingly encouraging. He was still at work when I got home from taking my Hebrew final, but he'd left a Post-it note on our front door: "Congrats! Jeffy is the best!"

My frustrations with seminary were compounded by my troubles in my denomination, the Reformed Church in America (RCA). While I wasn't sure I wanted to become an ordained minister, I'd begun the ordination process when I started seminary anyway. It was called a "discernment" process for a reason: The three years that it typically takes allows time for both the candidate and the church to listen for the call. I wanted to keep my options open.

One day, a church official came to Princeton to meet with me and other RCA students at the seminary. The RCA has long had an ambiguous stance on homosexuality. Nothing in our official rules and regulations prevented me from pursuing ordination or being ordained, yet at nearly every step in the process questions had been raised, because of my marriage, about my "fitness for ministry."

"Jeff, I'm going to be frank," the official said to me. "I don't see a good way forward for you in this denomination. It would probably be less painful, for you and for everyone, if you thought about finding another one."

I briefly entertained the thought of dropping out—out of seminary, out of the ordination process, out of this whole messy institutional Christianity thing. Honestly, I probably would have, were it not for my stubbornness and my overdeveloped sense of shame. If I didn't see this through, I would be doing the gatekeepers' job for them. If I didn't graduate, I would prove that I didn't belong. If I dropped out of the ordination process, I'd let the bigots believe they had won.

The only other things that kept me going were the farm and the small cluster of students who frequented it. Away from the tidy, historic buildings of the main campus, I could breathe. Sometimes I'd do chores, but other times I'd just sit on the stone bridge and let my legs dangle over the stream. Hana and I could spend hours in the hoop house, even in midwinter, weeding the spinach and the scallions while Lincoln roamed the grounds, popping in occasionally to check on us and make sure we were still there.

Often I'd visit the compost pile. I'd take a shovel and pick at the outermost layers, studying what had decomposed and what hadn't. Then I'd plunge the shovel in as deep as I could to make a gash, hoping to see a puff of steam rise in the cold winter air. Every time it happened, I saw it as my own personal pillar of cloud—a visible reminder that transformation was still in progress, and a clear sign that the pile was still preaching good news to me about the possibility of life, death, and resurrection.

I wasn't the only one who felt adrift on the rest of campus and found respite on the farm. Wes had a deep interest in the intersection of theology and design, and we had long conversations about the ramshackle architecture on the farm. We liked that there was no Wi-Fi, which helped us focus on the land. There was even an unusual hospitality to a barn that wasn't hermetically sealed; it was normal for a field mouse to sneak in during a potluck dinner, skittering along the rafters to see if it might be able to snatch a snack. All were welcome, right?

But even in my Farminary classes, I struggled. When I met with Nate to discuss his feedback on a final paper I'd written for him, he looked at me glumly and said, "Well, Jeff, this was not your best." That's devastating critique from a gentle Mennonite.

Just past the halfway point of seminary, two significant things happened.

First, Nate decided to create the first formal farm team—four students paid to tend to the garden and help with the Farminary's operations. Pearl, of course, would be on the team, along with Cogan, a reserved, irenic Lutheran from Indiana, and Emily, a Presbyterian from South Carolina who had an effervescent manner and a keen interest in social justice. Would I, too, he wondered, want to be a farmhand?

The commitment wasn't much: just a few hours of chores

each termtime week. But come summer, and the height of growing season, the demands would ramp up. And when he and his
family went on their summer vacation, we'd have to run the
farm ourselves. The pay was the standard rate for a student
worker: minimum wage.

Of course I said yes.

Then Tristan and I decided to leave New York.

Almost every weekday, I'd been doing the exhausting commute back and forth to Brooklyn, spending way too much time
on the New Jersey Turnpike. The drive took an hour and fifteen
minutes on good days, much more on the bad. One evening, I
circled our neighborhood for over an hour just to find a parking
space, spewing emissions and curse words all the while.

Tristan had wearied of his commute on the subway and the
grind of his corporate job. The work itself wasn't the problem.
He'd studied architecture and urban planning, and he geeks out
on buildings and cities. He has a remarkable ability to pinpoint
the decade in which a building was built; often, in Manhattan,
he can also name the architect who designed that skyscraper or
rustle up a bit of trivia about its current or former occupants. He
led a research unit at a commercial real estate company; what
better job for someone like that than studying buildings and trying to understand the patterns and trends driving change in a
city? But he's also a gentle soul, and commercial real estate in
New York is a hard-edged business. He was tired, and he was
ready for a break.

"What if we moved to Princeton just until you finished
school?" he wondered.

His question stirred both worry and exhilaration within me.
I still couldn't see where my seminary experience would take
me, still didn't know what any of this was ultimately for. But
Tristan still believed in me—in us.

Was he really quitting his job? Were we actually going to pack up our Brooklyn home? Were we moving into student housing, at our advanced age? Were we saying goodbye to the life we'd built in the city?

"I'm ready," Tristan said.

It was time for a new season.

spring

wilderness

The news that we were leaving New York sparked a range of reactions among our friends. My friend Rachel texted to say she was thrilled. She and her husband, Dan, had bought twenty-five acres in the rolling hills of East Tennessee. "After you're done with seminary," she said, "you and Tristan can come farm the land."

She insisted she wasn't joking. I replied that while society had changed a lot, I had a hard time imagining Tristan and me in the rural South. Anyway, was there anywhere within reasonable driving distance where I could buy Chinese groceries? She conceded the point.

"A bold move!" another friend wrote.

"Whoa," another texted.

"!!!!!!" another said.

How exactly does one respond to "!!!!!!"? Or "!?!?!?!?!?!?"?

A few people acted as if leaving New York City were akin to going off-grid. We were moving fifty miles away, to a town with an Ivy League university. That only counts as abandoning civilization if you're the snobbiest, most intransigent Manhattanite. Even if it were the wilderness, though, was that so bad?

"Wilderness" can carry an implied sense of banishment, of exile, even of punishment. I've often wondered whether that betrays an implicit bias: The city is the place of cosmopolitanism, sophistication, and success. Everything else—whether you want to call it the countryside or the wilderness—might be fine for a stroll or a hike, a pleasant day out, even an extended camping trip. In other words, it's okay if you choose to go there, but it's no place you'd want to be sent.

In the biblical record, though, the wilderness is often depicted as a place of divine encounter and spiritual restoration. There, an angel found the enslaved Hagar and gave her encouragement and good news. There, the Hebrews wandered for decades, but it was also where they received manna and found their way to freedom. There, Elijah fled for safety, and after he prayed that he might die, he was awoken to a miraculous loaf of fresh-baked bread. There, John the Baptist modeled the benefits of a foraged diet long before urban hipsters made it trendy.

Then there is Jesus. Though the wilderness was where the devil tempted him at the beginning of his ministry, it was also where he communed with the wild animals and was cared for by angels. According to Luke's Gospel, later on, as his fame grew and people clamored for his attention, "Jesus himself would often slip away to the wilderness and pray."

I don't think Luke's inclusion of this line was accidental. Surely he was telling us something about Jesus and what it means to be human.

I imagine Jesus out for a hike, Jesus catching his breath in the shade of a boulder, Jesus listening to the birdsong and the howls

of the beasts and the whoosh of the wind instead of the pleas of
the ailing and the wails of the desperate and the nattering of his
feckless disciples, Jesus collecting himself away from the endless
demands of his everyday life and the people around him, Jesus
resting. If Jesus himself needed the respite of the wilderness,
why not us? For all our fears of the alleged wilds, perhaps we all
sometimes need some space and a radical change in scenery to
reflect and reset. For all our worries about leaving the city, perhaps Tristan and I would find some respite and clarity in the
wilderness . . . of New Jersey.

In the Bible, the wilderness never seems to belong to anyone, at
least not in the long term. Armies might try to conquer the
land, and colonizers might build their citadels. But in the ancient prophecies, nature serves as a patient agent of justice, ever
ready to reclaim the bricks and turn them back to dust. The old
oracles that warn of hyenas taking over a military tower or owls
and ostriches finding places to nest can be read as warnings to
humankind: Don't see yourselves as more powerful than you
actually are. Don't think your structures are more permanent,
your systems more resilient, than they actually are.

"Mine" might be one of the most dangerously alluring words
in the English language. We guard our possessions jealously. We
seek deeds and titles to houses and cars, showing off what we've
earned. Our societies celebrate the self-made billionaire, rarely
examining the lie of independent wealth.

After we sold our house and moved into a seminary apartment with a lovely little balcony overlooking woods, Tristan and
I discovered the freedom of not owning the place. In exchange
for our (heavily subsidized) monthly rent, we had precious few
responsibilities beyond the electric bill. If something needed fix-

ing, we went online and logged a request. A maintenance worker would show up within a day.

Tristan found work at the indie bookstore in town. Make no mistake: It was still a job, one that came with some of the minor annoyances of customer service. But there, also, he felt the ease of lessened authority. There were no emails to answer, no work to take home with him at day's end, no burdens to be carried through the night and into the next morning.

The farm, too, had never been mine and could never be mine. While I might be able to find belonging there (sometimes) and while I felt a growing sense of responsibility to tend it well, it could never belong to me. Fidelity could never be mistaken for ownership.

To emphasize what's mine can be to underplay the importance of what's ours. The temptation toward self-sufficiency, self-importance, and indeed self-absorption is age-old and universal; hence all the detailed rules and strikingly specific regulations about how to treat one's neighbor, not just in the Torah but also in the holy books of so many religions and the writings of so many philosophers.

The idea of self-sufficiency can be such an alluring trickster. One day the previous fall, we had a surplus of produce on the farm, and I went around to some of the seminary offices, asking secretaries, deans, maintenance workers, and cleaners if they wanted any green beans or tomatoes or peppers. "They're from the Farminary!" I said, feeling like a door-to-door salesman. "They're free!"

While a few people were delighted, I was surprised how many responded with skepticism. Some looked askance at my overflowing basket; were there signs of rot in the produce? Or they quickly brushed me off, as if I'd insulted them by asking if they wanted free vegetables.

"I don't need any food," one said, looking at me as if she wished she had a door to shut in my face.

"Okay," I replied. Though really, I wanted to say, *Do you know how sweet these tomatoes are? And these lunchbox peppers? They're delicious.*

I couldn't find enough takers, so eventually I left the produce on a table in the library's café, with a sign that said, "Free! Help yourself." Maybe when nobody else was looking, someone would take them.

potato

On a drizzly Friday in early spring, we went out to the farm to plant potatoes.

Planting potatoes was an excellent excuse to think about eating potatoes. As we stood in the barn quartering our seed potatoes, my mind raced ahead to all the delicious things we could make some months in the future.

I love potatoes in pretty much any form—potato chips (but not Lay's, which are too thin); french fries; jacket potatoes, which I ate almost daily in my income-deprived days as a young journalist in London; hash-brown potatoes (both the McDonald's- and Denny's-style ones, especially if you order them extra-crispy). My dad often made his own version of breakfast potatoes on Saturday mornings—grated, flattened in a pan, and cooked until crispy on both sides. I guess you could call them a Chinese latke. Potatoes in breakfast tacos? Yes, please. Potatoes in beef stew? Of course. Once, Tristan and I had breakfast at a diner in Milwaukee where they served a dish called hoffel poffel: chunks of potato, parboiled and then crisped on the buttered griddle, scrambled with egg, onion, and salami, and then topped with American cheese. We still talk about it years later.

While potato plants do flower and produce tiny seeds, the typical—and much easier—practice is to chop up the tubers and plant those. You just have to make sure that each of the pieces has an eye—a growth point from which a new plant can sprout.

We planted our potatoes on Good Friday. I remember that it was Good Friday, because after we'd quartered all the potatoes and were squatting out in the garden, dropping the pieces into the ground and tucking them into little hillocks of compost-enriched soil, my friend Annalise said, "Burial mounds!"

We buried the potatoes in their mounds, in hopes that they would send their sprouts both upward and down. The ones that rose above the ground would become stems and leaves and eventually flowers. The ones that remained down below would form tubers—or, as I saw them, premature french fries.

Around that time, I opened the crisper drawer to see what in-gredients we had for dinner. I noticed three or four potatoes I had left to languish for too long. The skins had wrinkled, and the potatoes had begun to sprout.

On each of the potatoes, I could see little, white bumps. One particularly advanced specimen had grown several two-inch-long shoots. It was almost as if the potatoes were saying, *If you're not going to eat us, we're going to do what we know how to do.*

A couple of weeks later, I noticed the potato plants in the garden had pierced the surface of the soil, deep green leaves unfurling toward the sun. I considered their living testimony: dismembered but not dead. Each piece of potato was its own little Easter story, every one the embodiment of resurrection.

This is my body given for you.

I loved, too, how the potatoes reminded us that darkness can be good. "Burial mounds," Annalise had said, except the tomb was also a womb. The potato needed the darkness to grow. And so many other plants also require sufficient protection from sunlight to take root and blossom—rice, poinsettia, chrysanthemum, primrose.

As the potatoes grew, we had to watch the plants closely. As the stems and leaves rose above the ground, we needed to add soil, building up the mounds to ensure the nascent tubers growing from the roots weren't exposed to the sun. If those tubers saw too much light, a toxin would begin to form that would turn the potatoes green and inedible.

Darkness can be a friend.

worm

The creation of compost is a strange thing. Nate had taught us that it was important that we set the right conditions: a mix of "brown" materials, which are dry and carbon-rich, such as wood chips and fallen leaves, and "green"—nitrogen-rich contributions including vegetable scraps and eggshells. Beyond that, though, very little of the work fell to us.

One day, I called Jean Bonhotal, a compost expert who directs the soil and crop sciences section of Cornell University's Waste Management Institute. I wanted to understand what exactly was happening in the compost pile.

Those of us who tend compost piles "are microbe farmers," Bonhotal said. "They are taking care of something, just like any pet that needs the same things we need—air, shelter, food, moisture. Microbes need all that."

Healthy compost will typically feature plenty of bugs and beetles, but the real workers are the microbes—hundreds of millions of them *per gram*. As the visible creatures break the waste down into ever smaller bits, the bacteria continue the decomposition process. Some bacteria species thrive in cooler conditions, when composting is slowest. As they digest what they can, their activity raises the temperature of the pile, which creates ideal conditions for heat-loving species. These specialize in breaking down hardier debris, including bark and papers. Fungi—mainly molds and yeasts—are present, too, and collaborate with the bacteria to decompose the toughest materials, such as lignin, which gives wood its rigidity and vegetables their crunch.

Bonhotal began learning about this when she was four years old and playing in her grandmother's Catskills backyard. Her grandmother was a talented gardener who saw beauty and glory where others could only see trouble and waste. "She taught me more about weeds—what others would call weeds—than anything else," Bonhotal recalled. "She would take them and put them in her garden, and they produced beautiful flowers."

Bonhotal's grandmother always kept three compost piles in the yard—one active, to which she added her kitchen scraps; one curing, meaning that the microbes had nearly completed their decomposition work and the new soil was cooling and settling; and one finished, which she used for planting and gardening. Today, Bonhotal continues that tradition. She told me that composting is much easier than many people think. She recommended a two-inch layer of wood chips or other carbon-rich material on the bottom "so that it can absorb any odor and allow air in. The microbes have got to have air. If the pile is too wet, you'll have an anaerobic pile and it will stink."

Good compost shouldn't smell bad. The rot is only rank if you've been too lazy to turn your pile properly or if you haven't achieved the right balance between carbon-rich contributions and nitrogen-abundant ones. The earthy, slightly musty smell of good compost is itself a sign of invisible labor being done by the microbes living there.

If you dig into an active compost pile and spot some white or gray threads that resemble dog hair or mold, they're likely acti-nomycetes, an essential form of bacteria. They're especially gifted at digesting the cellulose in plants, and they also produce enzymes that help neutralize toxins in the soil. Actinomycetes, too, need optimal conditions to thrive. They are the reason we're typically taught not to put citrus in the compost pile. It's not that lemon rinds and orange segments will necessarily ruin the compost, but if conditions are too acidic, actinomycetes will work more slowly or not at all.

The most visible residents of the compost pile are the earth-worms.

When I first got to the farm, I didn't want to touch a worm. I blame the great but flawed Reformed theologian John Calvin, who turned the worm into a theological object lesson. "And what can man do," he famously wrote, "who is but rottenness and a worm?"

A version of this story of rotten humanity still thrives in some precincts of Christianity today. To its credit, that worldview seems to be reinforced each time we look at the news and absorb the latest reports of people's cruelty, the endless ways in which we have hurt one another. It's easy to believe that there is indeed rottenness in the heart of humankind. But this narrative, some-times labeled "worm theology," has also been weaponized against many of us: women who claim their full personhood, queer peo-ple, trans people, people who are for some reason labeled "other."

Unfortunately, Calvin had no idea what he was talking about

when he appropriated the worm for his rhetorical purposes. He was a big-city lawyer, not a farmer. His father was a church official, his mother an innkeeper's daughter. He had no firsthand knowledge of the land or its ways, no intimate familiarity with the life of the soil.

Calvin thought he was condemning humankind by describing man as "a five-foot worm," but here is the truth, which offers a richer and worthier reading of the metaphor: God empowered worms to take refuse and transform it into redemption. Worm castings, the fancier term for worm poop, are one of the richest forms of fertilizer we have. In the compost pile as well as in the fields, worms play a crucial role in the production and maintenance of good soil.

We are only just beginning to rediscover the power of worms. There are three thousand species of earthworm. Some are surface feeders that prefer the cooler temperatures of a compost pile in which the microbes have already done much of the work. They continue the processing that has already been begun by bacteria, which they eat along with the broken-down waste. Others, like the red wigglers that are familiar to folks with indoor worm-composting boxes, delight in higher temperatures and kitchen scraps. We are still learning—or in some cases, relearning—about the diversity and scale of their work.

A few years ago, scientists working in tropical wetlands in Colombia and Venezuela discovered the secret behind thousands of odd, lumpy dirt towers that dotted the landscape there, some more than six feet tall. Some researchers had speculated they might be remnants of an ancient agrarian civilization. Eventually, they realized these constructions were mostly built from the excrement of worms native to that region—in particular, the genus *Andiorrhinus*, which often grow to be three feet long.

Not every ecosystem is a good place for worms. In recent

years, some scientists have grown increasingly concerned about North American soils. For unknown reasons, the earthworms native to much of the United States and Canada went extinct at least ten thousand years ago. Today's American earthworms descend from European immigrants that arrived in colonial times, along with some Asian cousins that snuck in more recently, probably in the soil of imported plants. Our vegetable gardens do well with these transplants, but North American forests rely on more acidic soils than the ones these worms leave behind, and the worry is that the earthworms might be transforming those ecosystems to the detriment of native plants.

I said "rediscover" and "relearning" because many of the ancients understood the power of worms. Cleopatra was one of the first known rulers to honor the earthworm. During her reign over Egypt, she forbade both the harm and the export of earthworms, declaring them sacred and asserting that they were one of the blessings the god of fertility had bestowed on the Nile River valley.

Charles Darwin's final book, published not long before his death in the spring of 1882, was devoted to earthworms. He was awestruck by the abundance of worm castings in the world around him. And he rejected the conventional belief that worms were lowly, largely useless creatures. "When we behold a wide, turf-covered expanse, we should remember that its smoothness, on which so much of its beauty depends, is mainly due to all the inequalities having slowly been leveled by worms," he wrote. "The plough is one of the most ancient and most valuable of man's inventions; but long before he existed the land was in fact regularly ploughed, and still continues to be thus ploughed by earth-worms. It may be doubted whether there are many other animals which have played so important a part in the history of the world, as have these lowly organized creatures."

My own people also believed in the special power of worms. The traditional name of the earthworm is *dei long*—literally, "earth dragon." In other words, we named it after the creature that is more respected and honored in Chinese culture than any other, mythical or real.

For millennia, traditional Chinese doctors have harvested earthworms, dried them, and ground them into a medicinal powder. If live earthworms, they reasoned, are skilled at making their way through difficult terrain, aerating the soil, consuming pollutants, and cleansing the earth, maybe dead earthworms can do the same within the human body. Worm powder was said to help clear internal obstructions, assisting the function of the liver, bladder, and spleen. Because of the worm's accordion-like movements, Chinese apothecaries also prescribed the powder for another use: to temporarily lengthen a man's penis.

Not to insult my people, but the earthworm's agricultural powers were more than enough for me. When I spotted my first wriggling worms in the garden that spring, I was delighted. The warming soil had stirred them from their slumber. They felt in their bodies that it was time to get back to work. What an ordinary miracle!

Around that time, my friend Rachel called to ask me to preach at a spiritual retreat she was organizing. This was an unwelcome invitation. I still get nervous sitting at a table talking with one or two strangers—something that has never changed in all my years in journalism. While I'd forced myself to do some public speaking and, after I started seminary, even some preaching, I so dreaded standing up in front of any audience that I avoided eating for hours beforehand, for fear of publicly vomiting.

I told Rachel no.

Though she was several years younger than me, Rachel had never hesitated to take on the cheery yet unmistakably bossy mien of an older sister. She'd heard me speak before, she said, and had no doubts about my abilities. She told me just to be myself. Then she said that she had to go breastfeed her baby, and she hung up.

I'd always admired Rachel's ability to self-differentiate—to say what she needs, to do what feels right to her, to be resolutely her own, humble person. This was true when she was at home even more than while traveling. A stalwart liberal, raised in an extremely conservative town, she stubbornly stayed in the community where she grew up, not minding at all how out of step she was with the prevailing political and religious mores. "This is home," she said, over and over.

When I visited her and her husband a few years before, I'd been struck by the fact that they still ate at the same aged dining room table they'd had their entire marriage, and that this dining room table sat on the same aged linoleum that had been in the house when they'd bought it shortly after their wedding. This was not a sign of inertia. Rachel knew how to look around and know what was enough.

Rachel's gathering was designed for people who were wrestling with their faith, questioning the beliefs with which they'd been reared, or wondering about their place in the Church—or maybe all of the above. For weeks, I struggled to think of anything to say. Eventually, I realized I actually had plenty of thoughts; I was simply afraid to say them. So I decided to talk about fear—and about the compost pile.

But first, I asked everyone in the audience to do two quick little writing exercises. I gave them just fifteen seconds to do each exercise. On one scrap of paper or index card, I told them to write their fears and pass them up to me at the front. On another scrap or card, I asked them to write their hopes, which they held on to.

I had a hunch that many of the fears would be held in common, and they were: These folks were afraid of rejection, failure, being wrong, disappointing God, being alone, not being loved. Person after person wrote the same things down, and they could have been transcribing my own thoughts. "I feel those," I told them. "I fear not belonging, not being enough."

Then I told them about the farm, and in particular, the compost pile—how that pile had become a place of meaning and significance to me. "The more time I spend at the compost pile, the more I wonder whether one thing we might need is a robust theology of compost," I said. "Isn't the story of compost really just the story of God? Turning fear to courage, sorrow to joy, death to life. . . . A robust theology of the compost reminds us that death and the things of death, our sin, our suffering, the ways we hurt one another, the ways we harm ourselves: These things are never the end of God's story."

At the end, I told them that they could go home with the pieces of paper on which they'd written their hopes—to hold and to remember. But I'd take their fears with me, back to the Farminary, where I'd send them all to the compost pile. "There, these ideas, these little bits of death, these fears that are not of God, they will go to die," I said. "And in their death, they will give new life and new soil and new growth."

I think that was a pretty good sermon.

killdeer

One spring day, I spotted a killdeer sprinting across the farm's parking area.

You'd be overly generous if you thought I knew it was a killdeer. I didn't. With its spindly legs, though, I did know enough to think it was a shorebird. As it propelled itself across the gravel in a leggy blur, it reminded me of the fleet-footed plovers I'd seen on Cape Cod, except a bit taller and with a darker body.

Its movements enchanted me. It could go from perfectly still to a full-on sprint just like that—and I wanted to know who it was, what to call it, where it came from, and what it was doing. I downloaded an Audubon bird identification app and answered the prompts until it gave me a few pictures to pick from. That's how I figured out what the killdeer was.

The app told me that while killdeer are typically thought of as shorebirds, they are skilled foragers, too. When not at the beach, they prefer farmed fields, because the plants aren't too tall. They don't particularly mind humans, and have even come to find us useful: They've been known to trail after a tractor or a tiller, digging into the disturbed soil as if it were a buffet. Earthworms, beetles, centipedes, snails, grasshoppers, grubs—all make for a fine killdeer meal.

The efficiency of the killdeer's movements charmed me. It seemed at once to be super-quick and easygoing. To watch it traverse the gravel of our parking lot was to observe a creature that seemed to be in full sprint while retaining the effortless air of someone out for a stroll.

The name for a group of killdeer delighted me too: a season.

I began to keep watch for the killdeer.

One afternoon I went to the farm by myself to do some weeding. I was walking toward the garden when I noticed the killdeer standing by the garden gate, as if waiting to be let in.

I stopped and pulled my phone out, trying to find the bird app as quickly as I could. The app has a collection of bird calls, and I started playing them as loudly as I could. To my surprise, the killdeer began to respond. Every time my phone fell silent, even if only for a moment, the bird would chirp.

The killdeer got its name from one of its calls, which I guess sounded like kill-deer to someone important. I didn't hear that one, but I heard plenty else. Centuries ago, ornithologists noted how vocal these birds are, and took to calling them "noisy plovers."

The killdeer and I went back and forth for a good twenty, twenty-five minutes. I appreciated its attentiveness and its willingness to engage with me. But eventually, it seemed to get bored, and I certainly don't blame it, since I was just playing the same five calls on repeat. Then it occurred to me that I had no idea what I'd been saying to the killdeer. Was I seducing it? Warning it of danger? Did it regard me as some idiot who just kept repeating himself? Even worse: Was I making promises I couldn't keep?

There's a lab in Minnesota where a scientist designed an "anechoic chamber"—a room with steel and concrete walls and fiberglass insulation all designed to make it absolutely silent. In the absence of other sounds, you hear your own body at work: stomach churning, heart beating, air moving in and out of your lungs. It's said that people can't handle being in that room for more than a few minutes at a time.

In nature, as in the body, there is really no such thing as silence. Nowhere am I reminded of this more than the farm. The nonhuman creatures that call this place home, whether temporarily or permanently, are never quiet. The Canada geese in the pond constantly honk in conversation with one another. As the heron dips its beak into the water in search of a minnow, there's a gentle *plink* as it pierces the surface. I rarely see the deer, but I can often hear them, pushing their way through the woods, rustling the underbrush and cracking branches underfoot. That pitter-patter in the barn? Probably a mouse traversing the beams.

When the wind blows, the trees clap. In the springtime, a gentle rustle of soft, newly unfurled leaves tells us that a breeze has arrived, sometimes before we can feel it; by fall, it has grown into a clatter as the leaves have dried. If rain has just come through, the ground crackles as the soil sucks up the water— and if it's been a big storm, it's more like a steady *whoosh*. What can't be absorbed follows the guidance of the terrain, ushered toward the stream and onward to the pond.

My favorite sounds at the farm are the burble and babble of that stream. I like to sit on the stone bridge and listen to the water's incessant progress—the subtle but constant slap against the rocks that reside within the water's path.

I wonder sometimes what life must be like for the aquatic plants that hold on against this current. You can spot them just below the surface—these little green hangers-on that lean constantly in one direction. To me, they look as if they spend their entire lives sideways. Does the world above the surface look sideways to them? I suppose it's a matter of perspective.

The stream never, ever stops moving. It is never, ever silent.

So often we perceive God to be silent.

Or maybe I should be more honest: I have felt God to be silent.

I rarely pray the way I was taught to anymore. I suck at praise, I'm only marginally better at gratitude, and it seems strange, often, to go to the divine with a to-do list of my requests. Instead, prayer has become a running conversation—more questions than answers, and occasionally a plea that God would show up.

This conversation can feel so one-sided. Any hosannas I might muster feel hollow—rote, even insincere. And what hopes I still have seem foolish. Often, the most honest thing I can do, the most heartfelt prayer I have, is to echo the ancient chorus of the lamenting psalmists: "How long, O Lord?"

Usually, there seems to be no answer.

Some of our most respected theologians argue that God is never silent, only failing to speak in a timbre that we can register or acknowledge. The British author C. S. Lewis wrote in *The Problem of Pain* that "God whispers to us in our pleasures . . . but shouts in our pains: It is His megaphone to rouse a deaf world."

This is so unsatisfying to me. That notion of God seems cruel, even sadistic. Lewis suggests that our pain is God's intended tool. Perhaps that was how Lewis chose to make sense of his own significant losses: the death of his dog, Jacksie, when he was four, after which he insisted on being called by its name; the death of his mother when he was nine; the six months he spent on the front lines of World War I in France, which ended with his being wounded and two fellow soldiers being killed by a wayward shell.

For a time, Lewis thought that God seemed cruel, even sadistic, too. He left the Church of Ireland, in which he had been reared, and became an avowed atheist. In *Surprised by Joy,* he quotes the Roman poet Lucretius, who, according to Lewis's translation, wrote, "Had God designed the world, it would not be a world so frail and faulty as we see."

Lewis made his claims about divinely sourced pain years later, in 1940—after his return to Christianity and in the midst of the Second World War. He and his wife were helping to resettle children away from the threat of enemy bombs, and he was well acquainted with many forms of grief and loss. Still, it seems nervy, even impudent, to tell other people that God makes them suffer for their own good. I can't reconcile it with my understanding of a loving, nonviolent God.

That isn't to say that God can't accompany us through pain and suffering—indeed I believe God does. In dire circumstances, we might even find ourselves listening for God in new and different ways, because of our acute awareness of our vulnerability as well as our need for salvation. (I don't mean salvation in that grand cosmic sense so much as in that intimate need for a steadying hand in the midst of grief, or a whisper of solidarity in the throes of trauma.) Who can afford the pretense of independence then? We quiet ourselves because there may be nothing left to say, because we have prayed all the prayers we know how to pray. We do not have words anymore.

It became my habit to listen for the killdeer every time I came to the farm. Some days, afraid that I might misremember its calls and songs, I'd sit in my car and play them on my phone before going to the garden. Most times, I didn't hear the killdeer, which only made me want to hear it more.

When I finally did catch its song one day—*pee-pew, pee-pew, pee-pew,* like the sound effects of an old-school video game—I felt a rush of pleasure. I couldn't see the bird, but somewhere in the distance, I could hear it: *Pee-pew! Pee-pew! Pee-pew!*

It was astounding that such a tiny bird—an adult killdeer weighs no more than five ounces—could sing like that. Which leads me to another thing I don't understand in Lewis's framing of God: On the farm, at least, I can find no evidence of a deity who whispers to us in our pleasures. Here, the delights shriek and shout and cry out, mounting up in a glorious oratorio.

Calvin, in his *Institutes,* considers the ways in which the created world proclaims the glory of God. "It were, indeed, a strange defense for man to pretend that he has no ears to hear the truth" of God and God's presence, he writes, "while dumb creatures have voices loud enough to declare it." He explains that we ought to gain something from "that bare and simple, but magnificent testimony which the creatures bear to the glory of their Creator." Yet we continuously fail to give it our full attention, such that "we either so obscure or pervert [God's] daily works, as at once to rob them of their glory and the author of them of his just praise."

Truth is, I wasn't sure I was willing to listen to those testimonies, let alone join their chorus.

According to a legend among the Yokuts, a Native people of central California, the killdeer is a guardian of the underworld. It keeps watch over the sacred river that separates this life from the next, and there is one particular cry—a shrill *kat-kat-kat*—that it uses to try to deter those whose time has not yet come to cross over.

I never heard that particular call, though I listened for it.

For some weeks, I regularly spotted the killdeer. Often I would stop and talk to it through the app, still not knowing what I was saying, but insisting on trying to make the connection anyway. If the bird had time and nothing better to do, it might humor me for a few minutes. Other times, it wouldn't.

Adaptable as they might be, killdeer are also beautifully, tragically naïve. One day, we found four killdeer eggs in a nest of sand and gravel. To a killdeer's eyes, sand and gravel provide excellent camouflage, protecting its eggs from the seagulls that love to feast on them. That might be true if that sand and gravel were, say, amid some seaside dunes. Less so here, at the edge of the Farminary's parking area.

I checked on the eggs for a few days, and soon I found they had disappeared. We didn't know whether they had hatched (unlikely) or whether they had been crushed by an unknowing car (no evidence) or whether they had become a meal for some lucky predator, maybe one of the foxes that lived nearby (most probably).

I didn't hear the killdeer after that.

It's funny how I kept thinking of it as *the* killdeer, not *a* killdeer, as if it were the same bird the whole time—yet another manner in which I imposed my desired narrative on a story that was probably messier than I wanted to believe. What really happened to my killdeer friend? I hoped it had flown off to spend the summer somewhere beautiful. But just as I won't ever know what I said to it, I won't ever know where it went.

horseradish

The fenced-off garden where we did most of our planting wasn't the only growing space at the Farminary. Back behind the Christmas trees, there was the plot where Nate had first planted, which we'd come to call the Old Garden.

We were poking around the Old Garden one afternoon, trying to decipher what was weed and what was not, when Nate said, "Oh, look! There's the horseradish."

The horseradish wasn't just any random horseradish: It came from a patch tended by Nate's wife's uncle, Harvey, on his farm in Oklahoma. Nate met Janel in college. "The first time I went and spent the holidays with Janel's family, it was like a rite of passage: You had to have the holiday ham with the homemade Jantz family horseradish sauce," Nate told me. The test: "Can you handle this horseradish sauce?"

Of course he could.

After starting the Farminary, Nate asked Uncle Harvey whether he could take some horseradish root back to New Jersey. "We dug some roots out and took them back, and they sat in a plastic bag until things thawed out in the spring," Nate said.

Now here it was, growing on its own, an edible piece of Midwestern Mennonite family lore on a Presbyterian farm in New Jersey.

During Nate's first semester of seminary, a professor made a comment in passing that etched itself into his memory: "White people don't have culture," she said. "They're just American. There's no ethnic identity."

It was a wild statement. Everyone has a culture—customs, social practices, etiquette. To believe that white Americans don't have one is to exoticize the concept of culture as well as to see the dominant culture as normative.

The statement struck Nate as particularly inaccurate in his case. "I do think every family has one, but how many generations back do you have to go before you unearth some of this stuff?" he told me. "And I realized that I had an ethnic identity that was quite unique."

In the seventeenth century, Mennonites from Switzerland, France, and Germany began moving eastward across Europe. Some were fleeing religious persecution. Others, because they were pacifists, left because of military conscription. Nate's ancestors were part of the latter wave. By the late eighteenth century, they had settled in Volhynia, a region then under Polish rule but which was then annexed by Russia. (It now sits in the northwestern corner of Ukraine.)

In the early 1870s, word came that Czar Alexander II was instituting universal conscription. (Previously, only certain classes of peasant had been forced to serve in the military.) So Elder Jacob Stucky led seventy-three families on a long journey from the village of Kutusufka, westward to Liverpool, England, then across the Atlantic, to New York City.

Fourteen of those families went onward to South Dakota, where they already had family. Fifty-nine, including Nate's, took the train to central Kansas.

At the start of the journey, Jacob Stucky composed a hymn, called "Emigration Song."

If by Thy wisdom Thou willst show
What seemest best, where we shall go.
For this we too shall bring Thee praise
In thankfulness our voices raise.
Is it Thy will? Shall it so be?
To leave, and go across the sea?
So Lord, our will shall be Thine own
We'll go the way which Thou hast shown.

The Mennonite émigrés took with them not only their faith but also their culture, including the seeds of what's now known as Turkey Red wheat. This hardy variety, which is planted in the fall and lies dormant through the winter, thrived on the Great Plains. The climate in Kansas was not that different from the one they'd left behind, with long, cold winters and hot, dry summers.

That wheat went into so many of the dishes Nate grew up eating, including verenika (sometimes spelled varenyky)— dumplings stuffed with dried-curd cottage cheese, egg, salt, and pepper. "I don't know whether our people picked it up in Prussia or current-day Ukraine, or if it was more a German thing. But you can boil it or some will fry it," Nate said. "My people are boilers." In some families the dumplings were bathed in ham gravy, but the Stucky household favored a sauce made from fried breadcrumbs and heavy cream.

Another seed that Nate's ancestors brought with them: poppy. He remembers going to his grandparents' house, climbing atop the machine shed, and looking down at the garden. By late spring, an enormous area would be ablaze with the brilliant petals of blooming poppies. In early summer, as the flowers faded, they were left to dry in place. Then Nate's grandparents brought them into their garage, which became a poppy-processing facility. "They would spread newspaper across the floor of the garage, and the entire thing was covered with poppy seed," Nate said. "One head at a time, my grandma would break it open and dump out the seed and put it in a five-gallon bucket. That harvest would last for a year, and they'd save some of it for seed."

Part of that harvest would go to make a cake called mack-kuchen. A few years ago, Nate found some mack-kuchen at a farmers market near Princeton: "Terrible compared to Grandma's." She would grind the poppy seed, add heavy cream and sugar, and that would be the filling. Then she'd make a yeast dough—"this one bread dough that Grandma used for everything"—spread it as thin as possible, layer on the poppy seed filling, roll it, then bake it. "There was always that swirl," Nate said, "and the competition between my grandma, Ethel, and her sisters was the filling-to-dough ratio. The more filling, the less dough, the better the poppy seed roll."

These flavors, these ingredients, these bearers of heritage and journey, so marked Nate's upbringing that when he married Janel, his groom's cake was a poppy seed cake.

Maybe I gravitated toward Nate because he stood just a little distance from his peers. There were no other Mennonites on the seminary faculty, nor were there any others who had both "youth pastor" and "farm manager" on their résumés—or even just the farm manager part. As the farm's director, he wasn't a tenure-track professor, but he also wasn't a regular seminary staff member. In a hidebound academic environment, he was not only trying to do something different; he *was* someone different.

From my early weeks at the farm, I knew the bare bones of the Farminary genesis story. I didn't know that Nate had edited the grief out of that story.

He and Janel always intended to move back to Kansas after he finished his studies. Even after a two-year MA morphed into a PhD that took him eight years to complete, the plan had always been to return to the soils they knew and loved.

In 2014, he and Janel sought the counsel of a friend named Marcus Smucker, a retired Mennonite pastor and spiritual director. He met with them several times, and he kept asking them a question that made them uncomfortable: "What do you want?"

Nate struggled to form an answer. Part of the difficulty was that he had been reared not to give voice to what he wanted. "You just make do with what you have," he told me. "You don't ask for more." To name what he wanted would be to ask for more.

Smucker wouldn't be deterred, and eventually, Nate and Janel named it: They wanted to go home. They wanted to raise their kids around their grandparents, aunts and uncles, and cousins.

"I have no idea what God will do with your desires," Smucker replied. "But I have to believe that God cares very much about what you want."

Not long after that conversation, Nate got a call from Kansas. A dear mentor from his college was retiring, and he wanted Nate to take his place. Everything seemed perfect: He and Janel had bravely named their desire, and now it seemed as if the dream were coming true.

But after Nate interviewed for the job at his undergrad alma mater, it became clear that he was not going to be a good fit. That night, he fell into bed and was brutally honest in his prayers: "I'm sorry, God," he said, "but this just seems cruel."

He has never forgotten what came next—a message that was unexpectedly clear, though not audible: *I am not cruel. And you have no idea where this is going.*

In the death of his dream of going home, Nate was pointed toward a new life as the steward of the Farminary. Instead of returning to the horseradish, the horseradish came back to New Jersey with him.

chicks

For several seasons, Nate had been wanting to expand from flowers and vegetables to raising animals. Now, with a full complement of farmhands, he was ready to give it a try.

On May 17, he went to the local post office to pick up our twenty-six chicks. (Buy twelve, get one free.) He had set up makeshift housing in his garage, spreading sawdust across the bottom of a big cardboard box and installing a heat lamp to radiate the steady warmth the little birds needed in the early stages of life. This would be their home for the first few weeks.

When I went to visit the next day, I saw that one little guy immediately stood apart from the rest. (I don't know why I call him a little guy, because it was impossible at that stage to tell whether they were male or female.) I do not mean that he "stood apart" figuratively: While the others tested their legs and stumbled into one another and staggered around their new home and nestled against one another, this one stayed in a corner of the box, all alone and barely moving. When he finally did decide to move, he plopped himself right in the chicks' drinking-water dispenser. I pulled him out and placed him on the saw-dust, but he didn't even try to shake himself dry. He just stood there, blinking slowly, as if struggling to comprehend how he'd gotten here. How did it come to this?

He and the rest of the chicks had been born in Iowa two days earlier. The idea that you can go online, order a flock of birds, and have them in your mailbox forty-eight hours later seemed absurd to me. But here they were.

All of us come from agrarian roots, though some have to go further back to unearth precisely where they are. Like Pearl, I am a child of many soils.

I spent most of my childhood in the suburbs of San Francisco and then in the outskirts of Miami. I don't really belong to ei-ther, though—neither the golden California hills nor Florida's swampy, subtropical dirt.

I've always struggled to answer coherently when people ask where I'm from. Sometimes I say I'm from California, which is, according to my birth certificate, absolutely true. But then I'll often get this in response: "Where are you *really* from?"

This is a question my people would never ask. Instead, they ask who your people are and where your 鄉下 ("heung ha") is—literally, "Where is your countryside?"

"Where is your countryside?" is not a question about nation-ality or ethnicity but one of heritage and tradition. Where is the dirt from which your people sprang? What soil did your people tend? Where is the earth where your ancestors were buried?

The idea is never that you were born in your heung ha, nor that you have remained there. My parents were both born in British-ruled Hong Kong, and like so many Hong Kong families, our relatives have scattered all across the globe: the United

States and Canada, Switzerland and Australia, Malaysia and New Zealand. Still, we have never forgotten our heung ha.

From the time I was little, I knew that our home village was Chek Lai, about thirty miles northwest of the southern Chinese megacity of Guangzhou (Canton). The name of my grandfather's home village, which is therefore my father's and my home village, even though I have never been there, translates to "red-brown mud." Nobody will ever be able to accuse us of false advertising or over-romanticizing the place.

I was brought up as a child of Chek Lai even though I was born an ocean away, in California, and even though I've never set foot in Chek Lai.

When my father was young, he returned to the village with his family several times. He remembers languorous journeys from Hong Kong that involved multiple modes of transportation—bus, foot, boat—to get to the streamside hamlet a couple days' walk from old Canton. When I asked him recently whether our people were farmers, he said he didn't know. He remembered that his grandmother tended crops in the soil outside her small house, including the vegetables that American seed catalogs call "Asian greens," which we call greens.

Here's an extra wrinkle: Chek Lai is our heung ha now, and has been for as many generations as we have in recorded memory. But we also know that it isn't our true or original home. I do not mean this in the annoying evangelical way that insists on heaven as a Christian's true home. Though we are classified as ethnic Han—the group that makes up the vast majority of the Chinese—our people, our "tribe," is called Hakka (客家). The characters literally mean "visitor family" or "guest household," which alludes to an ancient journey that took us thousands of miles from our ancestral homelands in northern China southward to what is now Guangdong Province. Some historians say that war was the push factor; others attribute the move to famine. In truth, the two are so often braided together that it seems pointless to try to tease out which is which.

My mother's people are Teochew, sometimes spelled Chiu Chow. By stereotype, the Teochew are an opportunistic, adventurous people. Their homeland sits on Guangdong Province's eastern flank, facing the South China Sea, and they have long been tempted by the possibilities of the oceans and lands beyond. My mother's father was born in Singapore, then also a British colony, while his own parents sought a living there as traders. In their native dialect, the Teochew call themselves "our own people," as if they had to remind themselves, once they were scattered, whom they belonged to—who they were and whose they were.

On both sides of my family, then, our story is one of displacement and migration, of war and colonialism, of the propulsive effects of greed and survival, all pulling us away from the land, all moving us farther and farther from our native soils.

While Nate and his family were the chicks' chief caretakers while they lived in their garage, I tried to visit as often as possible. I'd never had any experience caring for poultry, though we did have two canaries when I was a kid. (They were both named Bird.)

Nate taught me how to clean out the water dispenser, refill the feed, and layer fresh sawdust over the birds' poop. When he and his family went out of town, I served as chicksitter. Twice a day, I had to make sure the little guys weren't starving or dying of thirst. As the days grew warmer, I monitored the outdoor temperature to make sure they didn't roast under the heat lamp. Some days, I'd grab some pellets and tempt the chicks to eat out of the palm of my hand.

I've read plenty about how chickens aren't really that smart, but I'm convinced they grew accustomed to me and might even have known who I was. I wondered why they would peck so eagerly at the food in my palm while shunning the food supply on the other side of the cardboard box, which was never empty.

I suppose it's one of the temptations of the novice farmer to speculate about the unprovable inner lives of farm animals. My version of this meant wondering not only whether they recognized me but also if the chicks knew where they had come from and where they were now. Did they even understand "near" versus "far"? It seemed impossible that they would have any memory of Iowa or the industrial hatchery where they and their siblings had been born—or that they would even know what the human-imposed geopolitical construct of "Iowa" was. It seemed ludicrous that they should have any notion of their bloodlines either.

Still, they carried within their little, feathered bodies a story.

All of these birds were Cornish Cross, an American hybrid. One day, I decided to spend some time in the library digging into these chicks' heritage. Turns out the story of the Cornish Cross is also the story of colonization and imperialism, immigration and globalization.

Chickens aren't native to the Americas. The first domesticated birds were believed to have been cultivated in Southeast Asia at least a thousand years before Jesus's time. From there, they slowly dispersed both eastward and west, along trade routes to Mesopotamia and China, then Ethiopia and Europe. Archaeological excavation tells us there were chickens being raised for meat in what is now Chile hundreds of years before Christopher Columbus landed. These birds are believed to have been imported across the Pacific Ocean by Polynesian traders.

Our birds were bred from British and American stock, hence

the name Cornish Cross. But while the Cornish chicken does have some roots in Cornwall, it's really as Cornish as I am American. Its other name, Indian Game, hints at its background. It was bred by Sir Walter Gilbert, an English aristocrat who served as an officer in India, and descends from fighting birds chosen for their well-muscled bodies. Shipped to England during imperial times, these birds were crossed with local breeds, including the Black-Red and the Old English, to maximize meatiness. The Asil, a new arrival from Punjab, was feisty, famed for its cockfighting abilities. But after cockfighting was banned in England in the mid-nineteenth century, the bird's pugnacious spirit became a notable but unmarketable trait. So these savage instincts were bred out of the bird by crossing it with tamer, more overtly domestic breeds.

The other side of the Cornish Cross's family tree, the Plymouth Rock, emerged in Massachusetts in the 1800s. As with so many Americans, the full heritage of the Plymouth Rock is lost to history. But in the mid-nineteenth century, the breed became popular because they were relatively docile and very useful—nourishing whether you wanted a steady supply of eggs or plenty of tasty meat.

What we have now in the Cornish Cross is an extremely white chicken in all senses of the word. Its dark meat has been minimized, its white enlarged to the point that, if you let the chicken live too long, its legs won't be able to support its breasty bulk.

I, too, am a crossbreed.

This chapter in my family's story is set in Macau, the old colonial port established by Portuguese traders in the mid-1500s on the southeastern Chinese coast. For a couple of centuries afterward, Macau thrived, its narrow streets bustling with local merchants and colonial bureaucrats sent from Lisbon. The Portuguese built gracious homes decorated with blue-and-white azulejo tile, erected magnificent churches that blended Baroque architecture with Chinese roof tiles, and paved the streets in calçada—black and white ceramic painstakingly laid by artisans into gorgeous, swirling patterns.

As Portugal's empire faded, so did the colony's fortunes, along with its tiles. In the late nineteenth and early twentieth centuries, relatives of mine still went to trade in Macau. But in the shadow of nearby British-ruled Hong Kong, the city continued to molder, its economy sustained largely by its casinos, which began opening in the 1960s. By the time I was a kid, the only reasons to visit were to gamble or to eat.

Macau's Portuguese heritage endures most powerfully in its distinct cuisine, which is flecked with the spices and scents of other outposts. One of my favorite dishes as a kid was galinha à Africana ("African chicken"): grilled chicken, preferably on the bone, drenched in a heavily spiced, glowingly yellow sauce that soaks into the bed of fluffy white rice. A mainstay of the Macanese menu, there's nothing particularly African about African chicken, except for maybe the hint of peanut and the hot peppers in the sauce. The heat in the marinade, which echoes the fiery piri piri of Portugal's African colonies, has been tamed for the Cantonese palate, which prefers subtler flavors. The coconut milk, also not a typical ingredient in Cantonese cooking, whispers of Goa.

For many years, my personal connection to Macau did not extend beyond a love for dishes like these and an affinity for the architecture of the city, which was just a forty-five-minute hydrofoil ride from Hong Kong. Then, when I was in my early twenties, I began to hear passing references to the origins of the enviable waves in my maternal uncles' hair as well as vaguely European features, including bigger eyes and double eyelids, on the faces of some relatives on my maternal grandmother's side.

By eavesdropping on my elders' conversations, I pieced together that, sometime in the mid-1800s, a Chinese man fell in love with a Portuguese woman in Macau.

I know little of the Chinese man's story. I don't know his name, nor how he ended up in Macau, though I'd guess he was just trying to make some money and find his way in the ever-widening world. Did he have to defy his parents and surrender some semblance of filial piety to marry a foreign woman? We know he was a man of some social status, or at least ambition, because he had the feet of his daughter—my great-grandmother—bound, a status symbol most common among the upper classes. That these women were forced to hobble was a (painful) way of demonstrating that they didn't need to work in the fields.

Unusually for those times, he also equipped that daughter with some education. My great-grandmother became an expert in Chinese medicine. She bore fourteen children, giving birth to all of them without assistance.

I don't know much of the Portuguese woman's story either. Was her father garrisoned at the Portuguese fortress that still sits watch on the hill over the city? Was he an official sent from Lisbon with rubber stamps to mark his authority? Was he a teacher, dispatched to raise up a new generation of pliant locals ready to perpetuate the colonial bureaucracy? Did she have to defy her family's wishes to marry this local? How much wealth did her family have? There must have been some, because her daughter—my great-grandmother—ended up with a sizable inheritance, nearly all of which she eventually gambled away at the mahjong tables.

All I know for sure is that a son of China married a daughter of Portugal, and it was this great-great-grandmother who gave me the 3.125 percent of my ancestry that isn't Chinese. Everything else has faded, much like those Portuguese tiles.

I didn't get the wavy hair genes.

Well fed and properly watered, a Cornish Cross chicken is ready for slaughter in about six to eight weeks, less than half the time it takes an heirloom bird to grow to market weight. This shockingly short timeline helps to explain why it has become a mainstay of industrial meat production in America.

It can be unnerving to see how Cornish Cross chickens are described by breeders. In their catalogs, you'll often see adjectives like "efficient" and "fast-maturing." They "have been selected for fast feathering, steady growth, optimal feed conversion ratios, and broad breasts," one hatchery's website says. These are the birds "that single-handedly changed American eating habits," another boasts. "The best choice for a person who wants to quickly produce delicious meat," adding the ominous warning that they are "nonreturnable."

This hardcore emphasis on hyperproductivity is intertwined with America's hunger for chicken. A century ago, the average American ate about ten pounds of chicken per year. Then, in 1945, the A&P grocery store chain, seeking a fast-growing, affordable source of protein to sell, held a contest called the Chicken of Tomorrow. Farmers were invited to submit eggs. These were incubated, hatched, and raised by the contest organizers so there wouldn't be any variations in diet or growing conditions. The birds were slaughtered when they were twelve weeks old, then judged for their "carcass characteristics"— bigger breasts, fatter thighs, and smaller bones meant higher scores. Also considered was their "economy of production," the amount of food required to achieve this ideal body. Total prize money: $10,000, about $175,000 today.

Forty chickens made it to the national finals. The one entered by Henry Saglio of Connecticut won in the carcass characteristics category. The Vantress brothers of California took top prize for economy of production. Those two birds were crossbred to produce the ancestors of most of the supermarket birds we eat today.

By 1979, annual per capita chicken consumption had soared to thirty pounds per person; by 1989, it was at forty pounds. Today, it's an astonishing ninety pounds per person. Some nine billion birds give their lives each year to be turned into nuggets and tenders, Buffalo wings and fried chicken.

We have taken a creature, a living thing, and optimized it for our purposes, juicing productivity and slashing costs. Intent on getting our chicken as quickly and as cheaply as possible, we have rebuilt these birds. To pick up a shrink-wrapped package of wings or thighs or skinless, boneless breasts or to pull a plastic bag of prebreaded, precooked nuggets from the freezer section is to have only the most distant relationship with the animals that had to surrender their lives to satisfy our consumerist whims.

Nate told the farmhands that our attempts to raise chickens were an effort to recognize that chasm and bridge it a little bit. We'd raise—and slaughter—these crossbred birds as humanely as we could. We would reconnect the chickens to the land, allowing them to roam free and help fertilize our fields. We wanted to be just a bit more aware of what has happened in our food system in the name of convenience, of what might have been lost in this process of hybridization and optimization, packaging and repackaging.

"But why Cornish Cross and not an heirloom breed that

hadn't been subjected to all these refinements and modifica-
tions?" I asked Nate one day.

"Hmm. Good question," he replied. "Availability, price, and
the guidance of the Holy Spirit."

As a Chinese kid growing up in a predominantly white community, I learned quickly to minimize the aspects of myself that
made me stand out.

On the days when my mom packed fried rice or marinated
beef sandwiches in my lunch bag, I'd privately scarf this food
down where other kids couldn't smell it or see it. Sometimes I'd
ask her to give me pizza rolls instead. As I got older, I learned to
emphasize what was wanted, whether on a group project in college or on assignment at work—mainly, my compliance, my productivity, my efficiency, my work ethic, and my utility.

Before I got to the Farminary, I spent most of my days report-
ing and writing magazine stories, yet English words could still be
a struggle for me to form, let alone play with. Not long after I
became a professional journalist, I tried to be a little unortho-
dox and creative with my syntax and diction. After reading an
essay I'd drafted, an editor asked me, "Oh, is English your second language?" (Actually, it is; I spent most of my first few years
in the care of my paternal grandparents, who spoke Cantonese.
I didn't learn English until I went to preschool.)

What I lacked in art, I tried to compensate for in mechanics.
I would show up in the newsroom long before anyone else did; I
would leave later. I wasn't a proofreader, but I read the proofs
anyway. I wasn't any more skilled at finding mistakes, really. I
just tried harder.

In conversation, I lacked the fluidity of my peers, with their allusions to movies I'd never seen and music I'd never heard. I didn't have their language either. In fourth grade, I got disciplined for repeating the phrase "bull crap," which had just been uttered by another kid on the bus; I'd never heard it before, I didn't know what it meant, and I couldn't understand why I was in trouble.

So I learned to compensate with my relative silence and by making myself useful by other means. At parties I gravitated toward the kitchen, where I could chop and pour and arrange things neatly on platters and spare myself most of the awkward small talk. At the office, I never stood around the water cooler chatting; even in my twenties I'd mispronounce words, and I never forgot the uproarious laughter when I did. (How was I supposed to know how to say "Gaia"?) But I was glad to be able to put a home-baked loaf of cranberry-walnut bread on the communal table. Food was a currency I could trade in, and people always seemed to want to fill their stomachs with something.

I longed to be respected, but I settled for being useful—and some days I fooled myself into thinking these were the same. In becoming the thing that is useful to other people, though, what do you lose? In conforming yourself to what the system wants and most values, what are you forced to give up?

summer

slaughter

Nate killed the first chicken.

He gently pulled it from a yellow crate in which we had transported five birds from the pasture where they had spent the last month of their lives. As it flapped and squawked in protest, he cradled it, tail up, until it stilled and quieted. Then he put it headfirst into one of the four metal cones on the slaughter stand.

He took a sharp knife and quickly drew it across the bird's neck, severing the carotid arteries and initiating a gush of blood. Then he stepped back and bowed his head.

He, Cogan, and I formed a silent semicircle around the stand. I wanted to look away, wanted to run out of the barn, wanted to be (almost) anywhere but here. I'd been thinking for days about this moment, and still I wasn't prepared. I wanted to pray, but for what? I didn't have words. I just willed my eyes to stay on the dying bird, counting silently as an act of discipline.

One, two, three . . . fifteen, sixteen, seventeen.

About thirty seconds later, the bird started jerking violently, shaking the metal stand. When it finally stopped, the barn was silent. I don't remember saying anything as Nate demonstrated the rest of the process to Cogan and me—scalding, defeathering, gutting, plopping the carcass into an ice bath. The word "process" feels too clinical to describe how a living, breathing creature becomes a piece of meat.

I've never been squeamish about recognizing that what we call "meat" is a dead animal. I was raised with no illusions: Every visit to Chinatown meant at least a little time gazing in the windows of roast-meat shops, where poached chickens and roasted ducks hung whole, skin glistening and lacquered in soy. On childhood visits to Hong Kong, I'd go with my grandmother to the local markets, where fishmongers thwacked live grouper and wrasse with mallets. Long before "whole animal" cookery became trendy, cultures including mine were practicing it. If we had duck for dinner, my mom would deposit the remnants of the bird back into a pot along with leftover rice, the bones and fat imparting their seasoning and meaty depth to the next morning's porridge.

I learned early on that this was abnormal in America. I was one of those Chinese kids who grew up enduring the lunchroom ritual of opening my lunchbox to a chorus of *eeeews* from the other kids. They had their chicken tenders; I had my soy sauce chicken on the bone. They had their pepperoni pizza; I had slices of pork shoulder that my mother had marinated overnight, stir-fried first thing in the morning, and then tucked into a bun.

In elementary school, on the days when a kid named Derek didn't manage to steal my lunch and throw it away, I learned, when asked what my mom had packed, to puckishly respond, in my braver moments, "Pig." It was a little jab against a culture that loved its pork yet hated thinking about where it came from. It was an act of juvenile resistance against people who claimed to appreciate Chinese food yet mocked the real thing—and the people who made it.

For all my own culinary sanctimony, though, I'd never raised an animal for meat, nor had I killed anything bigger than a two-pound flounder.

In the two months that our chickens were with us, even the ardent meat-eaters among my fellow seminarians questioned why we were raising broilers, not layers. Friends and family, too, had their wonderings: Why not eggs? Are you really going to kill these birds?

I had my answers ready, which I trotted out in conversation after conversation:

It would be nice to have eggs, but we don't have someone at the farm every day year-round to care for layers.

We're giving these birds a much better quality of life than they might have had at a factory farm.

If we're going to eat meat, we should understand what raising chickens entails—and we should be willing to kill them. If we're not, then maybe we also shouldn't be eating meat.

Even as I said these things, I felt unconvinced by them. They were all true, technically, but they felt too tidy, too pat. I wished for rationales and responses that were more deeply intellectual, and certainly more theological. But this was the best I could come up with.

A few weeks before the slaughter, an envelope had arrived in the mail from my mother-in-law, with whom I'd shared many a happy conversation about the delights of fried chicken and to whom I had texted cute pictures of our fluffy chicks. When I opened it, I saw that it was a Father's Day card.

"What's this for?" I asked my husband. We have no children.

He glanced at it, then instantly replied: "The chickens."

A few days later, I texted my mother-in-law a photo of a fat hen.

"Name?" she wrote back.

"Haha no names!! That will make it harder to eat them!" I replied.

"Exactly," she said.

Two birds in the flock had acquired nicknames during their time with us: From infancy, Gimpy had had an unexplained limp. And Lumpy had remained nameless until she developed a large, goiter-like growth just below her neck. After that, she was easily identifiable by her dramatically lopsided breasts.

I avoided Gimpy and Lumpy when it came time for me to choose my first bird to slaughter. Instead, I took one of their nameless white sisters out of the crate and tucked her into the crook of my right arm. "It's okay. *Shhhh,*" I whispered, stroking her head with my left hand. "It's okay. It's okay."

What an absurd thing to say. This was absolutely not going to be okay for the chicken. The words were more for me—a litany of self-justification to crowd out my guilt.

My first kill, which Nate supervised, went as smoothly as these things can go, but you can sense my severe discomfort in the very fact that I am calling this "my first kill." Any confidence that might have grown in me, any attempt to claim that I had some natural-born slaughtering skill, disappeared within five minutes, when I slaughtered my second chicken. Maybe my knife-wielding hand was shaky; maybe my nerves overtook me: I still don't know. But I did not get a clean cut.

I drew the knife across her neck, and within a few seconds, the chicken began writhing and convulsing and squawking. I glanced nervously around the barn, to see if either Nate or Cogan had noticed, but they were focused on gutting birds. I went in for a second cut, pushing harder this time, which increased the blood flow but didn't quiet the hen. Finally, not knowing what else to do, I broke her neck.

"I didn't get a clean cut," I said to nobody in particular. "I didn't get a clean cut. I didn't get a clean cut."

It was a confession in search of absolution that could not come soon enough. My eyes filled with tears of guilt and regret. I felt that I had made the chicken suffer more than absolutely necessary. Before the hen closed her eyes for the last time, I swear she gave me a look filled with disdain.

After that, I couldn't see much of anything through my tears. I swiped at my nose with my sleeve. A minute or so later, I pulled the dead chicken out of the metal cone and went numbly through the next steps: in and out of the scalder, in and out of the defeatherer. Then I flung the naked body onto the stainless-steel butchering table and ran out of the barn.

Cogan gave me a sympathetic half smile when I walked back in a few minutes later, but neither he nor Nate said anything.

Finally, Nate asked, "You all right?"

I didn't answer.

"You don't need to be all right," he said.

I don't know how much time had passed before I noticed a red, boomerang-shaped gash across the inside of my right forearm.

The blood had already clotted. I'd done what I'd done to the chicken; it seemed only fair that she had left her mark on me.

I cleaned the cut, applied some disinfectant, and put on a bandage. Then I got on with the work. Within a couple of hours, we had all the birds but one bagged in plastic and chilling in the refrigerator. We slaughtered Lumpy, too, which was when we learned the weird tumor was actually a big blob of food that, because of some chronic digestive misrouting, had accumulated and festered within her body.

"Should we confess?" Cogan asked after we were done.

I froze. Confess for what? To whom?

His question made me uncomfortable. Part of me felt that we should, but I couldn't really tell you why. Was he suggesting we might have done something wrong? I couldn't stop thinking of the poor job I'd done on that one bird, but did he mean for this whole project?

I shrugged, because I didn't really have any answer.

Should we confess?

In the Reformed tradition, a worship service always begins with the liturgist reciting the Votum, an acknowledgment of who God is and who we are in light of that conviction. Usually, it's taken directly from Psalm 124:8: "Our help is in the name of the Lord, maker of heaven and earth." Everything else proceeds from that profession, that God is God and we are not.

In confession we elaborate on that recognition, naming aloud the ways in which we have forgotten where our help comes from: individual sins as well as collective ones, personal wrongdoing as well as systemic injustice, passive neglect as well as active harm. We not only admit our ungodliness but also acknowledge our un-Godness.

I didn't grow up Reformed. In the Baptist churches of my childhood, there was no ritual of collective confession. Instead, it was something you did alone in your seat, silently, head bowed and eyes closed, as you waited for the communion tray to be passed. In the churches I attend now, you usually go to the bread and wine instead of it coming to you, but I guess I still get a little Baptist in those precommunion moments. As I move up the church aisle, I sometimes run down a little list of what I think I've done wrong—which typically includes most if not all of the seven deadly sins. (Unsurprisingly, gluttony is my favorite.)

I never get to the end of the list, though. Instead my mind inevitably goes on walkabout: *Is my shirt tucked in? . . . I don't want to trip . . . I left my bulletin in my pew so I don't know the words to this hymn . . . I'm hungry. What kind of bread are we serving? If it's challah, I hope I get a big piece.*

Self-absorption, greed, gluttony: I cannot even get through the act of approaching the communion table without accumulating more impurities. Which makes the absurd grace of the spiritual trade imbalance—Christ's body and blood in exchange for my sins—all the more evident.

Should we confess?

Perhaps not, if the ritual is about self-consciousness or self-soothing. Not if the act draws me further within myself instead of moving me toward all that is holy. Not if the exercise becomes more about self-flagellation than gratitude.

Perhaps also not if it means I focus on my impurities instead of the liberating God who calls me to surrender them. Not if I'm wallowing in my own shame instead of receiving these divine gifts, not least of all the life that has been given so that I might live more abundantly. Not if I'm still standing at a distance from the never-ending story of life, death, and resurrection.

Perhaps not if I'm still unwilling to admit that I don't have to be all right.

keys

Here's what I didn't say earlier about the chicken slaughter: Midway through the morning, Emily and Pearl had arrived. They were taking Greek classes during the summer semester, so they could only join us for a brief time during their lunch break.

Nate, Cogan, and I had spent the morning working in near silence. The chickens—squawking, trilling, sighing—provided the soundtrack. Then we heard tires crunching on the gravel outside, and, moments later, Emily and Pearl burst into the barn.

Emily seemed to struggle to take everything in. She strained to keep a smile on her face.

Pearl wandered around the barn, clapping her hands and squealing. "Amazing!" she kept saying, as she surveyed the blood-splattered slaughter area. "Amazing."

A complicated mess of feelings simmered under the word "amazing": Worry about Emily, who had narrated her nervousness throughout their entire drive to the farm. Pride at having helped tend to this flock of chickens. A sense of sacred importance at having witnessed nearly their entire life cycle. Sadness, though Pearl knew that slaughter had been the plan all along. It was all, she said, "so wild and so special."

All this she channeled into more chatter and joking, and with every word of their cheery banter, I felt my anxiety rise. As Nate walked them through the slaughtering process, Pearl never stopped talking and Emily kept giggling.

I knew it was a nervous giggle because Emily and I had discussed beforehand her mixed emotions about the slaughter. Emily was flirting with vegetarianism at the time, but she took her commitment to the work of the farmhand seriously. She felt it was important to kill at least one bird.

She slowly lifted a chicken out of the crate, holding it as far from her body as her arms would allow. Even as she turned the bird upside down and placed it headfirst into the cone, I could see the tears welling in her eyes. She slashed the bird's neck as quickly as she could. Then, hand trembling, she replaced the knife atop the stand.

Pearl told me later that Emily had sobbed their whole drive back to campus and all through Greek class that afternoon. "It looked like someone in her family had died. . . . She was bawling the entire time, and people were like, 'What's wrong?' It was awful. She looked devastated. And honestly, I felt robbed."

"Robbed" struck me as an odd word to describe the experience. Sure, Pearl had more farming experience than any of the other farmhands, she had felt personally invested in the cultivation of the chickens, and she was frustrated that she hadn't been able to participate in the entirety of slaughter day. But "robbed" seemed to suggest ownership that could never have been hers.

Nate knew that each of us was wrestling with our own particular mess of emotions, so a few days later, he scheduled a debriefing. We met on the patio behind his house.

As we sat in the dappled shade, Pearl could not stop gushing about what an "amazing" experience the slaughter had been. There was that word again! She went on and on about the joy and the wonder of it all, and with every sentence, I felt my glower harden.

I could have—probably should have—let her sunniness be. Perhaps I could have even let it pierce my own gloom. But I didn't want to be moved; I wanted *her* to move. I wanted her to see me. I wanted her not only to see me—because maybe she did, and that was why she was being as insistently upbeat as she was—but also not to rush me out of my pain.

I could have just said that, except I didn't know how. Instead, as Pearl said one more time that the chicken slaughter had been "just amazing," I blurted out, "I resent that."

She shot me a hurt look, and then she didn't say anything else.

A few days later, just before he and his family left town for their summer vacation, Nate handed me the keys to the farm. Neither he nor I knew just how consequential that simple act would be.

Pearl grew more and more distant. Some days she would walk to the farm from her room on campus, which took forty-five minutes. She would always say she needed the exercise, and, anyway, she didn't want to burden anyone by asking for a ride. Other days, she just didn't come, and if I texted to ask where she'd been and whether everything was okay, the messages went unanswered.

I suspected this was a way of asserting her independence, of signaling that under no circumstances should I imagine myself to be in any kind of authority over her. You only needed the keys if you were in a car. Arrive on foot, and the keys didn't matter: You could just walk around the locked chain and right down the driveway.

Even though I kept putting Pearl on the work schedule, her presence diminished until her appearances became a surprise. When she did show up, she seemed a shadow of the joyous self who had once delighted in the farm. I never found the courage to ask what was bothering her. In truth, I was afraid to know. So I reminded myself I wasn't her supervisor; I was just the guy who did the schedule. So I kept doing my thing and I let Pearl do hers.

Throughout the summer, a local food bank regularly sent trucks to the Farminary packed with produce that it couldn't give away; Nate had told the folks at the food bank that we could compost whatever they brought to us.

On the good days, something salvageable would arrive. Once it was a box of decent avocados, another time, a case of local spaghetti squash—all in such perfect condition that we invited our CSA shareholders to take as many as they wanted. The best? A couple pallets of heirloom tomatoes, nearly all of which were flawless or just slightly bruised. I took twenty pounds home and turned it into sauce for the winter months.

Then there were the not-so-good. The case of rotting frisée was bad. Worse: the hundreds of bags of spinach that had already partly liquefied; it took us a few hellishly hot July days to open all the plastic bags, empty the sludge into wheelbarrows, and cart it to the compost pile. The worst: fifty cases of bagged "sweet kale" salad kits.

Those salad kits were diabolical. Inside each big plastic bag were twelve ounces of chopped vegetables—kale, radicchio, brussels sprouts, broccoli, cabbage—as well as a smaller plastic pouch. Inside that pouch were two even smaller plastic packets, one containing salad dressing and the other dried cranberries and pepitas.

Pouch by pouch, packet by packet, we had to liberate everything that was compostable and discard the rest—an all-hands situation. To my surprise, the whole farm team showed up, including Pearl, along with a couple of other students who'd heard we could use extra help. Slowly, we picked our way through the hundreds and hundreds of plastic bags. It was an infernal afternoon. My eyes stung from sweat. The fruit-and-seed packets particularly vexed my slippery fingers, and as the temperature and humidity rose and rose, so did my irritation at the gods of convenience and the immense amount of waste they inspire. Was it really too much work to make a simple salad?

Around three P.M., Emily said, "Where's Pearl? I haven't seen her for a while."

Then we heard a burst of uproarious laughter and followed it to the side of the barn, where Pearl and the student volunteers were sitting in the shade. Though the rest of us kept working for a couple more hours, they never rejoined us.

When I asked Nate later why he'd given me the keys and not Pearl, he said simply, "I trusted you."

The devastating thing had been left unsaid, but Pearl felt it anyway. She couldn't—and didn't—name it, but I could read it in her body language, in her growing distance from me and the rest of the farmhands, in her increasing reticence on the ever-rarer days when she did come to the farm.

It took her months and months to tell me how much it hurt—and she never said anything to Nate. "You were given the keys to the kingdom and I one hundred percent was not," she told me later. "I was invited. It was like he was saying to me, 'You can stop by, but you can't have the keys.'"

She insisted she didn't resent any of the other responsibilities I'd been given. "Nate was one hundred percent correct that I would never have gotten the seed orders right," she said with a loud laugh. "All that other shit, I didn't want to do. The keys, though? It was the keys. To me, the keys meant you got to be connected to the farm in a way that I was repeatedly denied."

The thing I could never understand: Why hadn't Nate just made a second set of keys? One day, I finally asked him. He cocked his head in puzzlement and paused for a long moment. Then he said, "I never even thought about that."

body

Early in the summer, Nate texted to ask me to close the barns at the end of a workday.

I don't know if it was the rusty rollers or the way the thing was constructed, but the middle barn door felt heavier than the other two. I pulled. I pushed. I pulled again. I pushed some more. I got a splinter. I lost my balance and fell. After fifteen minutes, I'd moved the door no more than six inches. Finally, I gave up and asked Emily if she could help.

I felt a little humiliated, but this was nothing new. Most days and every night, I hate my body.

I hate my slightness—a body that isn't invisible yet goes unseen. Once, my pastor said to me, "How do you just slip in and out of a room like that? You're like a ghost! One minute I see you, the next minute I don't." But I hadn't moved. I'd been there the whole time.

I hate my shortness in a society that honors the tall. It's not just my whole body that's short. I had a suit custom-made once; as he measured, the tailor got a quizzical look on his face and then said, "Your torso is weirdly short!" (It does mean I can buy shirts in the kids' section, which saves money.)

I hate my eyelids, which lack the double fold.

I hate my coarse hair. A relative once touched it and exclaimed, "It feels like hay!" You can't flip this hair or toss it. A wind machine doesn't make it look sexy, just unkempt.

I hate, too, the blackness of my hair. When I was a teenager, I'd stare in the mirror at summer's end, satisfied that the sun had bleached my hair to something more resembling a chestnut brown, at least if you looked at it squinting, in the right light. I'd never be blond enough to be seen as all-American, but at least this got me a couple of shades closer to acceptable.

I hate the pain my body carries.

On the inside of my upper arm, just above my right elbow, there's an ache, stronger some days than others, where a tunnel containing a nerve has collapsed over the years. I wish it were some sports injury, something with a sexier backstory—maybe tennis elbow? But no. It's just another marker of my stereotypical Chinese American childhood—a reminder of the years that arm spent bent and contorted by Bach and Mozart, violin and viola.

I hate the fragility of my body. At twenty-seven, I was diagnosed with a colonic condition that left me uncontrollably dripping blood. A doctor said it was partly stress; he put me on a course of strong steroids, which to my dismay weren't the kind that builds your muscles but a kind that fed the acne I'd long struggled to control. Then a naturopath told me that my body doesn't like red wine, blue cheese, or mushrooms, which I'd been consuming in abundance; she issued orders for a strict diet of saltless poached chicken breasts and salad dressed with only lemon. I have a body that punishes me for delight.

I hate the weakness of my body, which sometimes feels like

little more than a carrying case for my brain, the only muscle my parents ever sought to develop. I remember going to Pride one June in London; all around me were the glistening, well-muscled bodies of shirtless white men—arms and pecs and abs with the definition of topographical maps, sweat coursing down the perfect hills and valleys. I wanted to buy myself a burka, but it would have been beside the point, given that nobody saw me anyway.

I hate this body, which can't even complete a one-person job—closing a barn door at the end of a workday—without another body's help.

Love your enemies, Jesus said.

Jesus's story was fleshy. We actually know very little about what happened within Jesus's soul; the Bible tells us far more about the experience of his body.

His body suffered. His body bore flogging and prodding. His body bled. But before that, his body hungered. I love that he once cursed a fig tree for not giving him the fruit he wanted—out of season, no less! I love that, after he rose from the dead, he asked his disciples for something to eat.

For all this, modern Christianity—or at least the American Protestant version of it—has done its best to free itself from all corporeality. I don't recall a single Sunday sermon from my childhood in which the preacher addressed our physicality in a positive way. If the body was addressed during worship, it was during the prayers of intercession, when we remembered Carlos's fragile heart or Kathy's swollen brain, Viola's weakened legs or Pat's failing organs. Of course you could talk about your physical aches and pains during coffee hour, but not too much, or else you'd quickly find your conversation partner edging back toward the cookie table.

Instead, we talked about souls.

The bifurcation of body from soul has a long history. While Augustine acknowledged that a human was both body and soul, he made clear which mattered more. "The corruptible body oppresses the soul," he wrote, "and the earthly tabernacle burdens the mind that muses of many things." Bernard of Clairvaux seemed to see the body in almost utilitarian terms. At its best, the body could be "a help to the soul that loves God," he wrote, "a good and faithful comrade for a good soul." If a person fell ill, for instance, the suffering of the body could be seen as "an aid to penitence," because it reminds the sufferer of the folly of self-reliance and compels them to turn toward God.

For those of us who read the Bible in English, this soul division results partly from inadequate translation. Pretty much every English version consistently renders the Hebrew word *nefesh* as "soul." But that's not exactly what it means. According to the literary scholar and Hebrew Bible translator Robert Alter, translating *nefesh* as "soul" "suggests a body-soul split alien to biblical thinking." He prefers "person" or "life" or "being"—all terms that encompass not just the spiritual but also the physical.

One semester, I took a class called Prophets from the South, taught by the eminent South African theologian Dirk Smit. He wanted to expose us to writings about God from a different space, place, and social location than our own. One of our assigned readings was the book *After the Locusts,* by Denise Ackermann, an Anglican feminist scholar and antiapartheid activist. In her late sixties, she felt a pull to collect her theological reflections and personal memories in a book accessible to a general audience. But how? Her writing had always been scholarly. She eventually settled on "letters to people who matter to me, about the themes that have been at the core of my search for healing and freedom." Letters, especially those to recipients including lifelong confidantes and her two young granddaughters, she explained, were "a vehicle to keep me from academic excesses."

Perhaps the most moving letter, addressed to her longtime friend Elfriede, dwells on questions about the body. Ackermann indicts the Church for how it has "failed to see the body as a source of knowledge." "Making love, giving birth, dancing, eating, wrestling with depression or arthritic joints—these are not only bodily realities," she writes, but also spiritual ones. An incarnational faith had to recognize that "our bodily experience is the fundamental realm of the experience of God."

Reading other people's mail has always given me secret pleasure, whether it was my mom's correspondence with my favorite aunt in Hong Kong or Paul's letter to the Romans. Here is Ackermann, commiserating with another woman about all that their bodies have had to bear, physically and symbolically. "If the body has been a source of pain," she writes, "one prefers not to be identified with it. One tends not to trust it. Besides that, we women do not want to be defined solely in terms of our female bodies in such a way that our anatomy is our destiny." And yet! "Our bodies are more than skin, bone, and flesh. Our bodies encompass the totality of our human experience, our thoughts, our emotions, our needs and memories, our ability to imagine and to dream, our experiences of pain, pleasure, power, and difference, as well as our beliefs and our hopes. Our bodies are, in fact, the intricate tracery of all that is ourselves, the good and the bad."

The intricate tracery of all that is ourselves.

I found this particular line exhilarating—and it thrilled me to think about bodies, in general, in such terms. But as soon as I thought of my own body, I realized: I still didn't know how to see this body as a gift.

I started hating my body when I was ten. Not long before, we'd moved from Northern California, where many people looked like me, to a small town in New Jersey, where almost nobody did.

There were three other Asians in the fifth grade. Dina, Chinh, and Laura had spent their entire childhoods in that overwhelmingly white town. Dina was the most popular; she had an easy laugh, a calm manner, and an open spirit that endeared her to everyone. Chinh, who lived on the less affluent side of town, had sharp humor and a winning wit he deployed to deflect and defuse. Laura had no friends; she spent recesses standing at the edge of the playground, wearing a long coat, no matter whether it was hot or cold, and a constant glower.

I also had three bullies that year.

Rick had a precocious and powerful physicality. Recess typically meant dodgeball, and if I dared to play, he would target me first, channeling his strength into that red rubber ball. He never missed. If I didn't play, no matter: The game became chasing me. He had the strength and speed of a tight end, and he used his entire body like a guided missile.

Kristin had a body that I suspect she loathed, too, but she, too, was able to use it as a threat. "Chu," she said again and again, "I'm going to sit on you."

My chief bully's name was Mac. He wasn't much taller than me, but his preferred brand of bullying was different from Rick's and Kristin's. It required only his perceptive eyes and big mouth.

Every fifth grader was assigned a kindergarten buddy; as the eldest students in our elementary school, we were to serve as mentors for the youngest. My buddy was Stephanie, a quiet, blond girl with lively, darting blue eyes and a defiant chin.

"Hey, Stephanie," Mac said one day. "Don't spend too much time with Jeff, or your eyes might start looking like his." He put his fingers to his face, pulled his eyes outward, laughed, and walked away. Stephanie's eyes widened. Mine filled with tears.

Multiple other days, Mac made fun of my bowl haircut. I'd never been to a barber; why spend the money? my mother thought. Once a month, she would get out her haircutting scissors, drape a nylon apron around me, and cut as straight across as she could.

The day of the fifth-grade holiday concert, our music teacher paraded us onto risers in the lunchroom to perform for those parents who either didn't have to work or had jobs flexible enough to let them do things like attend concerts in the middle of the day. Throughout the concert, Mac, who was standing next to me, teased me relentlessly under his breath while we sang "Jingle Bells." He mocked my appearance. He made fun of my voice. Finally, he asked where my mom was, knowing she was one of the few mothers in the class who worked outside the home and couldn't be at the concert.

It was all I could do to hold my tears in until we marched off the risers, at which point I began hyperventilating and sobbing. My classmate Dina's mom quickly pulled me into a hallway, away from the other students, and tried to console me. I refused to tell her what had happened—I wasn't going to be a tattletale on top of everything else. But I was glad for Mrs. Lee's warm, motherly hug—and at the same time I loathed it, because she wasn't my mom.

Here is what I learned in the two years I lived in that little town: It would have been better if I were taller. It would have been better if I were stronger. It would have been better if my eyes were shaped differently, if my hair were lighter and wavier, if my skin were paler. It would have been better if I had been born white.

Also, I still hate "Jingle Bells."

The scriptural equivalent of the coziest, Grandma-made afghan, always there to offer me some warmth even on the coldest nights, has always been the last little bit of Romans 8. In the winsome way of the King James: "For I am persuaded, that neither death, nor life, nor angels, nor principalities, nor powers, nor things present, nor things to come, nor height, nor depth, nor any other creature, shall be able to separate us from the love of God, which is in Christ Jesus our Lord."

I love that little comma after "persuaded." I know it's just in the King James, not the original Greek. Still, I like to imagine the apostle Paul saying, *Well, I could stop here, and it would be enough.*

I am *persuaded.*

I *know.*

I am *convinced.*

I *believe.*

I am *persuaded.*

Then he proceeds to explain exactly what he is persuaded of, an explanation that is one of the most gorgeous passages of reassurance in all Holy Scripture. Even during the years when I could go nowhere near a church, I would return to these verses. They were a perfectly formed little container that held what remained of my hope.

But here is the question I always asked, the one chip in that gorgeous (if true) little container: What if the thing that separated me most from God was not something outside me but rather my very self? What if it was this ramshackle assemblage of bones draped over with skin, none of which had been redeemed from the pollution of this world? What if it wasn't in fact "any other creature" but this one, this creature, this being that was reading these verses and struggling to believe them and picking at that chip in the container? What if I was the unlovable one?

Later in his letter to the Roman church, Paul explores the body of Christ and our sense of membership in that body. As I contemplated those passages in the late-night moments of solitude when there was no more busyness to distract my thoughts, I wondered whether the things I had done with my body, the things that had been done to my body, had negated the possibility of belonging, to God or to God's people.

I couldn't forget the alienation I felt when I came out—the *dismemberment.* As I tried to talk about my growing awareness of my sexuality with people who said they loved me, they responded by proclaiming not only their sadness but also God's disappointment. The brilliant persuasions of Romans 8 began to lose some of their shine. They began to seem less like reassurance than aspiration, less like aspiration than taunt.

Nothing can separate me from the love of God? This body seems to have done it.

The CSA pickup at the farm happened every summer Tuesday, between 4:30 and 6:30 in the afternoon. Only ten families, all with some connection to the seminary, had shares.

One sultry afternoon in August, just as the CSA pickup time began, the other farmhands and I were standing next to wheelbarrows, much as we had been for the previous three hours. We had finished preparing the farm shares early, so we were now at the other end of the produce life cycle, making what I like to call "compost salad." The local food pantry had made a delivery of expired produce. Moldy tomatoes. Withered fennel. And, worst of all, hundreds more bags of that prepackaged salad—spinach and lettuce and frisée so rotten it had essentially juiced itself.

The CSA pickup time was revealing, telling half stories about human behavior and relationship. Some shareholders would drive up to the farm and, ignoring the fact that the rubber of the tires against the gravel of the drive had loudly announced their arrival, they'd skitter into the barn head down, grab their stuff, and go. Others would glance around, even meet my eyes, but then look away. I don't know why. I can't know.

Jan Ammon, the minister of the seminary's chapel, and her husband, Greg, had a CSA share. When Jan showed up to pick up her share, she came over to the farmhands to say hello and offer hugs. I tried to evade her—really, to save her from my sweaty filth—but not even the stinkiest body would put her off. She wrapped me in a hug.

This might seem the tiniest thing, but it wasn't. In her insistence and in her embrace, I felt loved, just as I was—a rare and lovely thing.

Then there was a faculty member who showed up nearly every week. She had little time for me. If she spoke to me at all, it was only to ask a question about the week's share. More than once, this person walked past as if I wasn't even there. Though the professor greeted other students with great enthusiasm, I never even got that standard-issue question-but-not-a-real-question: "How are you?"

One day, she had a visitor with her. She decided to introduce me, though she didn't address me. "This is Jeff," she said to her guest, arms folded tightly over her chest. "He works on the farm."

I started avoiding the barn during the CSA distribution, at least until I saw the taillights of this professor's car. I'd squat in the garden and weed. I'd be especially slow with the last of that day's harvest. I'd just keep composting—and there was always composting to do. Better to make myself invisible than to open myself up again to a reminder of my invisibility.

One by-product of chronic invisibility is a heightened sense of attentiveness to the world and the people around us. "We were older than they in the sense of what it took to live in the world with others," the narrator says in Ralph Ellison's novel *Invisible Man*. We have not enjoyed the luxury of ignorance or the comfort of self-centeredness. We have had to understand what it means to navigate around others, to carve out our space around others and among others, to know our place and sacrifice appropriately—unjust as that may be.

Anyhow, I wondered sometimes whether I should be grateful for such candor on the professor's part. At least this person wasn't pretending to give a shit about me. Some days I feared that I was being overdramatic—and maybe I was. But my body was also telling me something: I had felt this alienation, this diminution before. My encounters with this professor were ricocheting off my memories. And one insidious aspect of this kind of invisibility is that I've been trained at times to see things that may not in fact be there: What had I done wrong? What might I have said to deserve this? In what way(s) was I insufficient?

Invisibility strikes me in my most tender place—a place that can't be mapped by physiologists. It's the spot Miller Williams writes about in his poem "Compassion": "What seems conceit, bad manners, or cynicism is always a sign of things no ears have heard, no eyes have seen. / You do not know what wars are going on down there where the spirit meets the bone."

I didn't know about that professor's internal warfare. What might have been going on where her spirit met her bone? What unspoken story did those folded arms hint at? What pain must remain invisible to me?

But if I didn't know about that professor's warfare, she also didn't know about mine. She had no idea about the wars going on down there where my spirit met my bone.

Sometimes I wonder what it would be like, just for a day, to be a tall, blond, blue-eyed white man. What do the tops of people's heads look like? What might it feel like to have to duck occasionally through a doorway, as if the built environment could not contain all of me? What might it be like to have a body that looked more like it could protect itself?

The year I turned fifteen, I returned to California for the summer to stay with my grandparents. They had a small, cluttered one-bedroom apartment, so I spent many afternoons wandering the streets of Berkeley by myself, dodging the clouds of incense on Telegraph Avenue and nesting for hours amid the musty stacks of its used bookstores. Once in a while I'd sneak a movie, hoping my grandmother wouldn't ask where I'd been, because she'd invariably remind me films were "of the devil." Occasionally, when I was feeling especially rebellious, I'd bum cigarettes from strangers.

One day, I saw a guy smoking on a bench in the courtyard of a small shopping center. He worked at the photo store. We made awkward small talk while we smoked.

I needed to pee, so I asked if he could unlock the shopping center's bathroom. He did. I didn't notice that the door hadn't fully closed behind me until, maybe half a minute later, I realized he had followed me in. He came up behind me and put his hands firmly on my hips—

He walked me to his store and into the back room—

Why did I go? Why didn't I run?

And then he pushed me to my knees—

Why didn't I yell?

The only thing I remember him saying was, "Doesn't it feel good?"

Why didn't I do something—anything—other than what I did?

Maybe if I'd been taller and stronger or looked less vulnerable or more imposing, maybe if I'd been a more obedient grandson, I'd have stayed safe. Maybe if I'd been braver or louder, I might have said or even shouted, "No."

In July we had nine days over ninety degrees at the farm. The trend continued into August. One afternoon (ninety-one degrees and 78 percent relative humidity), we were out in the garden harvesting tomatoes.

Sweat streamed off my arms. The bandanna around my neck was soaked through. My khakis felt heavy and wet, as if I'd been caught in a summer thunderstorm, except the sky was cloudless.

Emily asked me why I wasn't wearing shorts. "I never wear shorts," I replied. This wasn't much of an explanation, but she let it go. This also wasn't entirely true. I own shorts. I have worn them to the beach occasionally. Sometimes I will wear them in the privacy of my own home. But I never wore them to the farm.

Part of this was self-protection. Too many times, I'd seen the Pollock-like splatter of rotten spinach on other farmhands' exposed skin as we worked on the compost. *How do they bear it?* I wondered. *How can they open yet another plastic packet without washing that off?*

I'd be lying, though, if I said that my personal ban on shorts had much to do with cleanliness, or at least this version of it.

Try as I might, I can't remember that man's face. All I can come up with is a blur, a featureless blob—and perhaps that is a small grace, that I don't have to see his eyes again. I can still hear his deep, calm baritone, though. And I know that he was not tall—stocky, strong, like a miniature bull.

I do remember his legs. I saw them when he sent me to the floor. Patchy dark hair against pale skin. His prominent, sharply defined calves seemed abnormally large to me for someone of his height. The way they bulged out midway between his ankle and his knee. He was wearing cargo shorts that day.

My legs—spindly, thin—look almost nothing like his. I don't own any cargo shorts. (Nobody should, really; who looks good in cargo shorts?) It makes no sense, but this is the truth: I don't wear shorts in public simply because I remember that he wore them that day. I remember those shorts, those legs—and I want nothing to do with any of it.

Memories are funny things. They morph. They twist. They fester. They turn. Sometimes, absent the original perpetrator, whose name you'll never know but who remains with you nonetheless, you assume that role. You seek but never find absolution for the sin you never committed, for the sin that was in fact committed on you—in you—to you.

Sin is sin, though, right? Someone has to pay, even if "payment" comes in the form of a ridiculously convoluted relationship with shorts.

This is the body with which I kneel in the garden to weed. This is the body that opens the plastic bags of rotting produce and stumbles toward the compost pile with the wheelbarrow. This is the body with which I strain against an uncooperative barn door.

This body is housing—enclosure and infrastructure. Sometimes I wonder, *Can this body also be my home?*

Deliverance is not the same as redemption. And I refuse to believe that the deliverance God promises is merely a spiritual thing, or restricted to our thoughts. Too much sin in this world has been committed against our bodies. If there is such a thing as salvation, then healing has to come to these bodies, too.

I also can't imagine that I can do anything on my own to achieve it. Not with this body, which I did nothing to fashion and nothing to deserve. Tristan—my beloved Tristan—tries to help. We'll be lying in bed, trying to shed the weight of a day and surrender to night, and Tristan will turn to me. "You know I love you?" he'll say. "You know how beautiful you are?"

He knows the answer—my answer, anyway—and he knows I will never say yes, nor believe him entirely when he says it. But I think he also knows that each of us needs at least one person, one consistent and stubborn and faithful person, who will insistently name those truths we aren't yet convinced of but that we desperately want to believe. They hold on to hope for us when we don't know how.

In my better moments, I try to believe that, somehow, this thing I have hated can also tell me a better story—one about God's grace. I do nothing to keep breathing. I do nothing for my heart to keep pumping, for blood to keep coursing through my veins. I do nothing for the neurons in my brain to keep firing. I do nothing to keep my fingers typing these words.

Denise Ackermann writes that these ordinary graces are in fact extraordinary, if only we pause to consider them. "The very fact that we breathe, that the earth continues to spin on its axis, that the seasons follow one another, that communities are kept alive by uncountable, unnoticed, simple acts of generosity and kindness," she writes, "are due to God's grace, shed upon all creation."

Intellectually, I know all this. I know that everything my body does on this farm—and indeed the very land itself—is evidence of grace upon grace upon grace. To know is not to be convinced, though. Even as every fiber of my being strains to believe this is true, I can't quite be persuaded.

salt-baked chicken

When Tristan and I got married some years ago, my parents didn't attend our wedding. My mother wrote to say they couldn't, for theological reasons. The week of the ceremony, she emailed to say she was praying for good weather.

Then, some months later, she emailed to ask if she could come visit us in New York. Actually, that's not quite accurate: She wanted to know whether I might like for her to "come and cook a dinner for you for your birthday." She hadn't been to visit in years, not since Tristan and I moved in together. She'd met him only once, and that meeting had been incredibly awkward.

Food is the language my family speaks when Cantonese, English, and Chinglish all fail us. We can say with food what we can't with spoken words.

As a kid, on the too-common occasions when I got in trouble with my dad at the dinner table for talking back, my grandmother would just spoon another scoop of my favorite dish onto my plate. This is how she showed her solidarity. This was also her diplomatic way of suggesting that I just shut up and eat.

As my sister and I got older, my family began traveling more, and we fought constantly over where and what to eat. I recall spectacular meltdowns on the streets of Tokyo, Hong Kong, and Oakland Chinatown. We started taking cruises together partly because there isn't any argument about where to have dinner. Still, that left the problem of lunches; in Venice, one sibling conflagration only ended when my sister won the argument, and she led us to McDonald's for Chicken McNuggets.

I think we fought because we cared. More often than not, eating had made for happy childhood memories: Sitting in my aunt and uncle's laughter-filled kitchen in Hong Kong, the plastic-covered tabletop covered by a quickly shrinking mound of fresh lychees and a quickly growing pile of peels and pits. Waking one morning in a different aunt and uncle's home, in London, to the scent of ginger and scallion. A few days before, I'd said offhand that I didn't like scallops, which my uncle didn't believe—he speculated, correctly, that I'd just never had a good scallop. So he rose early to go to Billingsgate Market, where he bought fresh, in-the-shell scallops for my aunt to steam for our breakfast and my culinary education. Setting the kitchen table so many weeknights—me scooping the rice into the blue-and-white Qinghua bowls, my sister putting out the chopsticks, my mom finishing the dishes and calling to my dad that dinner was ready, my dad seemingly always needing to pee as soon as everyone else had sat at the table.

Food is the thing we can always talk about when we have nothing else. If I'm at a loss for something to say to my mother, I can always ask her what she and my dad have been eating. And I can always ask—genuinely, because I always want to know—how to cook a particular dish of hers.

Through food, my mother says things she can't in words. Sometimes a box will unexpectedly arrive on Tristan's and my doorstep. Inevitably it's packed with food: cans of abalone she has brought back from Hong Kong; dried scallops and dried mushrooms she worries I am too cheap to buy myself; preserved ginger, which is good for expelling gas and soothing coughs; bags of dried apple slices, made with fruit from a friend's trees, which she has sent regularly ever since I told her Tristan loves them.

When my mom arrived in New York to cook that birthday meal for me, one of the first things she did was to pull a gift out of her bag: an antique pair of ivory chopsticks. Everyone in our family has a pair, inscribed in red with our names. These were for my husband.

My mom told him it was my job to figure out where to get the inscription done. I reminded her it was also her job to help me come up with a Chinese name for the white boy.

Years later, I can tell you, she still hasn't. But we have those chopsticks.

We took my mother for so many other meals while she was in New York: In Koreatown, she happily picked at a whole fried fish and inhaled the fragrance of a pot of spicy, simmering tofu. In Brooklyn Chinatown, we had dim sum; her face radiated delight at a simple plate of fish balls. At our friend Adam's restaurant, Lunetta, she dove into a huge and fragrant bowl of mussels, carefully plucking the meat out and nodding in delight.

Those lunches and dinners, though, were appetizers and desserts. That trip was about one meal.

Eleven friends joined us, each carefully chosen for their impeccable manners and for the ways in which they had played their own supportive parts on our journey. All of them knew this dinner wasn't just about the food.

My mom taught me that you calculate the minimum number of dishes for a proper Chinese dinner, which is always served family style, by counting the number of people, then subtracting one. So, growing up, a weeknight meal for our family of four was always at least three dishes—two proteins and a vegetable.

But that was just the minimum. That Saturday, my mom had gone one better, preparing a dish for each of us. At five-thirty, her offerings began coming out of our tiny galley kitchen one after another. First, the starters: freshly griddled scallion pancakes; spring rolls stuffed with Napa cabbage, onion, and carrot; seaweed-wrapped sticky rice balls with Chinese sausage and dried shrimp. Then the mains: scrambled egg and tomato—a staple of Cantonese home cooking that is always a crowd-pleaser. A half-dozen types of mushroom, braised with abalone. Piles of Chinese greens, dressed simply in oyster sauce. Slivers of marinated pork, tossed with crisp triangles of two kinds of tofu. Two chickens, one steamed and one poached in soy sauce. Shrimp stir-fried with a multicolored medley of vegetables. Two whole black bass, steamed with ginger and green onions. A beef stew, with big, gooey chunks of tendon—one of my favorite dishes. Steamed spareribs, fragrant with black bean sauce.

This was her gift, her gesture of lavish love, her way of saying that she's trying.

She started cooking more than twenty-four hours before the first guest arrived, standing and rinsing and washing and stirring and chopping and tasting until her arms and legs ached and her own appetite was gone.

She watched us as we ate, scanning the overcrowded table, surveying our pleasure and ensuring there was never an empty plate. She wanted nothing more than for us to simply receive.

"Eat!" she kept saying. "There's more."

Did I tell you my mom's name is Grace?

I've been struggling to think of many functional, healthy families in the Bible. We read plenty of stories of sibling rivalry and abuse—brother killing brother, brothers throwing another brother into a pit, brother raping sister. There are depictions of marital strife, too, and plenty of evidence that advocates of "traditional marriage" aren't relying on the full biblical record: discord among Abraham, Sarah, and the enslaved Hagar; hapless Hosea pining after his unfaithful partner Gomer; barren Hannah getting picked on ruthlessly by Elkanah's other, more fertile wife, Peninnah. There's attempted reconciliation in the wake of rifts, but that gets messy, too. In the story of the prodigal son, a patient father's joy at one child's return ignites a jealous tantrum from the other son.

It seems as if Scripture has much more to say about how not to be a faithful family than how to be one. Yet in the churches of my childhood, people seemed to regard the Bible as a clear handbook for holy living, its pages a comprehensive to-do list for all forms of godly conduct. How?

The fifth commandment instructs us to honor our father and mother. Of the six commandments that have to do with how we relate to those around us, the instruction to honor one's parents is the only one expressed in positive language. Read the full set of ten commandments carefully and you'll see that the one about our parents is the only one that doesn't include the phrase "thou shalt not."

Kabbed, the Hebrew word that is translated "honor," derives from a verb that means "to be weighty" or "to be burdensome." This at least hints at the complexity of the task. But I didn't want mere hints; I sought clarity. Unfortunately, the voluminous pages that follow don't provide much of a helpful guide for what thou shalt actually do. There's little evidence that anyone has honored their father and mother all that well. And what does "honor" even mean in modern society?

Every year or two since that wildly lavish birthday dinner in New York, I've received a similar email from my mom: "Do you want me to come cook a meal?" she asks. "Let me know."

I always say yes. To say no would feel dishonoring—and honestly, given how good her food is, a little stupid.

We scheduled her latest visit for a few weeks after the chicken slaughter. Because this was her first trip to see us since I started seminary, theology was on my mind as we prepared. Her theology—on sexuality, on salvation, on heaven and hell—has not shifted, as far as I can tell.

Several years ago, during one of her visits, I noticed she had a copy of *Left Behind,* the apocalyptic Christian novel. This book is not on the recommended reading list in my household. Its prose traffics in fear; its theology fetishizes hellfire. In the spirit of honoring my mother, I censored the first dozen or so possible responses to the presence of this book in my house. Finally I asked her why she had it with her, since I knew she had read it years before, and it's not exactly a story that merits multiple reads. She explained that she was going to see another relative after visiting us, and she wanted to let this family member know what might happen if she didn't go back to church.

If the aspects of my mother's convictions that I find troubling haven't changed, those that give me hope haven't either. I see evidence of her theology in how she lovingly monitors my health and my workload and my diet. I see it in her conviction, expressed through her constant prayers. I see it in the meals she cooks for international students and the scarves she knits for

those living on the streets and in the parent-teacher confer-
ences she attended on behalf of friends who spoke little English.
I see it through her faithful witness to the beauty of becoming,
expressed through the cleaver's precise chop, the wok's transformative heat, and the rice cooker's steam.

Over the years, friends have told me they think I have chosen poorly. In their view, my parents are oppressive, even abusive. I should stop seeing them until they affirm my sexuality
and my marriage.

Those friends are still welcome at my table—just as my
mother is. My mom's example reminds me that I believe in a
difficult love. This kind of love doesn't shy away from discomfort, and it doesn't mistake discomfort for danger. It subordi-
nates our theological disagreements to the clear call to feed the
hungry and clothe the needy. It shows up, as courageously as it
can, even in the midst of confusion.

My mom's witness, distinct in some ways as it might be from
mine, nudges me once again to try to foster this kind of love in
my life. It rekindles my desire to lead a life of hospitality. And it
calls back to mind a conviction we share: that we live in anticipation of a greater feast.

The Episcopal priest Robert Farrar Capon has written beautifully about this hunger for hope. "To be sure, food keeps us
alive," he says in *Supper of the Lamb,* "but that is only its smallest
and most temporary work. Its eternal purpose is to furnish our
sensibilities against the day when we shall sit down at the heav-
enly banquet and see how gracious the Lord is. Nourishment is
necessary only for a while; what we shall need forever is taste."

"I hope I get to taste the chicken you raised," my mother
wrote me not long before her arrival in Princeton. "Are you selling them? If so, you should buy them all, haha!"

I promised I would not eat all the chickens before she came. I would save at least one. We would cook it together.

My mother wanted me to be a lawyer; she bought me an LSAT study guide after I graduated from college. My father never said what he wanted me to be, which was entirely in keeping with his taciturn character. When I finally told them I wanted to be a writer, he made it clear this wasn't on the Chinese parents' list of approved professions. "Investment banks need writers, too," he said. Then he walked out of the room.

My parents had slowly clawed their way into the American middle class. My mom paid her way through college by working as a motel maid and a casino money changer. My dad delivered pizzas and drove taxicabs; then he joined the army and eventually went to college, thanks to the G.I. Bill. Both sacrificed in that stereotypical immigrant way, clipping coupons and eschewing luxuries so they could invest in me and my education.

These memories all came to mind as my mother and I stood in the Farminary garden, next to the okra and the tomatillos, the morning after she arrived. If "writer" was of questionable value, what about "farmhand," which was surely nowhere on their list of hopes and dreams for their kid? When I got my first magazine job, which paid $40,700 a year, they had expressed doubts about my economic viability; how about $9.25 an hour?

My mother peered at the Chinese long beans we had planted in the garden, frowning slightly.

A staple of the Chinese kitchen, the long bean is an unfamiliar vegetable to most Americans. When it's ready for harvest, it resembles a skinny snake, purple or green, depending on the variety, at least a foot long, with a slightly puckered skin. When

I was a kid, my mom would dice long beans finely and either scramble them with eggs or add them to her fried rice. The long beans were new to the Farminary that season, part of our effort to grow crops that told the diverse stories of the students.

She stooped for a closer look, then said, "Why haven't you picked these yet?"

As she chided me for not recognizing that some of these beans were beyond ready for harvest, she pulled one off its vine. It was sad and shriveled, dried out and past its prime, and she tossed it to the ground.

It's funny how a few minutes in my mother's presence can bring out the dormant teenager in me. My face flushed. I felt embarrassed that I couldn't even grow this thing, and she knew it. I felt even more embarrassed that here I was, forty years old, allegedly an adult, and I still so craved my mother's approval. I just wanted her to say I was doing something well.

Soon, a white box truck from the food bank pulled up. The driver unloaded pallet after pallet of produce for the compost pile: sixty flats of Washington-grown apricots, sixty more of California cauliflower, twenty-eight forty-pound boxes of Granny Smith apples from Chile, and a case of spaghetti squash.

My mother was mystified. Our people didn't just throw food away: You trimmed the rot and cut around the moldy bits and saved the bones for the soup pot. She had worked in accounting and bookkeeping for most of her career, and I saw her mental calculator running.

A few of the apricots were moldy, but we quickly sorted at least fifteen pounds that were in perfect condition. At $2.99 a pound, she said, that was nearly $50 worth. I could take them back to my apartment and make jam.

Some of the apples were slightly bruised, but most were nowhere near rotten. Even on sale at $0.89 a pound, each box would be $36, and what sat in front of us had a market value of nearly $1,000. Plenty of applesauce, dried apples, apple pie, apple cake.

"So wasteful. So wasteful," she said to nobody in particular as she picked her way deliberately through the produce. When we had finished separating the salvageable fruit from those destined for the compost pile, she swiped at her sweaty brow and looked at the two nearly full boxes we'd saved. Then she nodded her approval.

Saint Paul often invokes descriptions of fathers and mothers, brothers and sisters to discuss Christian belonging. The Epistles use some version of *adelphoi*—"brothers," or more inclusively, "siblings"—more than 150 times. All these New Testament metaphors regarding family can be vexing to those of us who have had difficult relationships with our blood relatives—even more so in the West, where we often read these familial descriptions in a context that is markedly different from the honor-based culture of the ancient Near East.

Perhaps, though, Paul understood well all the baggage that comes with the metaphor, regardless of culture. Surely he knew the complicated feelings that it would stir up.

Jesus, too, gave injunctions regarding the way we should relate to our families. In Luke 14:26, he gives what might be the most difficult command of all: "Whoever comes to me and doesn't hate father and mother, spouse and children, and brothers and sisters—yes, even one's own life—cannot be my disciple."

The Greek word that most English translations render as "hate" is *miseo*. But the drama in the English might overstate the meaning of Jesus's original words, because *miseo* is perhaps better but less startlingly rendered "to hold in less esteem." In the context of a system that subjugated individual conviction to collective will, it was a profoundly radical statement to say that one should hold Jesus in higher esteem than one's parents. (Jesus did not seem to be any fonder of inordinate self-love, by the way; in John 12:25, he warns, "Those who love their lives will lose them, and those who hate their lives in this world will keep them forever." Again, *miseo*. Again, perhaps better to say "who hold their lives in this world in less esteem.")

It makes sense to me: If you hold Jesus in less esteem than you do those others whom you love, this whole endeavor of following Christ is not going to work. His ideas are countercultural to the point of absurd: Love your enemies? Really? They can only make sense in light of his solidarity and his self-sacrificial love. If you value something greater than the here and now, the here and now can be transformed into such greatness.

What he suggests seems not to be an abandonment of the fifth commandment but a reaffirmation of its proper context. He upends the honor/shame system that has been built up and reinforced over the generations. He questions the scaffolding on which human loyalty is built. He reminds us of the greater love that makes all the other loves possible.

My father built his adult life—and by extension, our family's life—by emigrating from Hong Kong to the United States in his early twenties. In Hong Kong he'd been an excellent athlete but a mediocre student; he and his brother bounced from high school to high school, eventually ending up at one called New Method. (The joke around town was that New Method was for all the students who couldn't hack it under the old method.)

He landed in the United States in 1967. He joined the U.S. Army, tempted by a recruiter's promise that citizenship would be quicker for those who served in the military. Then, the country in which he had arrived by ship—he was too poor to afford a plane ticket—sent him back to Asia by air, to fight in Vietnam. I don't know much about his time in Vietnam; it's something he has mentioned to me only once. My mother has said he re- turned to the United States a changed man, but she has never offered any details. I do know he came home with a deep patri- otism, an allegiance to this country that I have struggled to un- derstand, as well as a curiously strong affection for meatloaf. Yet his manner as a father has always been more stereotypically Chinese, relatively silent and resolutely strict.

There were times in my childhood when I wished for a father who was more stereotypically American. When I was maybe thirteen, we were in the midst of yet another argument, and I screamed at my dad probably the worst thing a kid could ever say to a Chinese parent: "You have to earn my respect."

I don't remember his response, but I do remember my mom's: A look of horror flashed across her face. Then she yelled one word at me: "*Run!*"

If I occasionally wanted a dad who was more stereotypically American, I bet he also wanted the same of his son. When I was in college, he came to New York for business and somehow got tickets to a Giants–49ers game. I was raised to be a 49ers fan, but I'm also not a vocal spectator. I cheer inside my heart.

I remember the fans around us loudly wondering what was wrong with me: *Why is he just sitting there? Is there something wrong with your kid?*

My dad neither defended me nor agreed with them. He just shrugged, laughed (nervously, to my ears), and turned his atten- tion back to the game.

My father hasn't visited in nearly twenty years, not since I started dating Tristan. He has strong theological convictions about sexuality—which we've only discussed, in painful, awkward passing, a couple of times—and I have mine. He has his understanding of how my childhood went, and I have mine. He has his sense of what is right, and I have mine.

That Farminary chicken I'd saved to cook with my mom: We decided to prepare it in the style of my father's people, the Hakka.

One of the central dishes in Hakka cuisine is salt-baked chicken. The whole bird is brushed with Shaoxing wine and dry-brined overnight, uncovered in the refrigerator, in salt, white pepper, and sand ginger powder. (Sand ginger, also known as lesser galangal or *Kaempferia galanga*, is more floral than the ginger root stocked in most grocery stores.)

The next day, you pull the chicken out of the fridge, let it come to room temperature, brush the skin with oil, and wrap it all tightly in parchment paper. You'll need the same amount of coarse salt as you have chicken—in other words, three pounds of salt for a three-pound bird. Heat a dry wok or frying pan, then toss the salt in, stirring it regularly for about ten or fifteen minutes until it just begins to turn golden.

Then, spread a layer of that salt at the bottom of the wok (if it's big enough and you have a cover), a Dutch oven, or, as is traditional, a Chinese clay pot. Pop the parchment-wrapped chicken in, cover it completely with the remaining salt, then roast it in a hot oven until it's just cooked and still juicy. (Traditionally, few Chinese families had ovens, and this would have been done on hot coals.)

As we cooked, my mom told me that when she was a kid in Hong Kong, her uncle kept chickens. This was new information to me. Her family was then living in Chungking Mansions, a famed apartment complex in Tsimshatsui, the densely packed

Kowloon neighborhood that would not seem to have space for such things. When she was a kid, though, Chungking Mansions wasn't the seventeen-story building that it is now. Then, it was a collection of shorter, ramshackle buildings with courtyards and outdoor spaces in which families, mostly working-class, grew things. When developers knocked that down, sometime in the 1960s, they kept the old name.

In my mind, the line between urban and rural has always been more fixed; my family's departure from our home villages in the Chinese countryside also meant a departure from our agrarian customs. But my mother's recounting blurred those boundaries. We were peasant people, and my great-grandparents and grandparents had brought their country ways with them to Hong Kong.

I asked my mom whether she had ever slaughtered chickens. No, she replied. But she said that her family had also raised pigeons. Sometimes she had to prep these for dinner, scalding them and plucking the feathers.

We left the Dutch oven in for about forty-five minutes. After taking it out, I didn't remove the lid, for fear of letting the heat escape. We just let the pot sit untouched and cool for about an hour.

When my mom and I finally liberated the chicken from its parchment, I saw that some of the salt as well as the paper at the bottom of the pot had charred. This wasn't supposed to happen, and I feared I had ruined the bird. But it turned out to be a happy accident. The chicken itself hadn't burned at all; it had an unexpected, gentle smokiness.

I put the bird on the cutting board, carefully found the joint between the chicken's thigh and the fatter of its two drumsticks, cut the leg off, and set it aside in a glass dish.

Many Chinese people consider this the best part of the chicken; in roast-meat restaurants in Hong Kong, you'll usually pay a premium for the leg. At our family's table, the best always goes along with the honor.

The drumstick would go home with my mom. It was for my dad.

long beans

July was all about the beans—yellow wax beans, green provider beans, purple bush beans, those long beans. We harvested them almost every day, and still there were more. Aside from the long beans, I rarely brought any home; neither Tristan nor I has ever much liked string beans.

Only at the beginning of August did our tomatoes begin to come in. Heirloom varieties hadn't done that well in the garden. Nate suspected the still-depleted soil, even enriched by our compost, wasn't yet robust enough for them. This year, we tried a type called Berkeley Tie-Dye—I'd been tempted by the pictures in the seed catalog of their intriguing striations of green and red—but they struggled.

The Sun Sugars, though, thrived as usual. Everyone loves these little orange orbs, which burst with sweetness. As we made our way down the rows, plucking the fruit off the vines, nearly as many ended up in our mouths as in the buckets for the CSA.

Our favorites among these favorites weren't the deep orange, textbook Sun Sugars. Once in a while, I'd spot one that was paler, more pinkish, a little less attention-grabbing. These tasted almost like little cantaloupes. We thought they were a different variety at first, something new that we'd planted without even realizing it. Then we realized Nate had saved seed from last season's crop. The thing about a parent hybrid tomato is that its seeds won't necessarily produce identical tomato babies. Genes can surprise you, lying dormant for a generation before popping up again. We hypothesized that the hybrid must have dehybridized.

Everyone wanted these tomatoes. Everyone wanted the string beans. Almost nobody wanted the long beans. On CSA days, shareholders would take them if we included them in their allocation, but who knows what they did with them once they got home. When we made the long beans optional, there was always a large, tangled pile waiting for me at the end of the day. The same thing had happened with the collard greens and the bok choy in previous seasons.

Why?

The long bean tells a story of trade and movement.

It is believed to have been bred in Southeast Asia, where it thrives in tropical heat and humidity. In the Philippines, they often lend their savory bite to a soupy stew called sinigang, balancing the fatty softness of pork and the tang of tamarind. In Malaysia, they are stir-fried with belacan, a deeply savory paste made from dried shrimp. In China, they're tossed in a hot wok with chili peppers, garlic, and ground pork.

If you trace the long bean's lineage back far enough, its roots are not Asian but African. A variety of cowpea, it's more closely related to black-eyed peas than the other legumes that we typically call "bean." The cowpea probably traveled via merchant ship and trade wind to Asia, where it was bred to produce the long bean.

On our farm, we grew three varieties: a pale green one called Gita and a dark crimson type called Red Noodle—both of which I picked out—and a deep-purple one planted by my friend Hana, who has Filipino ancestry. Like the cowpea, long beans don't need particularly rich soil, and ours flourished from the start. We sowed the green ones adjacent to the okra, and the vines of those bean plants quickly wound themselves around the okra's tall stalks.

I was struck by how the long beans used their neighbors as trellises. As much as we talk in modern society about individuation and autonomy and that wretched concept of self-care, we are communal creatures. We need others to lean on, borrowing their steadiness when we feel shaky. But how do we insinuate ourselves? To whom do we turn for support? How do they respond?

Long beans have no natural affinity for okra, which originated in Ethiopia, thousands of miles away. But here in our garden, they became neighbors. Here, one came to lean on the other. Did the okra feel burdened by the long bean? Did the long bean's weight take something from the flourishing of the okra?

We noticed no ill effects. But perhaps we just didn't know what to look for or how to perceive.

During the second week of August, a CSA shareholder showed up at the farm with two round, steel tomato cages. I should clarify that I didn't know they were tomato cages; I only knew they were tomato cages because she said they were tomato cages. She no longer needed them in her own garden, but she thought we might find a good use for them.

While our tomatoes were already trellised, the long beans were not. So I took the tomato cages out to the garden and stood there looking at the beans for a while, wondering whether they would react angrily to being retrained. I worried that stressing them might cause them to wither. Or maybe they'd protest by dropping the beans that were still growing and ripening. (After my mom's visit, I'd been a little more vigilant about harvesting the ones that were ready.)

Eventually, I decided just to risk it and set up the cages. I started with the vine most entangled with the okra. I slowly unwound the slender strands, letting them flop to the ground.

Stillness is my enemy on a hot afternoon in the garden. When I'm moving, I can generate my own breeze, windmilling my arms to feel momentarily cooler. But this stultifyingly tedious work allowed for little relief; it took me maybe forty-five sun-soaked minutes to extract most of the bean plant from its neighbor.

Then I carefully took one of the old tomato cages and placed it into the row, centering it around the beanstalk. It took me maybe another twenty minutes to wind the vines around the trellis. I hoped the plant would be happy on its new home.

Once I had done it, I stood back, wiped the sweat from my face, and examined my work. It was fine. But there was something puzzling about the trellis's design. On the one hand, it seemed perfect for the beans; I liked how it widened from bottom to top, allowing the maturing beans to hang free. But I didn't like the four sharp steel ends that just stuck into the air. This design seemed unusual, maybe even dangerous. If someone happened to bend over to harvest something without looking, or just weed in the wrong spot, it might mean metal piercing their eye.

Around three A.M. that night, I woke suddenly.

I can't remember if I had been dreaming. I wish I were the kind of person who wakes in the night because of brilliance and revelation. Nope. More often, I will be startled awake by some dream turning to nightmare, some worry that festered quietly in the daytime only to come alive at night.

I threw the covers off, trying not to stir Tristan. Then I lay there absorbing the aftermath of my flash of horror: I had installed the tomato cages upside down.

Idiot.

Idiot.

Idiot.

That design flaw, which threatened to poke out the eyes of an inattentive gardener, was in fact not a design flaw at all. If anything had a design flaw, it was my brain. This was entirely the folly of an inexperienced gardener who had neither useful knowledge nor the attentiveness to ask which end was up.

Fuck.

Fuck.

Fuck.

Early the next morning, I headed back out to the garden, tired but determined. It was already hot, but I can't tell you whether the worst of the heat was coming from the sun above or my shame within. All I know is that as I slowly unwound the vines from the trellis, my arms glistened from the labor, my hands shook, and my shirt, soaked with sweat and humiliation, oppressed me.

I wasn't gentle enough as I unwound one of the vines from the trellis. How the hell had they already made themselves so at home, so at one with the metal? In my carelessness, I snapped one vine off. Then another.

Eventually I managed to separate the cages from the vines without entirely destroying the plants, and I flipped them right-side up. As designed, those pointy bits slid easily into the soil. Whether Nate or anyone else knew what had happened, I still don't know. But I was ready to fire myself. I was the worst farmhand. Not knowing how to do things on the farm was not cute; it was a liability that could have cost someone their eyesight.

My parents taught me to embody a particularly high-functioning cog in the metaphorical machine. If mistakes were made, well, I wouldn't ever say "mistakes were made," because I would be compelled to acknowledge that I had made the mistake. But even before there was any opportunity for public acknowledgment—we do come from a shame culture, after all—it was my job to catch that mistake. I should fix the error before they—"they" being anyone else—even noticed. The high-functioning cog self-corrects.

On some level, this has always troubled me, though I haven't often had words to explain why it feels so wrong.

I once told a close friend I wanted to dress up as a sort of social experiment. I would put on one of my Chinese jackets, with its mandarin collar, and a rice paddy hat (culturally inaccurate, but whatever). We would spend the day in Manhattan, and I would play her Oriental manservant. We would go shopping, and I would be useful: carrying her bags, offering her water, always making sure to keep a step or two behind her. We would talk more loudly than we should, and I would call her "ma'am" in my best Hong Kong accent ("*Mem! Mem!*").

I don't exactly know what kind of response I hoped for. Maybe someone would say, "That's not really how you see yourself, is it?" and I could reply, "No, but isn't this essentially how you see my people, if you see them at all?" And in that deeply uncomfortable conversation, I wanted them to understand what it is to feel not like a full human but rather like a service provider. I wanted them to apologize.

No, that's not accurate. I wanted not only an apology but also a full embrace. Not a literal embrace, because I'm not really that huggy, but more of a metaphorical one. I wanted to be seen not as a cog or as a commodity but as a person.

My Chinese name is 朱天慧. The first character is my family name, Chu. Some fragment of family lore rattling around in my mind says there were Ming dynasty emperors named Chu. But I've wondered whether that imperial connection was just an aspirational figment in some relative's imagination.

My given name, 天慧 ("tien wai"), was chosen, as is typical in Chinese tradition, by my grandfather. It means "wisdom from heaven." Customarily, 慧 is given to girls, and more than once, during visits to Hong Kong, I'd share my Chinese name with a family friend or acquaintance, and they'd exclaim, in the blunt way of our people, "That's a girl's name!" I'm not sure what my grandfather was thinking.

Names matter. For my people, a person's name expresses the embodied hope that one's elders—in my case, my grandfather—have for the future.

In *The Christian Imagination,* a book that was assigned in several of my seminary classes, the theologian Willie James Jennings writes about ways in which names are used to map places, to form peoples, to shape identities, to build communal cultures, and to write histories. He mentions the Western Apache people, for instance, and how language expresses their deep connection to the land and all the stories to which it has borne witness. They endowed places with remarkably specific names: Shades of Shit, for instance, and Juniper Tree Stands Alone, and Water Lies with Mud in an Open Container. The speaking of a place-name "repeats the very words of the ancestors and invokes their presence and their actions on behalf of themselves and their progeny." It's a way of recounting what has been, and it can also be a means of expressing longing for what could be.

Names matter. Without them and the context they provide, something sacred is severed. Jennings links this brokenness with the commodification of bodies—particularly Black bodies during the colonial-era slave trade and Indigenous bodies during the brutal conquests of the Americas. Their names were often taken away, replaced by those of the people who enslaved them. Still, Jennings writes, those Black and Indigenous folks retained their stories, passed them on to their descendants, and remained "powerful witnesses to the struggle against cultural decomposition into commodity fragments as well as to the fight to assert narrative existence in the face of far more powerful storytellers."

Names matter. When I remember why my grandfather chose my name, I also recall all that my ancestors survived, all the journeys they made, all the hopes they invested in me, all the stories they've handed down to me. Even if others never showed any interest in those stories, they were still worth telling. Sometimes the storyteller is the one who most needs to hear that story again and to be reminded that it matters.

Most harvest days, it didn't seem worth the effort to separate the strands of the long beans and place them into the baskets for the CSA shareholders. Nobody ever asked what they were or wondered what you might do with them. Eventually I just took to piling them on a table to the side.

It baffled me that shareholders would *ooh* and *aah* over kale. Kale is fine, but it's also a diva among vegetables. I will always have mixed feelings about a vegetable for which massage is a legitimate cooking technique.

Then there were the beets. It puzzles me that someone should pay for something that tastes like dirt. If you want to eat dirt, can't you do it for free?

Anyway, the long beans: I think I would have preferred if someone had told me they hated long beans. Hate, at least, requires attention and engagement, and I suspect none of these folks had ever given much of either to the beans. The lack of interest and curiosity bothered me—but what irritated me even more was that I was so invested in others' opinions about a vegetable.

Why did I care so much?

Then I realized, with a flash of awareness and a flush of shame: I'd pushed Nate to plant them, wanting to see more of my story, my heritage, in the garden. I hadn't realized that, in doing so, I'd end up treating the long bean like a proxy for my very self. Their disdain didn't apply just to the vegetable. It extended to my culture and my cuisine. The rejection of the long bean felt like a rejection of me.

goat

Two goats arrived at the farm at the beginning of September. Daisy's coat was a radiant auburn. Her daughter August's was lighter, a shade paler than the straw we laid down for their bedding.

From the start, we could see their personalities were wildly different, too. Daisy kept a safe distance from us, hoarding her trust. August, who, as her name suggests, had been born a few weeks before, bounced and bounded up to everyone, braying happily and revealing herself to be a tireless extrovert.

Daisy and August were recruited as teaching assistants, borrowed for six weeks for a class on the society and culture of ancient Israel. Goats were one of the animals the ancient Israelites commonly kept, and the professor wanted students to experience just a tiny bit of what it might have been like to live in that pastoral culture. But there were only six people registered for the class, so the farmhands were asked to help out.

The responsibilities of caring for the goats were simple: Each morning, we were to replenish their feed, wash out and refill their water dish, check that they had enough hay, and milk Daisy.

This last task turned out to be the most challenging for me. Daisy and August were pygmy goats; as this name might suggest, everything is smaller on a pygmy goat, teats included. Also, Daisy had never been milked by humans before she arrived at the farm.

On the ninth day the goats were with us, I had to do the morning chores alone.

I wrestled Daisy onto the milking stand and secured the chain around her neck that was meant to keep her stationary. I put a red bucket under her and reached for a teat, and she immediately rewarded me with a sideways kick to my chest.

I tried again; her hoof shot out again.

There was milk in her udder—it felt full.

After a couple of minutes, I managed a long squirt into the bucket before she strained against the chain, attempting to turn her head to gaze at me in judgment.

I flushed: What did she think of me? She must loathe me. Did she identify me with discomfort? Invasion of privacy? Lack of consent?

Pretty soon, I was sweaty to the point of sopping, as much from my frustration as from the heat and humidity.

August had no intention of helping. Every time I squatted next to the milking stand, she tried to squeeze onto my lap. When I pushed her off, she would sprint a wide circle around the stand, then try again. If even a drop of her mother's milk landed on the ground, she'd get tangled up around my ankles, trying to get to that goodness.

The internet had told me that a pygmy goat can produce a

quart or two of milk a day. Before the goats arrived, I'd imagined how I might use the milk. I promised Tristan I'd bring some home. Maybe, I told him, we could even make some cheese!

How foolishly naïve.

There was, as usual, so much I didn't know. I didn't know that it's not easy to get a goat to adjust to being milked if that hasn't previously been part of her postpartum routine. I didn't know that it's usually wise to start milking a goat right after she gives birth.

That morning I got maybe an eighth of a cup, which turned out to be the high-milk mark of my time with the goats. Most other days, I got no more than a couple of tablespoons, which includes whatever was in the bucket when Daisy inevitably kicked it over.

I peered into the bucket, picked out a couple of pieces of grass, and then I drank the milk. I wish I could tell you it was luscious and creamy, a transcendent experience that redefined dairy for me. It wasn't. It was a little thin and kind of watery. To me, it tasted like a shot of success mixed with three cups of failure.

August and I fared better together.

We began regularly playing a game of chase. I'd freeze and she'd face off against me, then I'd suddenly take a big step toward her, and she'd take off, bounding onto the wheel well of the trailer and around the back. Then we'd do it all over again. She also loved peek-a-boo. I'd chase her in one direction around the trailer, then double back, and she'd either chase me around one corner or peek around another to see if I'd reappeared.

Some days, when nobody else was on the farm, we could do these things over and over, until she got bored and wandered into the trailer to munch some hay.

Or, if I wasn't feeling so energetic, I'd just sit. That's all I had to do. Because if I—or anyone, really—created any surface approximating a lap, she was *on it*. She'd leap onto her newfound platform with glee. She'd preen for a moment, maybe do a little dance, then she'd jump off and do another sprint around the enclosure.

In her presence, all the bad feelings disappeared: the worries that dogged me the rest of the day, the anxiety about things I had done or not done, all the shadows. My shoulders loosened. My spine straightened. My breath deepened.

I thought of the Hebrew tradition of the scapegoat. On Yom Kippur, one goat was slaughtered as a blood sacrifice. A second goat was sent into the wilderness, never to return. This goat was burdened with carrying the sins of the people away from the community, and its banishing symbolized the departure of these acts of wrongdoing along with all their consequences.

It might seem funny to think of this tradition in light of August's ministry—and I don't use the word "ministry" lightly. There was something about her that *was* transporting, that *did* do something of what a scapegoat was supposed to do. But whenever I'd read descriptions of scapegoats, I'd always thought of them as beasts of burden, not just figuratively but also literally. I never thought of a scapegoat scampering.

It was as if some invisible part of August's goatly spirit did play the traditional role of the beast of burden; when she scampered off around the trailer, it was as if she were carrying all the bad feelings into some wilderness. Yet the rest of her—enough of her—elaborated on the traditional narrative, remaining as reassurance and telling a new story: that our sins do not have lasting power to break fellowship. August embodied freedom.

I wasn't the only one who visited the goats for this strange solace.

Ashley, who had been my Hebrew study partner, told me August was the first farm animal she'd spent time with since childhood. "It felt like I was doing something rebellious, an activity that in my mind is normally reserved for children. Because petting zoos are for kids!" she said. "Being with August, I felt childlike wonder. I remembered that baby goats are fun."

Late one afternoon, I arrived at the farm to do some chores. As I walked toward the pen, I noticed the slight figure of one faculty member sitting on the grass near the goat enclosure. A friend had told me of a particularly acrimonious faculty meeting earlier that day, and I felt I should simply give this professor space.

Perhaps August felt the same. She was unusually calm and quiet that afternoon, as if she could sense that the most comforting thing to offer would simply be her presence. She didn't run. She didn't bleat. Mostly, she just stood nearby, as if to bear witness in silent solidarity to whatever was weighing her visitor down.

After a few minutes, I saw the professor rise and slowly walk back toward the parking lot. She spotted me, gave me a half smile and a nod, and kept going.

I couldn't tell you if August was an extroverted weirdo or whether she was quintessentially goatish. She seemed doglike to me—though every time I thought this, I felt a bit of shame. I wondered whether it was insulting, not to mention so typically human, to see a creature for what it was *like* instead of appreciating it for what it was.

I wanted to know how domesticated goats typically act, so one day I called Christian Nawroth, an agricultural scientist in Germany who studies the behavior and psychology of farm animals, especially goats. "What is it about baby goats," I asked him, "that makes us behave the way we do around them?"

He laughed. "Baby features," he said. "It's the huge head, the huge eyes, and they're fluffy."

Nawroth believes that domesticated goats have evolved their behavior in relationship to humans. "You think they act like dogs," he said. "No. They act like goats, but it's just that they do things you know dogs do." In other words, because we're more familiar with doggish behavior, we've created a mental category that we apply to any animal that knows how to relate to humans. But that doesn't mean goats are acting like dogs. Maybe there's a goatherd out there who thinks the dogs he encounters act oddly like goats.

Goats who are born and raised in captivity do develop relationships with their humans. In his experiments, Nawroth has found that if a domesticated goat couldn't solve a problem, "they looked at us and then they looked at the problem they couldn't solve. They were looking for help, basically."

He sees this tendency as a sign of animal intelligence. Rather than doggedly trying and then trying again, their appeal for assistance signals their capacity to switch strategies. In Nawroth's view, this is a reminder of yet another way in which we have underestimated animal intelligence, including "their abilities to cope with their environment and adapt."

One of those adaptations that he is still studying is play behavior. Nawroth has observed that domesticated animals play more than their wild counterparts. While it could be that we just haven't learned to recognize the kind of play that wild animals engage in, it might also reflect the ways in which humans have taken on the labor of ensuring the creatures' survival, giving them more space to play.

I'm not self-deceptive enough to think August reserved much of her heart for me. She was affectionate toward nearly everyone, and she revealed her extroverted self by jumping extra-high and running in circles extra-fast whenever a group of people came by to visit. Daisy seemed mostly to tolerate us, except when we thought to scratch that one spot between her horns or when I gave her some of the sweet grass that grew only outside their pen.

Whenever I was tempted to overthink August's affection, I remembered Nawroth's counsel. If we have underestimated animal intelligence, he said, "we also shouldn't overestimate their abilities." He doubted that goats could communicate something specific, such as empathy. He was pretty sure they cannot infer our motivations, nor could we know theirs.

A friend asked me one day whether my feelings had changed about eating meat. After all I'd experienced at the farm, from chicken slaughter to my time with the goats, had I rethought my omnivorous ways? I had to confess: I loved a good goat curry before, and I couldn't say I wouldn't eat a good goat curry again. I would not, however, eat August curry or Daisy curry; I prided myself on the ability to differentiate.

Three days before the goats went home, I went out to the farm in the late afternoon, when I knew nobody else would be there. I walked to their pen, grabbing some sweet grass on the way. August was her usual ebullient self, bleating her greeting as I neared. Daisy was Daisy, not giving me much of a glance.

I went in and sat on the ground, and August jumped onto my lap, as I knew she would. She buried her face in my chest, urging me to scratch her head and neck, as I knew she would. Then I just flopped onto my back and let August climb onto me.

She looked down at me—and I'm not going to pretend she was thinking anything other than that she wanted me to scratch her back or play with her, but I can tell you what was going on inside of me: For the two or three minutes that she was using me as a climbing platform, I felt happy. I felt joy. I felt lighter, as if August had noticed the worry, the anxiety, the doubts and troubles that regularly weigh me down and offered to carry all that for a few minutes so I could have a rest.

In my entire adulthood, I can count on one hand the number of times I've lain in the grass and let my head touch the ground. Always some fear had kept me from trying. Fear of impropriety, maybe, of doing something less than dignified. Fear of bugs. Also, fear of grass stains, which can be really hard to get out of a shirt.

What allows other creatures—our dogs, our cats, this goat—to unlock our vulnerability as they do? Some people will claim it is the purity of their feelings, something I refuse to accept, especially if we're talking about cats. Many of these domesticated creatures seem deeply transactional, trading affection and allegiance for food and shelter in a way that would be deeply objectionable were they humans. Yet we trust these animals with an openness we rarely show other people.

"There is no fear in love," 1 John 4:18 says, "but perfect love drives out fear, because fear expects punishment. The person who has been afraid has not been made perfect in love." The verb tense in that last bit is interesting. It isn't the person who remakes themselves as perfect, but rather, there is some outside agent facilitating or orchestrating this process.

For a few weeks, August was the embodiment of that for me. Don't get me wrong: As I gazed into her eyes, I did not see into her soul, and I cannot tell you that anything akin to love as we know it existed there. But she stirred in me an inexplicable love, and that love did something new in me. Whenever I was with her, I felt utterly unafraid, and not only unafraid but also free, which is to say: I felt more myself than I ever had.

heron

As I drove up to the farm the morning after the goats left, I braced myself for what would not be there. Every day for six weeks, my arrivals had been greeted by Daisy's throaty alto and August's juvenile soprano. Not this day. I don't think I even heard any birdsong. The quiet was so loud.

After getting out of my car, I started toward the goat enclosure, but then I thought better of it. Why go see what I already knew wasn't there?

Instead, I walked toward the pond and sat on the stone bridge. The sun was high enough in the sky that the oaks gave some shade, and through the dapple I could see a couple of geese. On the far side of the pond, there was a white bird with a yellow beak and long black legs, high-stepping in slow motion through the water: a heron.

My bird app told me this heron was a great white egret (*Ardea alba egretta*).

A group of herons, I learned, is called a congregation, which I thought was perfect for a bird that showed up on a seminary's farm. (They're sometimes called a siege or a wedge, alternative names that seem apt for American Christianity today.)

Some herons, I also learned, were once nicknamed "shite-pokes," for their unusual habit of pooping when disturbed. Considering all these terms together made them seem somehow a little less mysterious, a bit more familiar, certainly more relatable.

The great white egret, though: surely never a shitepoke. Too regal. The app did call it "common," by which it meant frequently seen. But in the nineteenth century, the feathers of the great white egret were so coveted that millions of the birds were slaughtered every year to keep the fashion industry supplied. Milliners could not keep up with the hat-wearing consumer's desire. By the turn of the twentieth century, an ounce of these plumes, which was four birds' worth, was selling for about $32 (about $1,100 today), nearly twice the price of gold.

Only federal legislation banning the killing of egrets and the harvesting of their feathers was able to save the birds from extinction.

In her poem "Some Herons," Mary Oliver describes the heron alternately as a preacher or poet—specifically, "an old Chinese poet." I believe she is writing about the great white egret's cousin, the great blue heron. No matter: I've never thought of such birds, white or blue, as preachers or poets.

If someone had told me that Canada geese were preachers, that would make sense to me; with their loud honks, they could be those street-corner barkers with megaphones. Crows, too, which many peoples have seen as messengers of misfortune.

The heron, though: What kind of preacher stays mostly silent?

I suppose Oliver's not wrong, though, at least according to my people. In Chinese lore, the heron is often regarded as a harbinger of goodness and a sign of a path forward. Its name, 鹭 ("lou"), is homophonous with a word that means "road" or "way." Some even believed it to be that rare creature capable of flying between earth and heaven, escorting the souls of the departed to the afterlife.

As I watched the heron, the thing that I admired most was its apparent ease. It seemed unfettered. It appeared to be free.

A few years ago, I got to talking with the theologian Kelly Brown Douglas about forgiveness and freedom. She had been studying forgiveness in the African American Christian tradition, and she'd been pondering it particularly in the context of the murders of the Mother Emanuel Nine. In the wake of the 2015 killings at Emanuel African Methodist Episcopal Church in Charleston, South Carolina, several family members of the slain had publicly voiced their forgiveness of the killer. These statements prompted waves of praise at their magnanimity but also criticism, particularly from those who wondered whether the killer should be so quickly let off the moral hook.

Douglas thought this act of forgiveness had largely been mischaracterized. "The media immediately talked about how great it was that they forgave, without really understanding what that meant," she said. Though she sympathized with critics who felt it was too soon to forgive, she didn't think they got it entirely right either: "It's not about cheap grace. It's not about ignoring anger."

In Douglas's view, true forgiveness is never primarily about the perpetrator. "Forgiveness is about letting go of things that prevent one from moving forward," she said. "There's an invitation to the party that is being forgiven—to repentance, complete turning around, recognition of the sin you've committed. But forgiveness does not hinge on their repenting."

To forgive is to declare that you will not be bound by that harm, by that hatred, she explained: "The only people it lets off the hook are the ones who are doing the forgiving." Forgiveness, in other words, means freedom for the one who has been hurt, not the one who did the hurting.

Of course, forgiveness is rarely a one-time event. It doesn't erase the past, and it cannot magically alter one's memory. Perhaps it isn't even an end. It's the means—for healing, for liberation, even for love.

After our conversation, I wondered: What were the implications of Douglas's understanding of forgiveness in other settings? What could it mean for those of us who have most struggled to forgive ourselves? What does it take to rejoin the congregation?

The heron's ethereal movements entranced me: Its mesmerizing strut. The S of its neck suddenly straightening, followed by the javelin strike of its beak at an underwater target. Its smooth, steady ascent into the air. Every silky motion reminded me of my grandmother doing tai chi.

Which way? I wanted to ask the heron.

Where was I supposed to go?

What did it think I should do?

I stepped into the pond, my boots sinking into the muck. The heron turned toward me. I took a couple more steps, but that was close enough. It lifted its wings and, with barely a sound, flew away.

autumn

parable

A farmer went out to scatter seed. As he was scattering seed, some fell on the path, and birds came and ate it. Other seed fell on rocky ground where the soil was shallow. They sprouted immediately because the soil wasn't deep. But when the sun came up, it scorched the plants, and they dried up because they had no roots. Other seed fell among thorny plants. The thorny plants grew and choked them. Other seed fell on good soil and bore fruit, in one case a yield of one hundred to one, in another case a yield of sixty to one, and in another case a yield of thirty to one.
—*Matthew 13:3–8*

With a few seasons behind me at the farm, I came to Jesus's parable about the seed sower with a different perspective than the guy who watered a plastic orchid and killed mint. I felt like I knew some things—and I had some questions: Who exactly was this farmer who haphazardly scattered seeds all over the place?

Where were his tidy rows? Where was his seed catalog and planting schedule? Who could afford such profligacy?

In the churches and Bible classes of my childhood, this parable was taught as a warning and a threat: *You have to be the good soil—or else.* God knows I tried. Tried to be the obedient son. Tried to kiss a girl and not hate it. Tried to pass off *not* kissing a girl as evidence of purity. Tried to be the tireless worker. Tried to pray and earn and prove and claw and strive and serve and confess and repent my way to goodness.

After I grew up and came out, I kept sinning and I kept struggling, and I was reminded again and again that I wasn't good soil. Then I stopped going to church, and I felt as if there were no hope of ever becoming the good and godly man of my family's—and my own—imagination.

Grief came to visit, as it inevitably does, but grace did, too. And all along the way, I never stopped dreaming about good soil. Good soil where I could simply lie down for a bit and rest. Good soil on which I might build a home. Good soil in which I could even grow something. Good soil where I might belong.

I kept dreaming about the good soil until it seemed as if even the dream was something that others could have but I couldn't.

Then I didn't dream anymore.

One day, Nate walked a group of us from the barn northward past the porta potty, past the pond, past a bald cypress tree, to a grassy clearing on the property. Then he read the parable of the sower aloud.

When he had finished, he shared some backstory about the farm that I'd never heard before. Decades ago, some utility workers had bulldozed their way from the main road to install some equipment not far from the pond. To allow access for their heavy trucks, they had carved a temporary path and brought in gravel. Sure enough, when we looked down, we could glimpse some bits of gravel amid the grass.

He was holding a shovel and asked for a volunteer: Who might be willing to dig? The first small scoop of the shovel yielded some clumps of grass and a puff of fine, dry soil. "Keep going," he urged. The shoveler put a little more muscle into the second effort. *Thunk.*

"Do you hear that?" Nate said.

Just two or three inches beneath the surface, the shovel hit rock.

In the few square feet surrounding us, Nate explained, we could see all the soil conditions described in Jesus's parable: hard path and rocky ground, thorny patches and fertile soil. They existed not in isolation but in relationship. They were not fixed states but dynamic phases.

What if the parable wasn't about categorizing good versus bad, healthy versus unhealthy, sinners versus saints? What if the parable were understood less as a prescription—*you need to be the good soil*—and more as a description of what was actually happening, both in the ecosystem around us and in our own lives? What if Jesus was describing the realities of both soil and soul, which were ever-changing and subject to outside forces?

The earth scientist George Fisher, who spent his career studying environmental transformation in Appalachia and who is also a Presbyterian elder, wrote a moving, ecological reading of the parable of the sower in which he reflects on the ancient knowledge that Jesus's largely agrarian audience would have brought to the first hearing of the story. The people of the Galilee had farmed the same territory for generations, but in Jesus's time, changes in land ownership wrought by the colonizing Romans were disrupting age-old patterns. "Thorny brush, once found only on hillsides, was appearing in valleys made desolate by owners who did not know the land. The parable begins in that scrub vegetation, where grazing animals have worn a path," Fisher writes. The seed that falls on that path "produces no grain, but birds eat it up, and replant some where it can germinate. Animals graze the brush, and leave manure that can fertilize worn-out fields. Even in this seemingly worthless habitat we find hints of the mutualism that is at the heart of ecological dynamics."

Fisher prods the reader to expand their lens, taking in information that Jesus's audience would have just known. The grasses that withered on the rocky ground? "The organic material they produced begins to transform that thin soil into rich humus." The thorns and thistles? They "keep humus in place and allow it to accumulate."

Nothing is wasted.

None of these soil conditions is permanent—not the hard path, not the rocky ground, not the thorn-choked earth—and nothing is guaranteed. The only constant is change. "When the harvest is good, the first three habitats seem to have no value," Fisher writes, "but when the rich soil begins to lose its fertility, the processes at work in those habitats gradually restore fertility."

Nothing is wasted—and everything has value.

The novelist Octavia Butler grew up in a strict Baptist household. While she disavowed any belief in God by her teen years, her groundbreaking novel *Parable of the Sower* and its sequels explore what, in a collapsing society, religion can be and do. As a Black woman whose grandmother had harvested sugarcane and done laundry for a white family on a Louisiana plantation, Butler understood the power of faith because she had seen its work among her own people. "Religion kept some of my relatives alive, because it was all they had. If they hadn't had some hope of heaven, some companionship in Jesus, they probably would have committed suicide, their lives were so hellish. But they could go to church and have that exuberance together, and that was good, the community of it," she wrote in 2000. "When they were in pain, when they had to go to work even though they were in terrible pain, they had God to fall back on, and I think that's what religion does for the majority of people. . . . They use it to keep themselves alive."

Butler once mentioned to an interviewer that, faced with the prospect of death, many people have to believe in an afterlife. They cling to that conviction, which fosters hope and offers comfort. The interviewer seemed puzzled and said she didn't need her religion to be comforting. "I said, 'Well, that's because you're already comfortable,'" Butler recalled. "It's those people who have so little, and who suffer so much, who need at least for religion to comfort them."

Comfort can come in different forms for different people. For some of us, it's rooted in being right—right about the facts, on the right team, on the right side of history. For many, it's an absence of some negative emotion, whether it's worry or pain, financial uncertainty or another fear.

For others—for me, I think—comfort comes in being reminded of possibility. Surely there is something more than this. Surely we will find redemption. Surely what's broken can be made whole, and what hurts will be healed.

———

Lauren Olamina, the protagonist in *Parable of the Sower*, plants the seeds of a new religion. "The only lasting truth is Change," she says. "God is Change."

I'm not a follower of Earthseed, the mythical religion in Butler's book, which some readers have adopted as a faith. Even Butler herself didn't imagine it to be a real religion, because she said it didn't offer enough comfort.

As I thought about Nate's reflection on the biblical parable of the sower, I was struck by the sharp contrast between my fixed interpretation and the fluidity of his. There was so much more room than I'd imagined, so much more hospitality in his reading than in mine.

There was another aspect of Nate's telling that challenged me: While the farmer seems a solitary figure, the story is actually a picture of relationship and community.

The parable depicts not a solo but a symphony. The birds do their part, as do the grasses and the thorns. Rain might not be mentioned, but surely it plays a role, too, gently wearing down the rock and watering all the plants that grow.

The farm was never mine, but I was just beginning to understand the degree to which its productivity was a collective effort. Nothing was wasted. There was such beauty in recognizing that—and in accepting the invitation, too, to participate in mutual flourishing. Each of us was invited to do our part, as were the goats that stayed for six weeks and the chickens that were here for a couple of months and the bean plants that flourished, then faded, returning nitrogen to the soil.

There was another layer of beauty, though, that only occurred to me much later: While I was just a visitor, to so many other creatures, this was home. In every moment, the soil existed in gorgeous precarity—always in process, always changing. Something was dying, something else coming to life. Worms burrowed. Microbes chomped. Ants scurried and scavenged. Roots grasped for water. The trees remained season after season, unfurling leaves, which then fell to become litter. Even the fox and the deer, which did their best to stay unseen.

An opportunistic bird plucked a seed from the ground and took flight. Where to from here?

trees

Several years before the seminary bought the farm, the previous owner had planted about two acres with conifer seedlings—some red and Norway spruce, but mostly eastern white pine. Fast-growing and native to the region, white pine had long been used by Indigenous people for all kinds of things. Its sap was useful for waterproofing canoes and also as the base for a medicinal salve. Its needles, rich in vitamin C, could be steeped in water to make a tea that prevented scurvy. During especially hard winters, its inner bark was dried and powdered into flour.

To the Haudenosaunee, who are sometimes also called the Iroquois, the white pine was known as the tree of peace. According to legend, a man named Dekanawida traveled among the five great Iroquois-speaking nations who were scattered on the shores of the Great Lakes. They had long been at war. Swayed by his prophetic call to peace, the five nations—Cayuga, Mohawk, Onondaga, Oneida, and Seneca—planted a white pine to signify an end to war and the beginning of the Iroquois

League. The needles of the white pine, which grow in clusters of five, became a symbol of their unity.

In 1605, English noblemen sent the *Archangel* across the Atlantic to explore and colonize. It landed on the coast of Maine. Along for the journey was a man named James Rosier, who was appointed to chronicle the expedition. In his "True Relation of the Most Prosperous Voyage Made This Present Yeere 1605," he lists the fruits and shrubs that he found: "Rasberries. Gooseberries. Strawberries. Roses. Currants. Wild-vines. *Angelica.*" There were birch and beech, ash and maple, as well as "oke, very great and good" and "firre-tree, which issue Turpentine in so marvellous plenty."

High in the hills, Rosier saw "notable high timber trees," which, in his mind's eye, he stripped of their branches and needles, seeing "masts for ships of 400 tun." Within decades, the Crown had claimed by decree all white pines larger than two feet in diameter. They became known as "mast pines," because their tall, straight trunks were perfect for the masts of the ships of the Royal Navy. What had, to the native nations, been a sign of peace became a fixture of war, and later, as forests of white pine were brought down for lumber, the raw materials for settlement: houses and bridges, shingles and cabinetry. As early as the mid-1600s, settlers in New England put the white pine on a flag, claiming the tree as a symbol of their own.

Drought-resistant and versatile, the eastern white pine can grow in all kinds of soils as long as it does not have too much competition from other hardwood trees. On the nutrient-depleted land that became the Farminary, they were intended to be Christmas trees. Once the seminary took over the land, though, nobody cut any of the white pines down. They grew twelve, fifteen, twenty-five feet tall, in stands four, five, and six trees deep, on either side of a grassy avenue. For those of us who were reluctant to use the single porta potty onsite, this man-made forest became our open-air urinal.

I was doing a shift at the farm one afternoon when I realized I needed to pee, so I headed out to the pines. I was tucking myself amid the branches, as far from view as I could, when my nose caught a strangely familiar scent. White pines tend to be less fragrant than other species, which is why people who suffer from severe conifer allergies often prefer them to other types of Christmas tree. Still, they're not fragrance-free. I stood there, sniffing the air. I picked up a faint whiff of piney resin but also a bit of musk (fox, maybe, or deer?). The smell triggered a memory, sending me spinning back in time and across an ocean.

When I lived in London in my early twenties, I was not out, even to myself, except sometimes after sunset.

My apartment was on the edge of East London, in Spital-fields, a neighborhood that hadn't yet gentrified. Small shops, some selling electronics parts, others with grimy windows through which you could see bold African-print textiles, lined the streets. Some mornings on my way to work, I'd stop in the café across the street, where the Moroccan-born proprietor made a decent bacon sandwich. Some afternoons, I'd visit the kosher butchery on the corner to buy a chicken. The Cohen family had opened the butchery in the 1890s, when there was still a significant Jewish population in the area. Nowadays, its clientele was largely African and Asian; the birds, which tended to be tough, demanded the patient simmering of a soup or stew.

At the end of my two-block street, the Petticoat Lane Market operated six days a week, much as it had for the previous three centuries. In the 1700s and 1800s, this neighborhood had been a hub of clothing manufacturing. Now, the clothes mostly came from China or Moldova or Bangladesh, but the market kept going. If my windows were open in the morning, I could hear the beep of trucks reversing and the clatter of wheeled racks, heavy with clothing, being trundled out of storage as I got ready for work. Some proprietors unfurled tarps over the metal frames that marked each stall and set out their wares—not just shirts and dresses but also kitchen goods and cleaning products and toys. By the time I returned each evening, all the merchants had already gone home, too. Only the bare skeletons of their stalls remained.

After dinner, I'd often wander down the block, take a left at the end of the street, then a right at the next corner. Soon I came to a parking garage. By day, it would be chockablock with merchants' cars and trucks. At night, it was nearly deserted, save a forest of concrete columns painted mustard yellow and the shadows they cast. If you stopped and stood and waited and watched, though, you might have noticed some shorter shad-ows, maybe a whisper of conversation, perhaps the orange glow of a lit cigarette. Always, it smelled slightly piney and a bit musky, a strange but unmistakable mixture of disinfectant and manhood. After dark, this was a gay cruising ground.

Most nights I just walked and walked and walked, doing laps around the garage, then wending my way through the nearby streets, then returning. I might steal a glance at someone, but I rarely mustered the courage to try out a pickup line, much less a conversation. If someone neared me, I'd usually lower my eyes and quicken my stride. Over time, though, I began to notice some of the regulars, and occasionally, I'd slow my walk, lift my gaze, even nod in recognition.

One of the guys had spiky blond hair, stiff with product. He looked a few years older than me, and he always wore a stone-washed denim jacket a couple of shades lighter than his frayed jeans, with paint-spattered construction boots.

One night, he blocked my path on the sidewalk next to the garage.

"Hi," he said.

"Hi," I said, frozen in place. I trembled as he drew nearer. Soon, he was no more than six inches from me, and I could smell his breath—minty from the gum he was chewing. He leaned in for a kiss, and without hesitation, I kissed him back.

After a few seconds, I pulled away, and he blushed.

"I'm sorry," he said. "I'm sorry."

"It's okay," I said. "I don't know what I'm doing."

"Me, too," he said, his cheeks reddening even more. I noticed his accent.

"Where are you from?" I asked.

"Poland," he said. "You?"

"The U.S.," I said. "But my family is from Hong Kong."

"Ah, Hong Kong! I've always wanted to go to Hong Kong."

He was from Warsaw. He had come to England to find work, and maybe also to get away from his family, and maybe also to find himself. As we stood in the flickering glow of a streetlight, I could see the deep dimples that emerged on his heavily pock-marked cheeks whenever he smiled. His name, he said, was Christoph—"but spelled the Polish way, with z's." So, Krzysztof. "You can just call me Chris."

"So, what are you doing here?" he asked.

"Just out walking," I said.

He cocked an eyebrow before extending me the sweet mercy of asking no more questions.

After that, I saw Chris every two or three nights. We never kissed again. Sometimes we chatted for a bit; he'd complain about his boss, and I about mine, and if he hadn't seen me for a while, he would ask whether I had been traveling. Other times, it was just a nod and a half smile before we both kept walking.

Either way, something about his continued presence reassured me. We never talked about sexuality. Neither of us ever said the word "gay." Once, I asked him whether he ever dated, and he just shrugged. Still, he knew things about me that nobody else knew. I told myself he understood something about me that even I couldn't understand.

I only ever brought one guy back to my apartment. His name was Mohammed—"my friends call me Mo." Slouchy, shambling, and a bit pudgy, he reminded me of a panda.

Mo and I kissed one night in a stairwell. Then I asked him if he wanted to come upstairs. As soon as he crossed the threshold of my apartment, he took off his shoes without having to be asked. When we got to my bedroom, I noticed he was trembling even more than I was. I handed him a blanket and we just sat on my bed and talked for a while. He told me he lived in a flat on a nearby council estate with his Bangladeshi immigrant parents and his sisters. It was tight quarters; at night, he liked to walk.

"Do you believe in God?" he eventually asked me.

I paused for a long moment before saying, "Yes. Yes, I do."

He told me he feared Allah's punishment and his father's wrath "for not being a real man." He had never gone home with another guy before. Always, he'd been too afraid.

"Shit," he said. "I can't stop shivering, man."

He covered his face with his hands.

"I get it," I said. "I'm scared, too."

We sat for a while in silence—not awkward, somehow.

"I should go," he finally said.

I walked him to my apartment door, and he pulled his shoes back on. I gave him a hug, and he gave me a defeated smile.

"Thanks," he said.

After Mo left, I took a long shower and realized I didn't know why he had thanked me. As the hot water ran over me, I scrubbed my skin as hard as I could. I was trying to wash away my shame, but I knew I couldn't. So I just stood there until my hands grew wrinkly, and I cried and cried and cried.

I'm not sure how long I'd been standing amid the trees when I finally came back to the farm and to my present-day self. I took a deep breath, brushed the needles of the nearest tree with my fingers, and smelled it again: pine and musk.

What had happened to Chris and to Mo?

I sent up a silent prayer for the two of them—a prayer not just for blessing but also of thanksgiving. When I thought of them, I felt only gratitude. They had encountered me in the wilderness of an East London parking garage, and somehow, in our mutual confusion, we found communion for a moment— a glimpse of peace and possibility even as our spirits seemed at war against themselves and the circumstances.

Then I shivered, but not from the memories. The sun had started to sink in the sky. As the cooling air snapped me to attention, I realized it was just about time to go home and cook dinner for my husband.

My husband.

My *husband.*

Twentysomething me hadn't been able to admit I was gay, let

alone imagine the possibility of having a husband. What did I know about love then? All I knew was fear and shame.

I pictured Tristan finishing his shift at the bookstore—Tristan, who hummed when he was happy; Tristan, who decided all on his own that my name was Jeffy, not Jeff; Tristan, who started dating a journalist and ended up married to a farmhand.

The breeze quickened. That scent was gone. I headed back toward the barn, and to my car, and to my home, and to my love.

zinnia

It's a weird and wondrous thing that you can go to the florist and find all manner of flower, no matter the season.

Occasionally, I will buy some gladioli. Each stem is so majestic, standing three feet tall and proud, with trumpet-like blossoms that unfurl progressively from bottom to top; every time I do, I remember they are my mother's favorite. Snapdragon looks so strange, and I want it just to say its name. If I'm feeling splurgey, I'll buy a peony, whose blossoms seem so grand. And if you see hydrangea on my table, it's probably a picture of my covetousness, an indication that I have been lusting not only after a full shrub heavy with blue and white blossoms but also the shingle-sided Hamptons mansion outside which they ought to grow.

I've always felt guilty about buying flowers in the off-season. They were grown somewhere far away, somewhere warmer, then flown across the sea to a country where I can buy them for a pittance. Whose hands tended these plants and clipped these buds? What soils do they come from? What are the cumulative costs of my season-defying desire for beauty? Who benefits?

Undoubtedly, it feels different—more gratifying, somehow—to have my own hand in growing the flowers. The ones we grew at the farm gently rebuked my consumerist conceptions of at-will beauty.

There was no way to manipulate the calendar: Daffodils and narcissi blossomed streamside during springtime, just before the weeping cherry let flow its pinkish veil. The dandelions ran rampant shortly afterward, growing wherever they willed. Then we waited for the rest of the flowers we'd planted, and those didn't even come when I thought they should, at the height of summer. Instead, they reached full flourish in late September, even into early October.

Every year, we planted delicate cosmos as well as hardy gomphrena: In the garden, the blossoms, in pink and purple globes rising from straight, sturdy stems, looked like a field of lollipops. That summer, we added marigold, whose deep oranges and blazing yellows echo the tomatoes among which they've been planted, and nasturtium, which creeps vine-like along the ground until it decides to send up a pretty red flower. Both of those have the extra benefit of being edible, the marigold offering a vegetal, almost minty zing, the nasturtium more spicy.

We'd planted sunflowers in the past, but not that summer. Still, we soon saw their thick, sturdy stalks rising from the ground, one row over from the okra. I double-checked with Nate to make sure he hadn't snuck any seed in. It must have been some dried and fallen seed from the previous year; what hadn't been snatched up by birds remained in the garden after everything faded away.

The sunflowers were pure grace.

Then there is the matter of what is honored as a flower and what gets dismissed as a weed, what work is seen as lovely and what is deemed less-than.

During the fall semester, Nate asked me to show up once a week to help his class with farm chores. Every week, he asked the twenty students to form groups to tackle the various tasks— one for compost, another for vegetable harvesting, one to weed, another to pick flowers and make bouquets for the CSA shares.

Two of the students always self-selected into the flower-picking group. One afternoon, I made this observation to Nate. He hadn't noticed. When it came time to divide into work teams, he asked those two students to join that day's composters. "Ew," one of them said, perhaps not as quietly as she thought. She slid sideways, tucking herself amid the flower team. Nate locked eyes with her and said, "Again, I would like to invite you to join the composting team."

I decided to join the flower harvesters. But as they took their shears and buckets of water and headed toward the cosmos and the zinnias, I straggled behind. In the end, I never made it to the garden, because I found myself in the weeds.

On the edges of the woods and along the overgrown fringes of the fields, so many different wildflowers and grasses sprang up entirely on their own: Goldenrod, its long, arcing stems heavy with their own sunshine. Queen Anne's lace, with its tiny white blossoms forming regal domes. Bulrush, which looked like corn dogs on a stick, but in an arrangement, among other flowers, added texture and visual interest.

When I returned to the barn, my bucket full of the things I'd collected everywhere but within the garden fence, the others asked, "Where did you get those?"

———

Early in my journalism career, I interviewed the artists Christo and Jeanne-Claude, who were famed for staging large-scale installations—say, wrapping the Reichstag in Berlin in acres of fabric, or surrounding multiple islands in Biscayne Bay, off Miami, with giant skirts of bright-pink cloth. All were temporary. After years of preparation, these artworks would be dismantled after merely two weeks on display. All that work, for just a few days!

When I asked why they didn't make things that endured for more than a fortnight, Jeanne-Claude replied, "We love what passes away." To her, life's fragility made it even more beautiful.

On her apartment balcony, my paternal grandmother nurtured some specimens of the queen of the night, which in Cantonese is called tan fa. The plant blooms rarely, and only under the cover of darkness, and shockingly briefly; the blossom will reach full flower after sunset, then fade before dawn the next day. Perhaps for that reason, tan fa has become one of the most treasured plants in the Chinese garden.

In the 2018 film *Crazy Rich Asians*, the wealthy matriarch, played by an imperious Michelle Yeoh, hosts a lavish tan fa viewing party. The scene accurately reflects the delight the Chinese find in these flowers. Is it because of their rarity that we cherish them? Do we quietly revel in the fact that we outlast them?

When my grandmother's tan fa were on the cusp of maturity, she'd sit out on the balcony at night, alone. She'd hum hymns and anticipate—waiting, waiting, waiting. What happened when it bloomed, I don't know, because every time I was either not there or asleep. She never took a picture of the blooms, either. But this I do know: It was one of the only things in my grandmother's life that was hers, and all hers.

My parents have since acquired the tan fa habit. Every couple of years, they will send me poorly lit cellphone photos of their blossoms. Once, they lamented to me an ill-timed vacation, which meant they missed the blooming.

This is, of course, a human-centric way of looking at flowers, and I know we are not the only ones who appreciate the blossoms, nor are we the only ones who benefit from the things we grow.

Flowers matter for pollinators. Bees rejoice in their presence. Butterflies and moths abound wherever the flowers grow. But even then, I regard their presence more often as a photo op than as a key link in an ecosystem's life. Occasionally, I'll take my phone out to snap a picture (or five) of a butterfly alighting on a blossom, but before I can click, the whir of its wings signals the end of the moment. It is gone.

For centuries, if not millennia, the flowers have preached their own sermons, and we humans have tried to echo them in our own language. I think, for instance, of the psalmist who contrasts the withering of the flowers of the field and the enduring presence of God. And then there's Jesus. "Why do you worry about clothes?" he asked, according to Matthew. "Consider the lilies. They neither labor nor spin cloth."

In the seventeenth century, the Dutch old masters added their own painterly variations on these ancient themes. They created fantastic still lifes that burst with color and vigor: rose and iris, chrysanthemum and daffodil, peony and lily, and, of course, tulip—red tulips and yellow tulips, orange tulips and purple tulips. Often, the tulips that stood highest in these artistic arrangements were the variegated blooms, striped and mottled and ruffled.

The paintings accomplished what neither nature nor even the most skilled gardeners back then could do: They made stunning arrangements of flowers that bloomed year-round, defying the seasons. In oil on canvas, these works of art offered a permanence that was both unrealistic and impossible.

That, too, was part of the point, because these works were part of a theological genre of visual art called vanitas painting. In emphasizing the glory of these rare and beautiful flowers, the artist invited the viewer to contemplate the brevity of life and the fragility of creatureliness. (Later manifestations of vanitas still lifes used clocks and skulls to make similar points, which feels a little too on the nose for me.)

One of the most celebrated vanitas painters, Hans Bollongier, often depicted a particularly valuable tulip variety called Semper Augustus ("ever exalted"). At the peak of the tulip market, in the late 1630s, one Semper Augustus bulb could sell for the equivalent of thousands of dollars, all to produce blossoms that lasted little more than a week. But those blooms! Deep crimson, verging on purple, streaked across the white petals, as if blood had been artfully splashed on bleached cotton.

We know now what they did not know then: The stripes were the work of viruses. These microbes were tiny painters that poured themselves into a gorgeous work of nature, the petals their canvas. In the first half of the twentieth century, botanists discovered that the viruses essentially interrupted the second color from being fully displayed on the petals. What merchants and artists alike considered the picture of glorious strength was actually a marker of profound fragility.

Of the flowers we grew in the garden, the zinnias were my favorite. You never knew what color they'd manifest: orange, red, yellow, magenta, pink, purple. Some were singles, the petals arrayed neatly around an open center. Others were double-flowering, as if a blossom had somehow implanted itself within another. Still others were so intricately layered there seemed no longer to be any center at all, just whirls of petals that befuddled the eye, forming a miniature dome more glorious than any humans have ever constructed on our greatest cathedrals.

The zinnia's native range stretches from southern Mexico up through the American Southwest. Much of this is dry, scrubby terrain, which built up the zinnia's resilience. What we have now is an easygoing plant that is not particularly picky about soil types. The one thing they want in abundance is sunshine, so we grew them in the middle of the garden, safely away from the shade cast by the tall sunflowers or the towering okra.

That they are today widely known as zinnias reflects a common narrative in modern horticulture: The flowers were named for a European. Though the Spanish were the first to bring specimens back from colonized Mexico, these early imported varieties were relatively scraggly blooms that did not demand much notice. Johann Gottfried Zinn, an eighteenth-century German botanist, is credited with being the first to describe the flower, and he is the one now memorialized in its name.

It's obviously absurd to claim that Zinn was the first to describe the flower. For generations, the native peoples of what is now Mexico would dry the petals and leaves of some zinnia varieties and brew teas for the treatment of indigestion and diarrhea. The Pueblo peoples upheld the zinnia as a symbol of wisdom; some particularly ambitious mothers and fathers forced their kids to eat the blossoms as if they were ethical vitamins. The Navajo treasured the flower and put it to multiple good uses—alleviating heartburn, soothing sore throats, producing natural dyes.

Unrooted from its native soils and original contexts, the zinnia was reduced to something simply lovely to look at. Generations of breeders have refined it since then, producing varieties that accentuate its superficial properties—more petals, more vibrant colors, longer-lasting blooms. Have these zinnia retained their medicinal qualities? I have no idea, because I've never seen a seed catalog mention anything other than appearances.

All this makes me wonder whether the many verses in the Bible that warn about the withering of the flowers of the field can be understood differently than we typically do. Where we read one-dimensional warnings about fleeting beauty and glory, perhaps there was also an admonition to consider more enduring purposes.

For instance, in the ancient cultures of the both Near and Far East, the lily—the flower most often mentioned in these biblical warnings—was held to have medicinal power. Derivatives of lily were variously believed to possess anti-epileptic and expectorant properties. Their bulbs were boiled to make ointments thought to combat tumors and tinctures said to heal burns.

In losing this knowledge, I wonder whether we have also misplaced a more holistic understanding. To consider a lily is to be attentive to the entire value of the thing that grows, not just its fleeting beauty, not merely its aesthetic appeal.

Perhaps the point was never to divert us from delighting in the flower but rather to encourage us to look even deeper. A single blossom contained multitudes—and maybe Jesus meant to prod us to honor the vastness of the life, death, and new life knit into the story of a little plant.

daikon

Daikon radish is not the most aesthetically pleasing of vegetables. It looks something like a fat, albino carrot. But it's the essential ingredient in lo bak go, a staple of the dim sum table that is often confusingly called turnip cake, even though it contains no turnip at all.

My mom rarely made lo bak go at home because it's somewhat labor-intensive and there's really no way to rush it. These little rectangular cakes are made from grated radish and rice flour that have been blended, then slowly simmered. Then you add minced dried shrimp, which burst with brininess, along with Chinese sausage, shiitake mushroom, scallion, salt, and white pepper. Steam the whole mix in a loaf pan, and put it in the refrigerator to firm up overnight. Then you slice and pan-fry until both sides of each cake are golden and crispy but the interior is still tender, even slightly gooey.

Mostly, we'd have it when we went out for dim sum. Lo bak go always tells you something about a restaurant. You can tell if they're cheaping out by using too little radish and too much rice flour. Poorly made cakes lack the radish's mildly bitter flavor. All you can taste is sausage, shrimp, and—if they're especially bad—the oil in which the cakes were fried. A lazy, rushed kitchen will put out lo bak go that has insufficient browning and no contrast in texture. If we're at dim sum and we order radish cake, I like to watch for my mom's reaction: She'll wrinkle her nose if there's insufficient radish or nod in satisfaction if there is enough.

As a kid, I didn't love lo bak go that was properly made. The ones that were overly heavy on rice flour were just bundles of starchy goodness, vehicles for salt and fat and umami. If they were well crisped, even overly so, I could eat them.

It was the bitterness that bothered me. But, like so much else, the palate changes over time. My taste buds have matured, gaining the ability to appreciate flavors that, when I was younger, just tasted foul. The daikon's bitter tinge didn't change. My ability to understand it as something delicious, something worthwhile, something good, did.

We sowed the daikon seeds in the soil at the farm early in the summer, knowing it could take a while for the radishes to attain their full plumpness and length. But the seeds sprouted relatively quickly, sending up shoot after shoot with abundant, pale green leaves.

As soon as the heat of high summer set in, though, those shoots seemed to gain inches overnight—and I began to worry. Not all growth is good growth: The daikon had begun to bolt. It was pouring its energy into making ever-taller stems and too many broad, fernlike leaves, rather than concentrating on its roots, down in the soil. A quick dig under the surface revealed none of the thick, white cylinders we wanted, just thin, wan things that somehow managed to keep the plants from toppling.

Planting the daikon among our summer crops had always been a risk, though I didn't know it when we planted. I had never re-searched their seasonality—one of the consequences, I guess, of growing up in a society where you can get what you want, when-ever you want, at the grocery store. Winter, spring, summer, fall: There the daikon were, always piled neatly, like white logs.

The cultural importance of the dish should have been my first clue: My people like to look for auspicious signs and lucky symbols everywhere, and we serve lo bak go during the Chinese New Year, when our year-round superstitions go into overdrive. In the northern hemisphere, the Lunar New Year always falls during the winter. Since lo bak go is sliced and fried to look something like little gold bars, they have come to symbolize prosperity and good fortune.

Daikon is traditionally planted in the autumn, and where the temperatures don't fall much below freezing, they keep well in the fields until January or February—perfect timing for the Lunar New Year. Elsewhere, daikon can be used as a cover crop in the off-season, because it effectively feeds nitrogen into the surrounding soils.

However unnatural it might have been, my attempt to culti-vate summer daikon still felt like a failure—of planning, if noth-ing else. We didn't need the real estate in the garden, so I just left the daikon to do its thing. This was less a strategic decision than a coping mechanism—a way of dealing, or not, with this little grief.

Anyway, there was so much else to do.

Saint Augustine wrote that "every change is a kind of death." Sometimes change happens because of our action. Other times, it results from our neglect.

Decay and death are written indelibly into nearly every aspect of the farm, from the peeling paint on the side of the barn to the seasonal metamorphoses of the plants in the garden, from the rise and fall of the waters of the pond to the comings and goings of generations of geese and heron to and from those waters. Yet I am often reluctant to speak of these changes as manifestations of decay or death. Even when I notice them, I'd often rather scurry past. With every death, there is something to be grieved. But grief is uncomfortable, grief is tiresome, and grief is unpleasant. Almost always, grief seems a terrible inconvenience. Who has time for all that mourning?

With so many deaths, there also comes new life. But if we can't even handle the grief, how do we then carry the complexity of sorrow alongside hope? There it is, throughout the garden—something always starting to fade, something else always beginning to flower.

The daikon kept growing until its green crowns were at least knee-high. Then it began to bud. Within days, the buds had blossomed into the loveliest little white flowers, many of them edged in lavender.

I was standing in the garden with Nate, puzzling over the bolting daikon one day, when I noticed the flowers for the first time. I took some pictures. And then I did what I do when I don't know what else to do: I googled "daikon flowers."

"I guess we're the kind of farmers who have to google things," I said to Nate.

He didn't reply.

A moment later, I added, "You can eat them!"

Turns out all parts of the daikon—flowers and leaves and roots—are edible. I plucked a blossom and handed it to Nate, then took one for myself and popped it into my mouth. We chewed, even though there wasn't much to chew. At first, it didn't taste like much of anything. Then, suddenly, a late hit of radishy flavor—slightly bitter, slightly savory.

The greens have somewhat more pungency, and they can be treated much like you would kale or bok choy. By that, I mean I am assuming you will cook them. In the Chinese kitchen, we traditionally frown on uncooked greens, which are for cows. The only time I remember my grandparents eating salad is when we went to Denny's on special occasions; a free salad came with the entrée, and they always got it with Thousand Island dressing—no idea why.

To me, the heat of the wok expresses culinary love, softening what's hard and imbuing it with flavor. Whether you're deep-frying or steaming, stir-frying or poaching, 鑊氣 ("wok hei"), the breath of the wok that the Cantonese venerate as near-spiritual, is present, eliciting the inherent goodness of the ingredients.

You can braise daikon greens with diced tofu and finely sliced shiitake mushroom, much as you might treat any other relatively robust green; for the liquid, just a bit of chicken broth or even a couple tablespoons of oyster sauce will do, since tofu will offer up its water. You can add some sriracha if you like heat.

You could simply sauté daikon greens, too, choosing to be generous with the garlic and salt. You could blitz them into a hearty pesto, with plenty of parmesan, basil, and olive oil balancing out the gentle bitterness.

Cantonese has multiple words to describe bitter flavors.

Some people say that 澀 ("geep," with a hard g, rhymes with "keep") is one. More properly, though, 澀 is a feeling, not a flavor. 澀 is the sort of astringency that dries the palate and makes your mouth pucker.

苦 (pronounced "fu," with a rising tone) is the most common kind of bitterness. Bitter melon is called 苦瓜 ("fu gua")—literally, "bitter melon." 苦茶 ("fu cha")—bitter tea—is a catch-all term for the medicinal infusions brewed up at the Chinese apothecary. 苦 is bitterness that clings to the palate, often until it's chased away by something else.

When I was a kid and I ate something that tasted even remotely bitter, I'd grimace and exclaim, "苦!"

Usually, my grandmother would sigh and gently chide me: "甘!"

甘 ("gum") has no precise translation in English. Some people have described it as a bitter start with a sweet finish. That doesn't seem quite right to me, but it hints at an important truth: The bitterness of 甘 doesn't linger. It's clarifying, not overwhelming. In its wake, other flavors taste somehow more vibrant. 甘 is a bitterness that doesn't smother. It never overstays its welcome. It brings a change of perspective.

苦 means "bitterness," yes, but not just in a culinary sense. It's also a word for hardship and suffering. In Buddhist-inflected Chinese thought, a virtuous human is taught to 吃苦—literally, "eat bitterness."

This has frequently been interpreted as an instruction to persevere through pain without complaint. After all, suffering is inevitable, but to protest it is a choice. In the cultural framework in which I was reared, one's personal feelings were real and valid, but they were also properly subordinated to the greater good, which was rarely, if ever, helped by one's moaning and groaning.

There are significant differences between Western and East Asian cultures when it comes to how people process and express emotion. According to a seminal 1991 paper by the psychologists Hazel Rose Markus and Shinobu Kitayama, these differences are rooted in our divergent cultural understandings of the self. For people from cultures that emphasize independence, they write, "not to attend to one's inner feelings is often viewed as inauthentic or even as denying the 'real' self." For those from cultures that prioritize interdependence, though, "it is the interpersonal context that assumes priority over the inner attributes, such as private feelings."

For people like me who have been reared amid two often clashing cultures, this can create no small amount of philosophical and emotional friction. We suffer, simply because we're human—and then we suffer a little more, because we don't know how we're supposed to reckon with our suffering. To give it voice would crystallize the blame and bring shame on important people in one part of our lives; to tamp it down would be to appear strangely stoic and even fake to those who matter in another.

Sometimes I feel myself ping-ponging between the two cultures—a flash of independence, then the pull of interdependence. Maybe someday the dissonance will resolve at last to harmony. I'm not sure how.

Perhaps, though, there's a way to extend the metaphor of eating bitterness in a way that feels like progression toward resolution: After you eat, you digest. A healthy body breaks down what's eaten into its constituent parts. It takes what's useful and nutritious and delivers it where it needs to go. Then it takes what is not useful and ejects it as waste.

I wonder whether eating bitterness could be understood—and experienced—not simply as an instruction not to express your pain or angst but rather as a healthy and even natural picture of how to process it. In that way, it's both a coping mechanism and a healing process: a means of taking the suffering that will inevitably come, extracting what's beneficial, and expelling what isn't.

Even here, the digestive system offers some help. The process of breaking down the food we consume is not something we do on our own. It happens in largely unseen community, with the body and microflora working in strange and symbiotic partnership. It takes time. It can't be hurried.

And what if "eating bitterness" were rendered not as 吃苦—not a bitterness that overwhelms, not a bitterness that lingers—but rather as 吃甘—a bitterness that clarifies and catalyzes? My Cantonese isn't good enough to know if that's grammatically correct. But theologically and philosophically, it feels right. In the context of the garden, too, it seems apt. After the bitter bolting of the daikon, I received the consolation prize of those delicate blossoms. Decay and even death are never the end of the story.

We left most of the daikon plants in the ground until they withered. This was less an intentional choice than an act of benign neglect: Absent any knowledge about how to rescue the floundering plant, we just ignored it.

We left the daikon for so long that its seed pods naturally dried. One mid-autumn day, I finally noticed that nothing had been done with the daikon patch. So I harvested the seeds and stored them in the barn, to be planted later.

In the root's failure to grow as I wanted it to, I eventually got those seed pods—little pockets of possibility. Maybe they contained the hope of a future harvest.

ax

Over the years, trees had fallen throughout the woods, and others were taken down because they'd been weakened by disease or lightning or some other unseen force. The seminary's maintenance staff had chopped the fallen trees—mostly maples and oaks—into large pieces, and gradually, a wood pile had grown behind the barn.

Nate bought an ax, and just after Thanksgiving, he invited me and a few other students to go chop some wood. When I got to the farm, Lincoln and Wes had already arrived, and Wes and Nate were taking turns whacking at logs. Most of the time they found their target, but sometimes they didn't.

Seeing them fail occasionally gave me some hope. When Nate asked if I wanted to take a turn, I said yes.

I had never chopped wood before.

He handed me the ax. I followed his careful instructions—how to hold the ax, how to draw it back, how to fling it forward over my shoulder and land it on the piece of wood on the chopping block. I tried and failed to make contact. I tried again, and only managed to knock the wood over. I tried again, and the ax bounced off the wood; it seemed to be mocking my weakness. My face grew hot, but it wasn't the feeling of physical exertion; it was the taint of failure.

I still have not chopped wood.

In the meantime, Hana had arrived. She'd been watching silently.

"Can I try?" she finally said.

"Of course," Nate said.

She took the ax in her hands and stood entirely still, eyes fixed on her target. Then, in one rush of elegant, unbroken motion, she lifted the ax and flung it in an arc that landed at the heart of the wood and split it perfectly in two.

"Before you got there, I said out loud to Wes, 'This is a safe space to fail,'" Nate told me afterward when we were sitting in his office. He was speaking as much to himself as he was to Wes. "It was me saying, *I am okay failing in front of you, Wes.* And I feel that. I've chopped a little bit of firewood in my life, but only a little tiny bit of it. And I'm supposed to be the teacher."

I told him that while I was flailing at the wood, some memories had suddenly—and unexpectedly—returned. It's startling how a seemingly innocent event can conjure ghosts. The ones that arrived unbidden while I was trying to chop wood were those of the childhood bullies who had made comments about my body.

After a long silence, which I appreciated, he said, "I wonder if it matters that it was me and Hana and Wes in that space."

"I'm sure," I said. To fail in front of those whom I know and love—those who know me and love me—somehow mitigated the failure.

"Can I tell you something else, Nate?" I asked.

"Of course," he said.

The story of why I don't wear shorts, of why I hate my body, came spilling out.

"I'm so sorry, Jeff," Nate said. "That story reflects a perversion of what the body was intended for. I'm so sorry."

Nate has a particular skill: Some of us, we begin to tear up and then there really is no intermediate step before we are full-on ugly crying. Others, like Nate, have this phenomenal ability to hold the tears in their eyes, until just that one perfect tear descends the cheek. It seemed not the right moment to ask him how he managed to do that, so I just sat silently as I admired that solitary trickling tear.

Maybe because I didn't say anything, he continued speaking. He began to talk about the pieces of wood in the wood pile. "We know they didn't all split with equal force," he said. "Some of them, we had to bludgeon the crap out of them to get them to split. There's the grain of the wood, and there are knots. And what might be imperfection to the woodworker is the strength of the wood."

He was right. A knot can form on a tree where a branch has been broken, where the wood has been attacked by a fungus, or where the tree has otherwise been hurt. It's a coping mechanism: The wood becomes denser as a means of survival. A knot signals not only weakness but also strength, not only injury but also resilience.

"Look, I don't want you to prematurely make the redemptive turn," Nate said gently, as if noticing that I wasn't finding his metaphor particularly helpful. I was still angry—angry at the return of memories I'd wanted to suppress, angry at the pain I still carried in my body, angry at my inability to heal. I didn't want to hear about redemption.

Maybe because I still wasn't saying anything, he once again kept talking.

"Somehow the tradition—the Christian tradition—has consistently affirmed the goodness of God, and creation is supposed to be a place that bears witness to that." My squirming in my chair bore witness to my discomfort at this entire conversation. "When we think of creation bearing witness to the goodness of God, we have 'purple mountain majesties' in mind," he continued. "But I don't think that's quite fair to the scriptural testimony. We've been farming long enough to know that there's more going on out there. So what do we mean when we say that God is good?"

I found his use of the word "we" a little presumptuous. Had I said that God was good? But I felt a nudge toward possibility when he said, "There's more going on out there." I could accept that reminder—perhaps even say a tentative "yes" to the invitation to search the terrain for some sign of ordinary goodness.

He asked if I might be willing to try to chop wood again. I said yes.

In *Presence in the Modern World*, the French philosopher Jacques Ellul writes about "an unresolvable tension" that he saw in society: "On the one hand, we cannot make this world less sinful. On the other, we cannot accept it as it is." This is the reality of life in a beautiful but broken world. "Just as we are caught in the tension between sin and grace, so always are we caught between these two contradictory demands," Ellul continues. "It is an infinitely painful position, it is very uncomfortable, but it is the only one that can be fruitful and faithful for the Christian's action and presence in the world. . . . The Christian life is a continual struggle."

"Struggle" suggests that we have choices, that we have freedom, that we have agency. Ellul writes that it is up to each person to use this freedom for the cause of grace, "truly working out how to embody their faith in the concrete forms of their life." He emphasizes that "concrete forms" include not just broadly visible gestures but also the small things, the tiny choices.

A couple of days later, I returned to the farm when nobody else was there. I found the ax in the barn, walked slowly out to the woodpile, and chose a large piece of wood. I placed it gently on the stump that was serving as our chopping block.

A few times, I totally whiffed. A few times, I made more solid contact. I never was able to split the wood into anything resembling a log that you could put into a fireplace or a stove. But I tried again, and then I tried again, and then I tried again. I did not succeed in the conventional sense, but I also didn't totally fail. Sometimes simply choosing to pick the ax up again, even if you whiff, counts as a win.

seeds

Before the last of the fall crops had faded away, we were already planning for the following spring. This was undoubtedly my favorite time of year, maybe even more than harvest. I'm not even a little embarrassed at how much pleasure it gave me to go over our seed spreadsheet again and again. There were columns not just for the plant name as well as the particular variety but also for the cost each year we'd ordered it, for companion plants (onions are a good neighbor to radishes and leafy greens, for instance, because they help deter pests that are drawn to those crops), and for combatant plants (sunflower roots excrete an acid that will stunt the growth of potatoes and beans).

If I loved anything more than the spreadsheet, it was the seed catalogs. They were my porn—temptation on every single page, photograph after photograph of plump turnips and fat carrots, juicy fruits and glistening tomatoes. Some of the cannier seed dealers went not with photos but with line drawings. These were even more powerful. I filled the white space in my imagination with not only vibrant produce but also my fantasies of being an old-time gentleman farmer. Every listing burst with promise, every seed packet shouted of hope. Nothing had failed yet. All was still possible.

In previous years, we'd planted plenty of beans as well as a couple of varieties of summer squash—two of the famed Three Sisters cultivated for generations by Native tribes all over North America, including the Lenape. Corn had never been planted, though. Online, we found an heirloom blue variety called Sehsapsing, which had traveled west to Oklahoma with the Lenape.

I wondered whether inviting Pearl into the seed-ordering process might be a chance for me to reconnect with her and let her know she mattered to me, so the next time I saw her, I asked if there was anything she wanted us to get. She recalled how, in previous summers, some CSA shareholders had made critical comments about both the collard greens and the bok choy in their farm shares: *Who likes them? How do you even cook them? They're just not my favorite.*

Maybe it was mischief, or maybe it was anger. Maybe we wanted to dare them to insult our beloved foods again.

"So I guess we should order more of them?" I said to her.

She cackled. "Yes, Jeff! Yesssssss!"

We added an extra variety of each to our seed order: Mei Qing, a Shanghai baby bok choy, with emerald leaves over jade-green stems, and Top Bunch, collards with large, slightly wrinkled leaves.

"What do you want?"

I had less than a year of seminary left, and I needed to start thinking about what would happen afterward. So Nate asked me this terrible question, and then he sat there in silence, staring at me with his ridiculous saucer eyes for what seemed like eons.

"What do you want?" he finally said again.

It was the same question his mentor had asked him all those years ago, the same question he'd found so difficult to answer aloud when he was still nursing the dream of returning home to Kansas. Now he was turning that cruelty on me.

"I don't know, Nate," I said.

He cast me a merciful smile before giving me the gift of the same words Marcus Smucker had given him.

"I have no idea what God will do with your desires," he said. "But I have to believe that God cares very much about what you want."

Even as he said those words, I felt the reprimand of a Bible verse that had inscribed itself on my childhood heart: "The heart is deceitful above all things, and desperately wicked." The words were the prophet Jeremiah's, and they had been deployed again and again by pastors and preachers and teachers in my childhood to warn against the temptation of chasing what we wanted.

Where Jeremiah had said *the* heart, I'd heard, "*Your* heart is deceitful above all things, and desperately wicked." Anything I wanted, whether it was a toy or a trip, a new book or just some time by myself, was probably bad or selfish or wrong—or all of the above. I began to doubt myself, wondering whether it was sinful even to say what I wanted to eat for dinner. Of course my hyperpersonal interpretation of the text makes no sense and might even seem shockingly arrogant: Why would Jeremiah have been targeting me? But to a kid growing up in an environ-ment where individual salvation was the dominant concern and where Scripture was the holy handbook for life, I didn't know how else to process it. Every time the verse came back to me, I believed, with all my heart, that I could not trust that same heart whenever it wanted something delightful or pleasurable.

To voice what I wanted would be to give that deceit shape and form—and to share that with another person would only be to heighten the shame.

Because I couldn't say what I wanted, I tried the next best thing: I emailed a small group of close friends and former colleagues to ask them what they imagined for me. What ideas did they have for my post–grad school life? What could they see me doing?

Most of the replies were generic. "Praying for you!" "Thinking of you!" "Sending you love and light!" "Hang in there!" I didn't want love or light or anything else that could have appeared either on a sympathy card or an inspirational poster with a dangling cat; I wanted concrete, actionable thinking.

The not-generic emails tended to be equally annoying, except in long form. Perhaps the most grating one came from an eternally sunny friend: "Put aside your unhelpful fears and trust in your knowledge and experience of the love of God." I immediately wrote back to tell him that, actually, my fears have historically been extremely helpful, because they have prepared me for even the worst disappointments. Then, before I could press send, I filed that email in my "drafts" folder.

My friend Rachel was the only person who replied with specificity—and who acknowledged that this wasn't just about my future but also Tristan's: "What a weird, uncertain, potentially transformative season for y'all."

As if divining my own doubts, she questioned whether I'd ever find the right place within the bounds of the institutional church, and she confessed that she didn't think I'd thrive in a traditional congregational setting. "One thought that I keep coming back to again and again is: teacher," she wrote. Again, she added, it probably wouldn't be a conventional classroom, but she felt this was as good a lead as any. "I get teary thinking about the impact your presence would have on students."

Then she added that she had asked her husband, Dan, for his thoughts. "Didn't Jeff kill a chicken?" Dan said. "He can do anything."

In the Gospel of John, Jesus goes to Jerusalem during a festive season and visits the Pool of Bethesda, where many disabled people would gather. Superstition held that whenever the water in the spring-fed pool bubbled up, the first person in would be healed of whatever ailed them. (Some archaeologists have identified a possible location in what's now the Muslim Quarter of the Old City.)

At the pool, Jesus encounters a man who had been sick for thirty-eight years. His condition is never clearly identified, only assumed, because at the end of the story Jesus says, "Get up! Pick up your mat and walk."

What intrigued me as I studied the passage was the question that Jesus asks the man before healing him. In English translations, it's usually rendered either as "Do you want to be well?" or "Do you want to be healed?"

My friend Noah, who is a pastor, pointed out to me one day that the man never actually answers Jesus's question. He talks only about not having help to access the pool. Someone else always got there first.

As I thought about Noah's observation, I went back to the Greek. The Greek word that's translated as "well" or "healed" is ὑγιής. And yes, it can mean "well" or "healed," but it's probably more precise to say "whole." In our modern understanding, healing might seem to be about finding a personal cure (the man picks up his mat and walks). But in the context of that time, such a condition would have separated the man from full belonging (he had nobody, for instance, who could help him to the pool). To be made whole isn't just to have one's physical affliction removed; it is to be restored to community and returned to relationship.

Anyway, the man has been there for such a long time that he seems incapable of imagining wellness or healing or wholeness. All he can describe is where he hurts.

While I knew that Nate was asking what I wanted in the big picture, I did manage to respond in a smaller way. A few weeks earlier, he and Kenda had ambushed me: Even though a thesis was optional for master's students, they decided I would be writing one. It was up to me what form that would take.

I knew I wanted to grow good things and cook good things for people I loved, because I've always been able to say things in the language of food that I couldn't manage in Cantonese or English. I can express myself in the kitchen in a way I can't anywhere else. And at my table, I can create the belonging I wish for elsewhere.

For my final project at the Farminary, I decided I wanted to cook a feast in which every dish would contain something grown on or foraged from the farm. Every person at the table would be someone who had been crucial to my journey.

Nate was immediately skeptical, not least because of the timing. We were already deep into the autumn and just six months from the end of my time at the seminary. His main concern was that grades had to be in the first week of May, when most of the seedlings normally hadn't even been transplanted.

I reminded him that he was the one who asked me what I wanted. All I needed, I said, was a hoop house. It could go over the rows where I'd already planted Chinese greens.

For weeks, he demurred. For weeks, I nagged. For weeks, he dodged my questions about why he was so reluctant.

One day, a text popped up on my phone: He'd gone and bought all the raw materials for the hoop house. We put it up a few days before Thanksgiving.

I started looking at the seed catalogs, trying to figure out what I could grow by late April. Then I went to the barn, retrieved the daikon seeds, and planted them, along with the nubby ends of some green onions.

winter

garlic

Late autumn drained nearly all the color from the farm, the growing season's lush greens ceding to yellows and oranges, then beiges, browns, and grays. As soon as the air began taking on winter's bite, visits to the farm dropped off. Almost always, I was there by myself or with only Nate. I understood. The place looked dead. After the first snowfall, everything was blanketed in white; it looked as if nature had spread dustcovers over the farm—a sure sign to come back another time.

People often said to me, "Nothing is growing!" This wasn't true. They meant there were no sunflowers to harvest, no bouquets to create, no cherry tomatoes to pluck off the vine, no leaves of basil in which to wrap those tomatoes, no peppers waiting to be transformed into hot sauce. That didn't mean the land was lifeless.

I was walking in the backwoods one afternoon when a flash of red streaked past me—it was one of the foxes I knew lived nearby but had never seen.

In the pond, a family of ducks appeared one day. I thought

they were mallards, but the green on the male's head looked more like a mohawk than a mask. My bird app told me they weren't mallards; they were American wigeons. This was too far north for them to overwinter. Most likely, they had just stopped for a rest and a snack before continuing southward.

In the herb garden, the chives were still persisting.

And, not long before, we had started next year's garlic.

The garlic was unlike any other crop we grew—and we didn't even grow it in the garden. It was the one thing we felt safe planting outside the fence, because the white-tailed deer roaming these woods and fields have never shown any interest in it.

This season, we had created a slightly raised bed just outside the garden, tucking clove after clove into the soil. It seemed a fishes-and-loaves-style miracle that each of those cloves would become six, seven, eight more.

We planted seven varieties, whose names and stories speak to garlic's global reach: Shantung Purple, a hot, striped variety from northern China; Russian Red, which migrated from Europe to Canada with Anabaptist refugees and is so called not because of regional political history but for its exterior blush; Pyong Yang, which is traditionally grown in the farmlands surrounding the North Korean capital; Nootka Rose, from Washington State's San Juan Islands; Godfather's Italian, which purportedly traces its roots to Italy but, as its name might suggest, is really more American; and Chesnok Red, which is also known as Shvelisi, for the village in the Republic of Georgia from which it comes. The final variety, elephant garlic, whose name hints at its massive cloves, isn't garlic at all, though it looks the part; native to southern Europe and the eastern Mediterranean, it's officially a leek.

There are so many things I love about garlic.

As a gardener, I appreciate how it grows on a different time-table than most other crops: planted in mid-autumn, harvested in early summer, hung to cure for at least three or four weeks after that. It reminds me that not everything matures at the same time. It disrupts my tendency to hew to a single calendar. It teaches me that seasons differ depending on the species.

As a cook, I applaud the supporting role it graciously plays in so many dishes. It can back up the basil in a good pesto, or enliven a wok full of stir-fried greens. Slivered and dried, it harmonizes with the poppy seeds, sesame, and salt on the outside of an everything bagel. Minced, it integrates beautifully into a simple egg fried rice. In all these dishes, it is rarely the star—and even when it might be considered one (roasted, for instance, until it becomes buttery, its in-your-face essence gentled by heat and time), it almost never shines alone.

On a cold afternoon just after Christmas, I went to the garden to do some work. I needed to shovel several wheelbarrows of finished compost to build the beds in the hoop house. When I got there, though, a wave of weary laziness overtook me. I looked at the empty wheelbarrow, and I just felt hatred. It had been raining for several days. I knew the soil would be sodden and heavy and I'd have to fight harder than I wanted to push through the mud.

So instead, I mulched about half of our garlic beds.

To mulch garlic in the early stages of its growth requires both careful hands and patient eyes. You want to smother the weeds, but not the garlic. Assuming you haven't weeded attentively—or, as in our case, at all—you have to search the weedy bed for the thick sprouts that have protruded through the dirt line in search of sky. Sometimes you see it right away. Sometimes you don't. Even if you're tracing the allegedly neat line of planted cloves, sometimes the fledgling garlic is just not ready to be seen.

This kind of garden work gratified me. It was similar to weeding, which likewise put me in a contemplative, almost meditative mood, but weeding sometimes sent me into thoughtless autopilot. Putting that first layer of mulch on a bed demanded a particular kind of attention. I had to focus so much, searching for evidence of the right kind of growth, seeking signs of the garlic's slow protrusion above the soil line, that, at least for a few minutes, it crowded the neuroses from my brain. To let the mind wander too far from the garlic bed in front of me might mean smothering a shoot that was asking for my care.

My friend Noah called me one day and asked a loathsome question, as our dearest friends tend to do: How near does God feel to you right now?

I struggled to answer.

What then came out of my mouth was mostly conversational filler—the kind of thing you say when you don't want to betray what you really think or feel. The truth was that God had felt mostly distant, like a star you struggle to see because of all the artificial light pollution. Was that a flicker? Or was that just my astigmatism acting up?

I'd imagined seminary would bring me closer to God; I was studying for a master's in divinity, so it doesn't seem wild to think the divine might be present in the process. What I hadn't considered was that reading books about God and sitting through classes about God did not necessarily engender encounters with God.

I strained to seek evidence of God's presence—and sometimes it felt as if I didn't have the energy to strain that much at all. But it was hard to say that out loud. I felt guilty about it, as if God's apparent absence were my fault. My fault for not being diligent enough in my prayer life, my fault for not being disciplined enough to read my Bible as regularly as my mom wanted me to, my fault for not being a better, less judgmental, more wholehearted person.

I thought of the English mystic Julian of Norwich, whose adoration of Christ, chronicled in her rambling masterpiece *Revelations of Divine Love,* has always humbled, baffled, and intrigued me. She is one of my favorite writers of faith, a medieval weirdo who, at thirty, fell ill and thought she was dying. A local clergyman was summoned and showed up at her bedside with a cross. As Julian regarded it, she felt the light in the room change: "It was all dark about me in the chamber, as if it had been night, save in the Image of the Cross whereon I beheld a common light. . . . All that was away from the Cross was of horror to me, as if it had been greatly occupied by the fiends. Suddenly all my pain was taken away from me, and I was as whole as ever I was afore."

Not just whole, but also, over the subsequent hours, gifted with a series of sixteen visions of Jesus, which she chronicles in florid prose. In one vision, she sees Jesus as a divine mother figure. "The mother may give her child suck of her milk, but our precious Mother, Jesus, He may feed us with Himself," she writes. "The Mother may lay the child tenderly to her breast, but our tender Mother, Jesus, He may homely lead us into His blessed breast, by His sweet open side, and shew therein part of the Godhead and the joys of heaven, with spiritual sureness and endless bliss."

I have never known spiritual sureness, and whatever bliss I've felt in my soul has been fleeting. Yet Julian's visions are graphic, even visceral. Perhaps that's why I find her understandings of God so electrifying. They are so foreign, so distant, so unreachable, like postcards from a faraway land. How is it that she, walled up in her cell in eastern England, could feel God so near?

It wasn't that she didn't allow for different experiences of God. She knew that many of us went through seasons of spiritual lack, and offered counsel for such times. She reminded us that Jesus "did not say, 'You will never have rough passage, you will never be over-strained, you will never feel uncomfortable.' But he did say, 'You will never be overcome.'" Elsewhere, she wrote, "Pray, even if you feel nothing, see nothing." But then she followed that exhortation with this: "For when you are dry, empty, sick or weak, at such a time is your prayer most pleasing to God, even though you may find little joy in it." Really? Does God rank our prayer that way?

It was all so strange, and maybe the strangeness is what kept me coming back. I wanted to understand. Would my joy grow just like the garlic, which is to say haltingly and slowly and over many seasons? Did I believe it would come? Was the growth that mattered mostly invisible to me yet still happening nonetheless?

I wanted to believe that could be true. I was also growing bored of my farm metaphors. But at least this much was right about this particular one: If joy did come, it would not mainly be my doing.

Who first noticed the garlic and decided it would be good to taste? What culinary adventurer realized it would delight in so many different ways?

Though it traveled far and wide in ancient times—cloves of garlic were mummified along with King Tut, and archaeologists have uncovered remnants of three-thousand-year-old garlic in the ruins of Crete—it's believed to be native to the harsh steppes and foothills of Central Asia. I wonder whether some ancient forager, amid the beiges and browns of winter, searched for a glimpse of green. And there the garlic was, rebelling against the seasons and sprouting possibility.

As I mulched the garlic beds, I thought ahead to the late spring, when we'd harvest garlic scapes. These slender curlicues would provide early evidence that something else delightful was growing beneath the surface. Minced and scrambled into eggs or chopped fine and stirred into fried rice, they were milder than the cloves, yet unmistakably garlicky—a gentle suggestion of the pungency that was still to come.

In early summer, we'd pull the bulbs themselves out of the ground, still attached to the long stalks. We could cook them then, sure, but if we wanted the fullness of the garlicky intensity, we had to wait. We'd bundle them and tie them together with twine. (Garlic farmers with greater skill might braid the soft-neck varieties.) Then we'd hang the bunches from nails high up in the barn so the air could wash over them and slowly dry them out, concentrating their flavor.

Of course, sometimes the garlic might rot before we could do any of that. Or we might leave it hanging for too long, until the cloves were just desiccated husks. We might have to wait longer than we liked to find out whether any of this had been successful. Sometimes it just didn't grow at all.

tomato skin

When almost everything is dead in the garden, new things are revealed.

Our heirloom tomatoes hadn't thrived the previous summer. While we'd enriched the soil with compost and added fertilizer made from fish emulsion (the liquid that's left after fish carcasses are ground up and strained), only the hybrid plants flourished. The heirloom vines quickly browned and withered, and what tomatoes grew tasted watery. Nate took this as a reminder that the soil was still not healthy enough. We still had work to do.

Months later, in one of the rows where we'd tried to grow the heirlooms, I noticed the remnants of a tomato. I only saw it because it hadn't decomposed completely. Amid the beiges of the dead stalks and stems and the dark brown of the surrounding dirt, the flecks of red, orange, and yellow jumped out—bits of still-vivid skin. Clinging to the skin were a few seeds.

Almost everything else had already been broken down and transformed. Why not this tomato?

———

Pearl continued to avoid the farm. Her repeated absences quelled whatever hope flickered following our brief moments of détente. Even after Nate said they'd discussed her commitment, she ignored my scheduling emails. When she did show up—for instance, when the farmhands met to start seeds in trays—it was a surprise.

One morning, I awoke to find an email from her. This was unusual, because she'd always been a texter. Her typical messages went something like this:

HAHAHAHA

lol

I'm dead

This email was of an entirely different genre. In careful detail, she laid out why she had stopped coming to the farm: I was too serious. I was too insistent on scheduling. I cared too much about organization and not enough about people. She felt hurt. Even more importantly, though, my presence at the farm was now "unsafe" for her.

Unsafe.

I read and reread the email too many times. Every time, my eyes lingered on that word.

Unsafe.

It devastated me to be told I had made her feel unsafe.

I was confused. I was only doing what Nate had asked. It wasn't like I'd clamored for control over the seed-ordering spreadsheet or that I delighted in reminding people about team meetings. Anyway, I thought I was doing an okay job. But as became evident through her email, a job has multiple layers to it. You can be a functional administrator and a relational dud, a competent clerk and a terrible jerk. But couldn't she understand that I was just trying to do my job?

"You have taken a place of joy," Pearl wrote, "and turned it into a place of unhappy chores."

To kill someone's joy is a crime against humanity. Part of me wanted to plead innocence, or at least be charged with manslaughter, not murder. But another part of me recognized that any attempted defense was irrelevant in the moment.

I wrote Pearl back and apologized. Even if I felt confused, it mattered more that she felt unsafe. I suggested we meet for a conversation, but perhaps it was a good idea to have a third party there to help facilitate.

Pearl agreed. We decided that Jan, the minister of the chapel, whom both of us trusted as well as adored, would be a good mediator. We set a time to talk the following week.

The conversation didn't resolve everything, but it was a start. We spoke as candidly as we could, and I think we both listened well: We agreed that more had happened over the years than we could put words to. We'd both made mistakes. We'd both held on to feelings that we should have communicated. We acknowledged that we both shared responsibility for the deterioration of our friendship.

Still, I left the conversation heartbroken.

I went out to the farm. It was cold and windy, and I did a big loop, past the Christmas trees, past the old garden, to the back of the property. On the marshy path that wound through the woods, my boots got stuck in the muck. I walked on through the empty field where, in warmer weather, we kept the chickens, and ended up back, as always, at the compost pile.

A thin layer of frost glazed the wood chips atop the pile, and it was easy to believe that nothing was happening. But as I started kicking at the compost with my boots, kicking and kicking and kicking and kicking until I'd sprayed wood chips all over the place and I was slightly out of breath, I'd dug something of a hole. And from that hole, a wisp of steam rose in the bitter air.

Did I actually believe in the theology of the compost?

On a sunny day, I could drone ad nauseam about the compost pile and its beautiful spiritual lessons: that nothing was wasted, that nothing was beyond redemption, that death was not the end of the story. Did I really believe that?

If I did, then I knew there was something I had to surrender. For my friendship with Pearl to endure, the friendship I'd imagined had to die.

When I say that friendship lives or dies, I suppose I'm making a claim that friendship is an organism. It might spring up unexpected, but then it requires nurturing—fed by candor, nourished by compassion. Vulnerability—our daring to *be* with one another, to be as much ourselves as we can—is necessary but also insufficient. There must also be mutuality, which isn't necessarily the same as equality. We have to be willing to meet each other wherever we are, and often, that means one person will have to move a little more than the other.

In the heady early days of blossoming friendship, when everything is fresh and new and exciting, it can be easy not to see the frailties or the flaws. Certainly with Pearl, whose tendency was to joke her way through tension or past pain, our laughter could hide so much else. Eventually, though, I began to understand that the friendship I'd been cultivating in my mind—the relationship I wanted—was sapping the lifeblood out of the friendship that existed in reality. I told myself Pearl trusted me; she didn't. This wasn't entirely her fault. It's not like you get to show the other person an inventory of wounds and scars you've acquired along the way; sometimes you don't even have access to that yourself. Despite her easy manner, trust was hard for Pearl.

I told myself I knew how to love Pearl well; I didn't. This wasn't entirely my fault. It's not like normal humans sit down for a conversation early in a friendship to chart the ways in which one gives and receives love. I thought I'd been communicating my affection in tangible, evident ways—cooking meals, surprising her with her favorite candy (butter mints). I hadn't understood her desire—no, her need—for encouraging words and explicit reminders of her belovedness, which would speak safety into existence for her. Or maybe I *had* understood and felt as if she should understand that's not how I usually operated.

I thought back to a happy recent afternoon when Pearl and I went together to check on the progress of the compost pile. She roared with laughter as I, in a button-down shirt and chinos, climbed the hill of rotting carrots and putrefying squash, my rubber boots sinking deep into the soft not-quite soil. The decaying produce made squishing, sucking noises with every step I took.

"*Disgusting!*" Pearl screamed in glee. "Jeff! No!"

This is one thing I loved about Pearl: Even in the midst of multiple layers of mess, she could still find delight.

We could have thrown our hands up, guarded our hearts even more, and walked away from each other. We could have just sat with what we had, stumbling toward graduation and that natural parting of ways. But I realized I still wanted to try.

Pearl's email laid bare the ways in which we had failed to see each other, failed to communicate, failed to compromise. I was tempted to say that the email threatened to kill our friendship. But that wasn't accurate at all. Her words simply put sinew and muscle onto the bones that were already there, fleshing out a thing I desperately wanted not to be.

It might seem odd to describe the faltering of a friendship in this way, in terms of a coming to life. But in the garden, I saw on a daily basis how the death of one thing was inevitably linked to the coming to life of another. The fading flower bears seeds, the withering grass nourishes the ground, the rot of the compost pile feeds good soil.

There was another way to read her email: Amid the pain and sorrow, she had sent me an invitation. By naming what she felt and saw, she had opened herself up to my response. She was daring me to show up as the friend she needed and wanted.

Then I remembered the remnants of that dead tomato.

I went back to the garden and found it again, still in the same spot in the soil. It had faded. The red was gone, but I could still see some orange and yellow. When I picked it up, it felt almost weightless, almost like onionskin.

I carefully swept all the seeds into my hand and dropped them into a cup I found in the barn. Then I took them back to the space where we did our indoor starts, filled a tray with soil, and planted them. I didn't know whether they'd grow, but it was worth a try.

spring

crickets

A busy morning: Nate and I had just finished planting three varieties of carrot as well as spinach and mustard greens when I was struck by the din around us.

"The crickets are so loud today!" I said to him. The chirping sounded like a neighborhood full of security alarms going off simultaneously. "We just started to hear them the other night."

"The crickets?" Nate said.

"The ones that sound like alarms," I said. "Listen."

He paused and smiled a half smile.

"Those aren't crickets," Nate said as he began to walk back toward the barn. "They're frogs. Peepers."

I had no idea what he was talking about.

"Frogs?" I said.

"They're called peepers," he said.

My face flushed. Then I did what I usually do in these situations: I googled "peeper frogs."

————

Two and a half years on the farm might as well be a millisecond: I still knew so little. So much of what I saw and heard and smelled and felt on this land remained mysterious to me. I still couldn't tell the difference between the chirp of a cricket and the call of a frog. On a cloudless afternoon, I might look up to find the sun in the southern sky, just to remind myself that I knew anything at all.

The machine told me that the frog's full English name is spring peeper and that, across much of North America, these little creatures have traditionally been regarded as loud heralds of a new season.

Spring peepers are tiny, typically no more than an inch and a half long. Each weighs in at about a tenth of an ounce—about the same as a penny. Despite their size, they are capable of generating a tremendous amount of noise. An especially intense peeper can belt it out at about ninety decibels, roughly the same as a gas-powered lawn mower.

The frogs sing not for entertainment but for survival: It is the males that sing, and the louder the song, the better that frog's chances of attracting a mate.

The frog owes its Latin name, *Pseudacris crucifer*, to Prince Maximilian of Wied-Neuwied, a German aristocrat who traveled across America from 1832 to 1834. Upon returning to Germany, he wrote up a formal, scientific description of the spring peeper and chose the name.

This isn't to say, of course, that the frog hadn't been given other names. The Lenape, whose historic hunting and foraging grounds included the land we were using as the farm, mark their calendar according to the signs of the seasons, and *tsquali gischuch*, "the time when the frogs begin to sing," has always been one of the markers of *siquon*, "springtime."

Prince Max's intricate notes detail nearly every aspect of the frog's physique, down to the relative lengths of its toes ("the second toe from the outside the longest"). But the peeper's most notable feature to Prince Max was the X on their backs, which he read as "a broad St. Andrew's cross," hence the *crucifer.*

Prince Max was a polymath. As an ethnographer, he wrote some of the most detailed accounts of Native American language and culture we have, which proved especially important for several tribes that were decimated by smallpox within decades of his visit. As a largely self-taught biologist, he chronicled a remarkable range of species that previously had not been classified by scientists. As a sociologist and anthropologist, he was scathing in his evaluations of what the European settlers had done to nature and equally unsparing in his critiques of white Americans' treatment of non-whites.

Prince Max managed to find beauty even in nature's most violent manifestations. During his trans-Atlantic voyage to the United States in 1832, his ship endured stomach-churning storms. "The sea rolling toward us like high mountains, we plunge from crest to trough," he wrote. "The entire surface of the frightfully seething ocean was lashed and torn into foam and spray. The sight is dreadful but terribly beautiful!"

As he traveled across America, Prince Max made a habit of counting churches. Allentown "has 1,700 inhabitants, three churches, and a court-house," he wrote. Reading "is a very pretty town on the Schuylkill, with 6,000 or 7,000 inhabitants; it has seven churches, and a new one was just then building." The "little village" of Richmont has "a mean-looking church, called Upper Mount Bethel."

Prince Max left little record, though, about his own relationship with God or Christianity. Though his travelogue indicates that he regularly attended church, only once does he hint at the importance of religious practice in his own life. During his stay in New Harmony, Indiana, he noted the general failure to observe the Sabbath among the community's "otherwise reasonable and educated men . . . [They] have no regard at all for outward religious practices and churchgoing. Moreover, they have a hatred for the clergy."

He was clearer in his critique of American values. In his published account of his travels, he expressed dismay at what human hands had done to the American landscape—calling it *Zerstoerungswut*, which historian Paul Schach translates literally as "destructive rage." Prince Max was horrified by the treatment of Black people, even those in the free North. "All menial offices must be performed by blacks, who, though free people, are still held in contempt by the Americans, who so highly estimate the dignity of man."

He was equally saddened by the state of the Indigenous population as he and his entourage made their way through the East—or perhaps it is more accurate to say the absence of an Indigenous population. "Instead of its former state of nature, this country now shows a mixture of all nations, which is rapidly proceeding in the unjustifiable expulsion and extirpation of the aborigines," he wrote from Boston. Later, crossing Pennsylvania, he continued his lament: "There is not a trace remaining of the aboriginal population. O! Land of Liberty!"

In his personal journals, which were not published during his lifetime and have only recently been translated into English, he draws a connective thread between American settlers' treatment of fellow human beings and their attitudes toward nature. "One can feel only disgust and revulsion at the sight of such a coarse population streaming in with its notions of freedom," he wrote as he traveled through Indiana. The Midwest was then being rapidly populated by newcomers from points east. "These people show neither feelings of humanity nor moderation in their treatment of the Indians, as well as in their mistreatment of the animal creation."

All the settlers seemed to care about was whatever could be used or exploited. Everything else just wasn't worth anyone's time or attention. While Prince Max was visiting New Harmony, for instance, he learned that none of the white settlers could tell him anything about the people who had inhabited this land before—a disregard for history that he found both startling and rude. What was the point of the past for a people so fixated on the future?

Prince Max didn't consider a lack of understanding and knowledge to be adequate excuse for disrespect or negligence. Near New Harmony, he noticed an ancient burial ground that had been desecrated during the excavations for a watercourse. The town's founders were German pietists who had studied the Native American burial mounds in and around their settlement, even building a cemetery that left some of those mounds in place. But the pietists were quickly outnumbered by other settlers who had little interest in what came before. "While the observer deeply regrets that he is wholly without information respecting these remarkable remains of antiquity," he wrote, "he feels that the present white population of North America may justly be reproached for neglecting or destroying them."

In other words, you don't have to know all that much. But you're responsible for seeing and trying to see your surroundings. An absence of data is no excuse for an absence of respect, of care, or of heart.

I wonder how Prince Max learned to see and listen. He filled thousands upon thousands of pages with notes that testify to his abilities. The cynic in me wants to suggest that someone born into wealth and high social status might simply have had more time to sharpen his skills. But I can think of myriad rich and/or privileged people who pay little attention to what passes before their eyes or hits their ears.

Somehow, some way, Prince Max learned a posture of openness, a sort of self-abnegation that allowed him to perceive so much beyond himself. He demonstrated that curiosity is a discipline. And he seemed almost offended that so many others he encountered showed little interest in even beginning to absorb all that was happening around them.

One never need go far to begin.

The spot where I stood in the garden, listening to the peepers' song, could be described simply as grass. But under my boots was an entire household of clover and vetch, fescue and rye. To crouch and observe it was to appreciate that it seethed with life—earthworm out from the dirt for a morning meander, little brown spiders scampering up and down the blades, centipedes propelling themselves into hiding.

I never saw any peepers, but I could hear their insistent chorus. Prince Max passed not far north of here, then crossed the Delaware into Pennsylvania. I wonder if he had heard these frogs' ancestors.

As the climate in its native range has warmed, the spring peeper has shifted its schedule. Temperatures in the mid-thirties begin to rouse it from hibernation, and as the mercury rises into the mid-forties, it begins to call. Warmth isn't all that matters, though. Scientists have noted that in times of drought, the peepers wait to emerge until the coming of a rain.

While the spring peeper is not classified as endangered, its abundance has been hurt by the loss of the wetlands it likes to call home. It breeds in shallow ponds, it hibernates in mud, and it delights in the cover of marshy woods. Widespread pesticide use has decimated the insects on which it depends for sustenance. The frog has already been listed as threatened in Kansas and it is also under protection in New Jersey.

Nate had some aerial maps of the farm and the surrounding lands, going back to 1940. Once, these were mostly fields, relatively low-lying expanses of floodplain laced with woodland-guarded streams. Flip through the images of the 1950s, 1960s, 1970s, and 1980s, and you can see the planting of subdivisions, as suburban housing became the most widely cultivated crop. As drainage ditches were dug and the land made more suitable for building, what became more hospitable for human habitation became less so for creatures like the spring peeper.

Prince Max described the spring peeper's song as "a clear whistle that rises somewhat at its finish." I wonder how attentive we are to its call, especially given that many of us don't even know it's there, hearing only an unidentifiable soundtrack for the coming of spring. Regardless, an alarm only matters while you can still hear it.

lemon basil

Midway through April, the temperature rose above eighty. A slight breeze from the west, maybe five miles per hour, tickled the cherry trees. They looked as if giant cheerleaders were shaking their pink pom-poms.

Springtime warmth can be deceptive. Winter seems to resist its annual exit; just when you think it's gone, just when your body begins to forget how to shiver, the cold season likes to offer a little reminder—a light frost, maybe, or a late snow. So, even though we were still a few days from our last frost date, we hadn't transplanted most of our seedlings to the outdoor garden.

The plants weren't happy about staying in the basement. The lemon basil looked cramped under the grow lights, the tops of the plants nearly touching the fluorescent bulbs and beginning to bend sideways. The nasturtium craved stretching room, too; one bloom had even opened, an unexpected burst of deep orange amid the greens and browns of the soil-filled trays.

A week before, at the farm, Wes and a few of his friends had constructed a set of raised beds and filled them with topsoil. I dithered for a while before loading the trays of lemon basil and the nasturtium and some other herbs into my car and out to the garden. "It feels warm," I kept telling myself.

I had barely begun pulling the seedlings out of the tray—not just the lemon basil and nasturtium but also some parsley and English thyme—when our honeybees arrived, drawn by the scent of the few precocious blossoms on a single lemon basil plant. We hadn't meant for them to flower. When the plant sends its energy up into the buds and blossoms, it sacrifices the leaves, which can turn brown and tough. But I couldn't bring myself to pinch off these flowers quite yet, eager as the bees seemed for some new flavor to taste.

Lemon basil is not native to North America. In Asia, where archaeological evidence suggests it was cultivated as many as five thousand years ago, it flavors curries and stews, its unique mix of mint and citrus invigorating rich, savory dishes. But it also works well in desserts. I like to infuse it into cream, cutting the fattiness of the dairy with its lightness and brightness.

Because lemon basil is a tropical plant, it was, of all the seedlings I transplanted that day, perhaps the riskiest to move into the garden. But I had checked the weather forecast and then checked it again. Every day going forward looked to be in the sixties and seventies, and evenings wouldn't see anything close to freezing. It was a gamble, but it seemed a safeish one.

The previous weekend, I had been in California, at a conference. My friend Rachel was there, too.

Because Rachel had two young kids and lived in eastern Tennessee, we pretty much only got to see each other on the road, when we were attending the same gathering. While texting with her was delightful—her pithiness made her a superb short-form correspondent—I'd always choose to share physical space with someone I love. Whenever we got to sit, eat, and just talk one-on-one, the conversations had a familiar rhythm: Stories about her kids and our spouses. Discussion of our work. She was much the same both online and off: Inevitably, she'd find an opportunity to crack some rude joke or tease me, we'd laugh and sit in amiable silence for a moment, and then she'd take advantage of my relaxation to delve deep into some theological dilemma or ask about my current feelings about the Church or probe my questions about vocation. I loved it.

That Saturday in San Francisco, we went to a mutual friend's house for dinner. Rachel seemed unusually quiet. We stood for a few minutes on the back deck, watching the serene orb of the sun sink into the roiling Pacific. "I'm just really tired," she said.

When we went inside, Rachel, whose introversion rivals mine, curled up under a weighted blanket and closed her eyes while the rest of us chatted. Occasionally she reminded us she wasn't really asleep, interjecting a witty aside or some commentary about the glories of weighted blankets. When we sat at the table for dinner, she stayed on the couch to snooze.

A few days after I returned to New Jersey and she went home to Tennessee, she texted to say she had the flu. She and I commiserated about the toll of travel. We assumed the trip had simply taxed her body like the social activity had her introverted spirit. We had no doubt she'd quickly rebound.

A couple of days later, she sent an update: Her fever had broken, but she was still "suuuuper tired." A couple of days after that, she emailed saying she'd checked herself into the hospital because of a combination of the flu and an infection and a bad reaction to an antibiotic. Still, she was her usual, indefatigably casual self. It was a Sunday morning, she had her HBO password and her phone, and there was no way she'd be missing *Game of Thrones* that night.

The wind began to quicken on Monday morning, still from the west, whistling past the barn. The weather reports warned of gusts up to forty miles per hour.

I checked the herbs I'd transplanted. They were all still upright but looked frazzled and stressed. I worried a little, because I knew forty-eight hours had not been enough time for them to get firmly rooted in their new soil. I piled more dirt around the base of some of the plants, tamping it down, trying to give them a little extra support.

The following afternoon, I realized it hadn't been enough. The lavender looked serene and unscathed, the nasturtium grateful for its low-to-the-soil profile. But the wind had stripped most of the leaves off the bee balm and even snapped a stalk. And every single specimen of the lemon basil, the tallest resident of the raised beds, had a discouraged droop. The leaves were more brown than green.

What could I have done differently? I had prepared for rainstorms. I had considered the possibility of cold. I had scanned the weather map, trying to anticipate whether the fronts dumping April snow on the Midwest would warm sufficiently before getting near us. But I hadn't thought about the wind.

Wind often has little regard for season, appearing and disappearing with insolence and caprice. On a hot day you can beg for its arrival, only to be slapped in the face with the infuriating stillness of the air. On a cold one the wind might mock you with its bitter, invisible bite.

The mystery of the wind might be one reason it is so often invoked in Scripture as a particularly potent form of God's address to the earth. "God releases the wind from its storeroom," Psalm 135:7 says. Isaiah likens it to the force of the wave of God's hand. Job testifies that only God can know the wind's weight.

Frustration built up within me. While one of my spiritual gifts is angst, this was an odd kind, an atypical species for me, and it took me a while to place it. I hadn't necessarily done anything wrong. I'd planned. I'd made an educated guess. I'd anticipated what I could anticipate. And that was the problem: I wanted more control than I possibly could exert.

I have never liked surprises. Nor am I fond of incomprehensible forces—things that defy research, that behave unpredictably. I wanted some sort of reassurance, some guaranteed outcome, some notion that if I did everything right, things would turn out just fine.

Rachel was just thirty-seven. The mother of a rambunctious three-year-old and a serene baby just shy of her first birthday, she was in the midst of weaning her daughter when she got sick.

On Maundy Thursday, I got word she was on a respirator. Some unknown thing was disrupting the circuitry in her brain and causing uncontrollable seizures. Her short-term memory had disappeared. The seizures wouldn't stop.

Nobody could figure out precisely why she was caught in this cycle, and nobody could devise any successful strategy for addressing it—neither her doctors, who had years of clinical experience, nor those of us who only had Google and prayer. All the doctors could think to do was induce a coma to give her body a chance to rest. Then, when her local hospital ran out of options, they flew her across the state, to a university medical center, for another try.

A thousand miles away from her hospital room, I texted a few mutual friends to ask them to pray for Rachel.

I could not pray without crying. Maybe the tears gave me some semblance of action, as if in the act of falling, they could summon something greater. "You have kept count of my tossings; put my tears in your bottle. Are they not in your record?" the psalmist says. It seemed almost as if he were daring God to respond. "Then my enemies will retreat in the day when I call. This I know, that God is for me."

I didn't particularly need God to be for me. I wanted God to be for my friend, because her situation was beyond me or her family or her doctors or any mere mortal.

So, on the day that commemorates Jesus washing the feet of his disciples, I asked God to bathe Rachel in similar healing. *Liberate her from the woeful evidence of this messy life. Lift her from that hospital bed and let her walk. Restore her to wholeness.*

There is risk, at a farm devoted to Christian theological education, of over-romanticizing the fragility of life—and I suppose I should use the word I have been resisting all the while: "death."

As Rachel was in the hospital, I was working on a final seminary paper about the things I'd learned at the farm. I was writing about how death was a prerequisite for the making of compost, but I and so many of my fellow students had distorted the image by rushing past what is—the rot, the ruin—so we could glory in what would be—the redemption, the resurrection. Of course, I knew there could be no compost without death, but I preferred to gloss over that harsh reality and fixate instead on the good soil, on the crops that would surely grow, on the life that was to come.

What was merely uncomfortable in metaphor became especially challenging in reality. As the doctors hooked up my friend to machines so that she might have a chance to survive, I didn't want to face the possibility of Rachel's death, especially not before what I deemed its proper time.

Even when Nate and I had examined the damaged lemon basil, we kept looking for signs of strength. Yes, the larger leaves were brown or fallen, but there! Some of the lower leaves, the littlest leaves, still looked robustly green. When that wasn't enough to reassure us, we turned to the neighboring sage, where new growth was even more abundant.

There is no logical rationale why death should not strike at any given moment, except that it just doesn't seem right. We have made our plans, and those plans assume growth, assume breath, assume life.

To minimize death, though, is, for the Christian, to short-change the resurrection—and surely it is the promise of new life that empowers us to stare death in the face and reckon with its current reality. The idea of resurrection is ridiculous. It's as wondrous as it is because it's not supposed to be. It's a rupture of the natural order of things, a disruption of what ought to happen. But even Jesus couldn't get to life everlasting without dealing with death first.

I wanted a miracle. I wanted a miracle that shouted of life irrepressible. I wanted a miracle in which health was restored to Rachel's broken body and the full force of survival cried out against premature death. But I can think of no Bible story in which the miracle comes without facing the terrible reality of suffering and human fragility and the hovering presence of death. Miracles are miracles because, by definition, they defy our logic and challenge what we perceive to be natural.

We had made our plans: Rachel was supposed to come visit the week after Easter. Through all our years of friendship, I'd never had the chance to cook for her, never had the opportunity to welcome her to our table, never had the pleasure of sharing contented postmeal silence in my home, never had the delight of showing her that form of my love.

I'd already imagined the menu: Chicken stir-fried with onions as well as red and orange bell peppers, because I wanted something approachable on the table and because my mom had taught me that vivid color enriches a meal. Fish with ginger and scallion and soy, because that alchemic combination had gotten me through so many moments of homesickness and sorrow, reminding me of belonging and goodness. Garlicky greens.

I'd already been savoring the conversation—the kinds of stories you share among close friends over never-empty glasses of wine (she liked Pinot Noir). She'd make some irreverent joke, tease me about the omnipresence of the writer who was my professional nemesis, ask me gently about what I might do and where we might go post-seminary. I'd ask about her work, tease her about the omnipresence of the writer who was her professional nemesis, and beg for another story about the kids. We'd tuck our inappropriate commentary into the vault of trust, never to be opened, except in the case of a mutual desire for public cancellation.

But instead of sitting with us in our dining room, Rachel was lying in a hospital bed. I scrolled through her text messages again. I suspected there would be no more, but I begged the universe—God or the devil, I almost didn't care—for another. Just one more late-night check-in, sent out of worry that something terrible had happened. Just one more snippet of beautifully brutal teasing. Just one more note about my nemesis.

I told myself I had to hold on to hope. But it might be truer to say I simply wasn't ready to succumb to grief. To grieve is to feel the fullness of our humanity—the depth of our love, the reality of our fragility, the precarity of our existence.

We can rebuke death all we want—yell at it to go away, pretend it is not standing just outside the hospital room door. Even then, because death is what it is, it can outshout us and push its way in and remind us we have not yet won. I could insist on making good things, tasty things, life-giving things, with what lemon basil leaves I might be able to salvage, but I couldn't change the fact that the herb also carried with it another story: In ancient Greece, lemon basil symbolized mourning.

feast

I did not get to cook for Rachel on April 25. But on April 30, even as I kept checking my phone for news from the hospital, I had to cook and serve another meal: the thesis dinner that was to be the culmination of my senior year of graduate school. This was the meal I had been working toward—growing for, thinking about—for months. But really, every meal requires months of preparation, from the sowing of the seeds and the fattening of the animals to the watering and the weeding, before you even get to harvest.

The previous summer, Nate had planted rye as a cover crop; I'd gathered the ripe grains, dried them, and pounded them into flour with a mortar and pestle. In the pantry, there was a jar of pickled fennel, made from some perfectly good bulbs I'd rescued from a food bank delivery destined for the compost pile. Two chickens from the autumn's last slaughter were defrosting in the refrigerator. Simple syrup made with sage and rosemary from the farm was in the fridge, waiting to be mixed into cocktails. The Jantz family horseradish that Nate had transplanted from

Oklahoma was in the crisper drawer, along with the daikon grown from the seeds of our earlier failures. Every single thing I served would contain at least one ingredient from the Farminary.

It was easy for me to cook a meal on my own, and it was also easy for me to forget that this wasn't just a special meal; it was an academic assignment. Months before, Nate had said that one of his hopes was that I might learn to ask for help, even when I didn't need it—a nod to interdependence and a rebuke of the lie of self-sufficiency. I'm not sure he knew what he was getting himself into: I asked him to help me smoke a chicken for the dinner.

The day before the dinner, Nate and I met at the farm. He had defrosted a Farminary chicken. I'd made a rub (galangal, white pepper, five-spice powder, paprika, black pepper, Sichuan peppercorn, salt). He rigged up a Weber grill to serve as our smoker. I grabbed some wood from the barn—the remnants of an old grapevine we'd cut down, which I'd saved for this very occasion.

It was a beautiful afternoon, the warmth of the sunshine defying the mercury, which told us it was barely above sixty degrees. While the bird was in the smoker, we talked and we harvested: pea shoots, carrots, other things I needed for the following evening.

The next morning, I returned to the garden with my high school friend Heather, who had flown in from Texas. We needed to harvest greens for the meal. Of course I could have done it the day before or even the day before that, but I also had a notion that the greens I served should never feel the adulterating cold airs of refrigeration. They would be artisanally harvested (which is to say, excruciatingly, unprofessionally slowly), then remain pure and unsullied by modern technology.

As Heather and I walked past the pond, we spotted not one egret, nor two, nor three, but four. I'd seen lone birds, and one time a pair, but never before a quartet. Watching them together, I could have sworn they were doing some contemporary dance for us, the way their legs rose out of the water in an unhurried prance, the swiftness with which their beaks dove toward their subsurface buffet.

Heather and I spent an hour in the garden, harvesting spinach and nasturtium, tatsoi and edible flowers. We didn't talk much, because we didn't need to. Over some thirty years, we've built that kind of relationship that doesn't require much conversation. She knew me when I had a bowl cut. And she has shown up, egret-like, at some of the most auspicious moments of my life. She was at our wedding when my parents and other close friends boycotted. She has written me letters—real, old-fashioned, pen-and-paper letters—full of encouragement, words of comfort and exhortation that arrived at some of the most difficult junctures. When Tristan and I moved into seminary housing, she was the only person to send a housewarming gift: It was an orchid, gorgeous with purple speckles on white petals.

I killed it within weeks. It was not fake.

I don't believe in omens.

After we left the garden, I dropped Heather back at her hotel and drove to the airport to pick up my friends Nate and Noah. Both are pastors—Nate in Indiana, Noah in Michigan. Both are straight white men reared in the Midwest. Both are married— Nate to a teacher, Noah to another pastor. Both have three kids. We'd met years before at a denominational conference, which we called "the worst summer camp ever," because we had been gathered to discuss human sexuality; they were theologically more conservative than I was, and on first meeting, neither would have said they approved of my marriage (not that I asked).

In the years since, though, both sat with me in moments of grief and celebrated with me in times of joy. They've seen me at my best and walked with me through the worst. They've listened as I've agonized over questions and waded through doubts about my call and my belonging—in our denomination, in the Church, in the world. They, too, have gone through some changes in their own theological convictions. They've sent me stupid GIFs and humored my remarkable lack of game in that department. Despite so much difference, we've forged beautiful friendships—and now, here they were, having secured the blessings of their wives and spent hundreds of dollars to fly to New Jersey, just to sit at my table.

It's not uncommon to make a new acquaintance at a conference. You might share a brief conversation, maybe even a meal or two, then you go your separate ways. How did things turn out differently with these two? Why have these men faithfully practiced the ministries of text message and music, of telephone calls and hard questions that you only dare ask a true friend? Why did they become not only my dear friends but also, near the end of my fourth decade of life, the brothers I'd never had as a kid?

Growing up, I had few friends. I didn't know how to open up, how to risk, how to trust. My parents never had many friends either; our emphasis was always on family. The ones they did have—well, I never witnessed anything resembling the kind of intimacy, the sort of deep spiritual understanding, that I craved.

It has taken me many, many years to learn how to receive

love. Though love might surround you and even bombard you, it can feel meaningless if you lack the capacity to believe that love could be for you.

The love of friendship can be like an unfamiliar plant in the garden, there waiting to be acknowledged. Perhaps it's edible. Perhaps it has some markers of beauty. But unless you believe it carries nutrition, unless you decide it offers aesthetic delight, unless you recognize all its goodness, well, it might as well be a weed.

In her novel *A Thousand Acres,* Jane Smiley writes about an Iowa farm family that comes to the table carrying all the tension, grief, and anxiety of the rest of life. But they have neither the words nor the ability to share the burden. They're painfully alone, together. "It was exhausting just to hold ourselves at the table, magnets with our northern poles pointing into the center of the circle. You felt a palpable sense of relief when you gave up and let yourself fall away from the table and wound up in the kitchen getting something, or in the bathroom running the water and splashing it on your face," Smiley writes. "We ate with our heads down, hungrily, quickly, because there was nothing else to do at the table."

The experience of the Chinese family—or at least my Chinese family—is different. In my early childhood, when we lived near my grandparents, we ate together as an extended family at least two or three times a week, sometimes on weeknights, always on Sundays after church. Later, when it was just my parents, my sister, and me, we sat at the table more evenings than not. A complete meal would be rice plus at least three dishes, two of which, by my father's request, would contain meat or fish; he saw this as a sign of his conquest of his childhood poverty, when meat was a rarity. When we gathered for family re-unions in Hong Kong, failure to show up for family meals was inconceivable, even if some of the relatives were mid-argument, which was often. And at the table, whatever tension we'd brought with us would inevitably dissipate, rising into invisibility with the steam from each dish.

This meal, though, had to be different still. It was the culmination of my time as a farmhand, during which I'd learned about not just survival but also flourishing, about not just history but also possibility.

When I was planning the menu, I considered my journey and the cultural traditions that gave me life. I knew I wanted the food to tell a story about where I had come from. I wanted it to share something about my heritage—Californian and Chinese. I also knew I wanted to speak of my life with Tristan—about the integration of his Texanness into my story and the creation of *our* story.

But I also knew it would have been foolish to be bound by tradition and history. The kitchen, like the garden, is never static. You learn new skills. You acquire new tools. You experiment with new ingredients. You incorporate new ideas. You might try to replicate a dish from a past season, but it will never be exactly the same. Your taste buds change. So do your moods, and even the produce. A chili pepper harvested in early autumn will likely be spicier than one picked in midsummer. Even two peppers grown on the same plant and harvested on the same day might not carry the same heat.

I'd always told myself I'd be a success in the kitchen if I could cook like my mother. As I stood at the stove that night, though, I realized that wasn't really true. I'd learned so much hovering over my mom's shoulder as she cooked, absorbing her counsel about how to contrast texture, how to play with color, how to amplify flavor. But I'd also tasted things she'd never tasted and been places she'd never been.

The real win, I realized, was that I had learned to cook like me.

Just past five P.M., our guests started to gather.

Tristan—my dear, faithful Tristan—had been cleaning the apartment nearly all day. Noah had pitched in, too, washing vegetables and drying dishes. Heather and Indiana Nate were soon joined by my two thesis advisers, Kenda and Farminary Nate, who, by saying "Yes!" to me over and over and over, had made this entire adventure possible.

Then came Jan, the minister of the seminary chapel, and Stacy, a theology professor whom I'd known before enrolling here. There were eight chairs at the table, eight seats of honor for eight people who had helped me imagine possibilities I couldn't imagine by myself.

We began with cocktails—a California Collins, I called it—made with gin, to honor the years I lived in London in my twenties, but a California-made one, to commemorate my birthplace. Farminary Nate and Tristan both love bread, so our hors d'oeuvres were a miniature Chinese spin on Parker House rolls. I made them with a bit of that Farminary rye flour and stuffed them with barbecued pork.

Then I asked everyone to sit at the table—and as I looked around at these eight dear friends, I thought about how that table had its own testimony of survival. It was my first major purchase when I was a young journalist in London. Crafted by an apprentice woodworker in Scotland, it was mostly elm, with a thin strip of ash inlay along the edges of the tabletop. Twice, its legs had been broken off during moves. Twice, it had been put back together again.

We began with what I called the "Western" part of the meal, because I served it tasting menu style: crispy chicken skin with hot-sauce aioli made from Farminary peppers; daikon radish cake; seared New Jersey scallop in a light spinach broth, topped with spinach gremolata; roasted carrot salad with a blood orange vinaigrette; and a New York strip steak, with sauce made from the Jantz family horseradish.

The chicken soup, made from a stock I'd started the summer before, was the bridge to the Chinese part of the meal, served family style: the chicken Nate and I smoked together; abalone my aunt had sent from Hong Kong; garlicky Chinese greens; a whole poached Gulf snapper, in honor of my Floridian adolescence; and, of course, brisket fried rice.

We ended with a lemon and thyme cream tart along with dipped chocolates. As they ate dessert, I asked if any of them had a favorite bite or a dish that had particularly delighted them. To a person, they named a different one: Noah said the radish cake, because he'd never tasted anything like it. Stacy chose the steak, because he loves a good steak. Tristan said the fish hit him right that night. For Farminary Nate, "it has to be the brisket fried rice."

It was humbling to look over the list of things the garden had given us: sage, rosemary, rye, baby leek, chicken, peppers, daikon radish, scallion, spinach, carrot, nasturtium, edible flowers, onion, horseradish, chive, tatsoi, bok choy, pea shoots, garlic, thyme, marigold, lavender.

Yes, we had sowed and tended, weeded and harvested. But so much of the work was done by others—the bees and the butterflies that provided pollination services, the sunshine and the rain, the inexplicable forces that rearranged cells and sent up shoots and delivered sugars to protect the tender plants from the elements, and of course the God who creates all things.

"We expect love to grow here," Kenda had said on that very first night of my very first seminary class. It had seemed impossible to me then. But more than any other crop, it had—and this feast was my testimony to that truth.

grief

Final papers were due three days after my thesis meal. I got to my usual coffee shop just as it opened. I had one last paper to write, for my class on the maddeningly complicated theology of Saint Thomas Aquinas. I'd spent the entire semester pretending I'd understood the week's readings, enduring presentation after presentation about dense prose that I'd barely managed to skim and that reminded me of the long history of impenetrable theological writing. The only things I'd gleaned were that Thomas had a low opinion of animals and a lot to say about love.

As I sipped a cortado and stared at my blank laptop screen, my phone began buzzing. I looked down to see the name that had popped up: *Dan.* Rachel's husband.

I stepped outside, my heart pounding.

"Hey, buddy," he said.

"Hey, Dan."

The silence that followed told me everything I needed to know.

Finally, he spoke: "If you want to say goodbye, you should come today."

We talked for a few brief moments. Then he hung up, and I called Tristan. Instantly, the tears I'd stifled while on the phone with Dan came tumbling out.

Tristan held the silence as only those who know how to love us well can do.

"What happened?" he finally asked.

I told him what Dan had said.

"Go," he said. "I'll be fine. Just go."

I cried quietly most of the flight from Newark to Nashville and then for the entire drive from the airport to the hospital. It's a minor miracle I didn't crash my rental car, given that I was navigating through a veil of tears.

I stepped into the hospital room and greeted Dan. His eyes were damp and red, his lips quivering.

"Hey, buddy," he said, as he always does.

We hugged.

Rachel's dad, Peter, whom I'd never met, was there. We shook hands—what a strange time and place to meet—and he thanked me for being her friend. "The honor is all mine," I said.

Is.

Because Rachel was still there.

Then I turned toward her, but as soon as I did, the machinery that was keeping her alive distracted me.

No disrespect to the doctors and nurses who work so diligently to save lives, but the ICU has always felt to me like a lifeless space: The whirs, hums, and beeps of the gadgetry. The wires and the tubes. The smell of disinfectant. Especially the godforsaken and unnatural fluorescent lighting.

I'd come to see Rachel. And there she allegedly was. What do we mean, though, when we say "alive"? Her body was in that bed, her chest steadily rising and falling. When I held her hand, it was warm and soft. But when I squeezed it gently, she did not squeeze back. It seemed as if my vibrant, vivacious friend were already gone.

The next couple of hours passed in an awkward mix of small talk and heartfelt reminiscence. In the absence of more extraordinary measures, the nurses had resorted to doling out sympathetic half smiles.

Finally, we gathered around Rachel's bed. Our friend Nadia prayed the *Nunc Dimittis*: "Now, Lord, let your servant go in peace. You have fulfilled your promise." I remembered those words originally were uttered by a very old man, Simeon, who had been promised he would not die without seeing the Messiah.

When Nadia was finished reciting the prayer, someone— I don't know who—started singing "It Is Well with My Soul." The others in the room joined in, one by one, but I couldn't.

The backstory for this hymn: It was written in 1873 by Horatio Spafford, who was something of a nineteenth-century Job. He was a wealthy Chicago property investor until the Great Fire of 1871 consumed nearly his entire fortune. Two years later, all four of his children died en route to England, when the ship they were on collided with another vessel. It sank in twelve minutes.

When peace like a river attendeth my way . . .

How did Spafford write those words? I felt absolutely no peace.

When sorrows like sea billows roll . . .

Accurate.

Whatever my lot, thou hast taught me to say / It is well, it is well, with my soul.

Well, I was also taught not to be a liar. So I didn't sing a single word of the hymn, because I couldn't in good conscience. Not those words.

I looked over at Dan. He wasn't singing either.

There was nothing left to do, nothing left to say, except one final goodbye to Rachel. Bleary-eyed and exhausted, I drove Dan to a friend's house to try to get some sleep. Rachel died a few hours after we left. I flew back to school the next day.

nugget

Whatever differences had arisen between Pearl and me, they faded whenever we talked about chickens. This was the common ground on which we could build not just détente but also genuine solidarity: For months, she and I had been badgering Nate, every chance we got, for some new chickens.

I understood his hesitation: A spring flock of chicks would arrive toward the end of the semester, just as his workload was ramping up. Despite all our promises to help, he knew he'd be the chicks' primary caregiver, since they spent the first few weeks in the nursery, which was also his garage.

To be clear, our interest wasn't just in getting new birds. We'd raised and slaughtered Cornish Cross; now, as we kept telling Nate, we wanted chickens of color. "It's a joke—but it's not a joke," Pearl said. "We need to break up the uniformity! We need to see something different! We cannot just have all white chickens."

Perhaps we finally exhausted him. Perhaps he realized the extraordinarily bad optics of rejecting diversity. Perhaps it was both. Whatever the case, Nate finally relented.

First, two dozen Barred Rocks arrived. As chicks, Barred Rocks are almost all black. Over time, as they grow, their adult feathers come in, striped, black-and-white plumage that looks as if a thousand UPC codes were cut up and pasted onto the birds' bodies—hence the name "barred."

Then, three weeks later, Nate picked up sixteen Blue Silkie Bantams at the post office. The choice of Silkies, an heirloom Chinese breed, particularly gratified me.

Marco Polo wrote in his journals about the Silkie, describing a strange "furry chicken" he'd heard about during his visit to China but never managed to see. Three centuries later, the Italian polymath Ulisse Aldrovandi wrote a survey of the world's known chickens and included a description of the "woolly" chickens in the "kingdom of Mangi"—an antiquated term for Southern China. He struggled to depict Silkies precisely, eventually deciding simply to say they "wear black hair like that of a cat."

To me, the Silkie looks like a weird, impossible cross between a chicken and a French poodle. They're fluffy, with feathers even on their feet. Nobody should be fooled by those voluminous plumes of gray and black: Underneath it all, they're very lean.

Practitioners of traditional Chinese medicine have long believed Silkies, with their midnight-blue skin, gray bones, and black-tinged meat, to have special healing power. But these chickens aren't much good for frying or roasting. We stew them or make soup from them.

The first time I saw one cooked, it was in my maternal grandmother's kitchen. I was maybe ten or twelve, and the dark flesh of the cooked chicken startled me. I had never seen chicken that looked like that.

My grandma and I spoke Cantonese to each other. She claimed to speak English, and did so with great enthusiasm, but it was intelligible mostly only to herself.

She gave me a hard look, then declared emphatically in English: "Good for you!"

The Iowa-born Blue Silkie Bantams had arrived in New Jersey on the same day I left for Tennessee to say goodbye to Rachel. The day after I returned, I went to visit the chicks for the first time. They were five days old.

Each one was just a gorgeous puffball, glorious in its floofiness and gray from head to toe, with the exception of some black on the face, as if nature's makeup artist had been liberal and a bit messy with the eyeliner. I admit: Though I knew they were from Iowa, I still spoke to them in Cantonese.

A few hours after I left the chicks, Nate called.

"I have some bad news," he said, his voice cracking.

He and his family had been watching the documentary *The Biggest Little Farm* that afternoon. In the film, the farmers struggle with predators attacking their poultry. Nate thought, *That really hasn't been a problem for us. We're fortunate.*

Just before leaving his house to pick up some pizza for dinner, he went into the garage to check on the chicks. Then he left the garage door open, which was not unusual. In the time he was gone—no more than twenty minutes—a fox had gotten in. As Nate drove up with his pizza, he saw the fox standing in the middle of the driveway, two chicks hanging out of its mouth.

Nate jumped out of his car and started yelling at the fox, which scampered away. When he went into the garage, "it was just carnage everywhere," he said. "Dead birds inside the brooder box. Dead birds on the floor."

Most devastating were the chicks that were gravely injured but not dead. He picked them up and, one by one, broke their tiny necks.

"I'm so sorry," Nate said to me after recounting the story.

I was, too.

Only half of our Barred Rocks and one of the Blue Silkie Bantams survived the massacre. That lone Blue Silkie was a paler gray than the others. Over the next few weeks, its foot feathers started to come in.

Because they were older, we moved the Barred Rocks out to the pasture in mid-June, leaving that one bird in Nate's garage all by itself. Eventually, Nate and his family decided to move it indoors, to their basement. I fretted over that bird, visiting whenever I could. It was unusually vocal every time: *cheep cheep cheep, cheep cheep cheep.* I wondered, was it telling me about the fox attack? What did it remember? How did it feel being alone?

The pastured birds lived in chicken tractors: mobile enclosures that we'd move to a new piece of ground every couple of days. That gave the chickens fresh grass and forage and allowed their poop to fertilize the soil. We transferred the surviving Blue Silkie to the fields sooner than we probably should have, motivated by the desire to give it some company. We gave it its own tractor—the Barred Rocks were much bigger, and we feared the larger, more aggressive birds would pick on this little one. Instead, we put one coop right up against the other, so the Silkie would always be nearby but safe.

It wasn't near enough for the lonely Silkie. It spent its days pacing right up against the edge, sometimes even throwing its little body against the chicken wire wall, constantly trying to get closer to its neighbors. Just about the only time I ever saw it settle down was when I'd pull it out of the coop and give it some time in the open pasture. It would peck at the fresh grass for a few moments. But then it would inevitably wander back toward the Barred Rocks. It always wanted to be part of a flock, always yearned to be on the other side of the chicken wire, always seemed to seek belonging.

Nate's kids named it Nugget. This was a canny gamble: Surely their dad wouldn't have the heart to see this one bird, this lone survivor, become an actual chicken nugget.

transition

A few months before graduation, I emailed my parents to ask if they wanted to come. My father's response gratified and surprised me: "I am very proud of your decision to enter seminary. I know God will lead you on the path that He has prepared for you. . . . I will be pleased to attend."

This was only the second time in my life that my dad had told me he was proud of me (the first was when I got my college acceptance letter). I read and reread the email, taking each word in. After all we'd been through, after years of tension and frustration—mutual, no doubt—this felt like an unmitigated win.

Not long after that, my mother emailed with a point of clarification: My father had no intention of meeting Tristan. They would attend only the ceremony. No other events, no other activities—though perhaps I could have a meal with them afterward. They would like that. But it would have to be just me, not Tristan.

I longed to tell my dad that he had no more chances, that his rejection of Tristan was also a rejection of me. I wanted my mom, who had at least made some room in her imagination to acknowledge Tristan's humanity, to stand up for me. I wished for my graduation, a day that was allegedly about celebrating a milestone in my life, to be about more than them and their theological misgivings.

As ever, Tristan came through as the voice of patience, faithful conscience, and almost shocking grace. Of course I'd welcome my parents, he said. Of course it would be hard. Of course we would do whatever we had to. "They're your parents," he said—the non-seminarian reminding the seminarian of the things he claimed to believe.

So many times, people have said that my refusal to cut off my parents was cowardice, not courage. A queer pastor told me my example was dangerous, because it told other people to stay in abusive situations and unsafe relationships. Peers who wore their progressivism loudly talked about me behind my back, always forgetting I am a trained reporter, and I keep a wide network of sources. They judged me too quick to compromise. I suffered from internalized homophobia and unhealed self-loathing, they said.

If any of them had chosen to engage me in deeper conversation, I would have told them there were two questions I'd spent years pondering.

First, what did it mean to honor my parents, not because some ancient scribe said I should but because I loved them?

Second, what power should their disapproval have over the love I believed enfolded me and empowered me as a child of God?

It's a running half joke among pastors and seminarians that each of us has just one sermon that we keep preaching for our entire lives. Mine seemed to be about the compost. "I believe in a God of second and third and fourth chances," I'd say when I preached at churches. "The compost pile tells a story of life and death and resurrection, testifying to divine grace."

Almost every single time, I reminded the congregation they were loved by a love beyond all other loves—a love that had formed them and breathed life into them, an emboldening love that enabled them to persist even through trial and tribulation, an unconditional love that freed them to live without shame, a patient and gracious love that was with them no matter their worst actions or their most profound shortcomings. I said this to them because I needed to hear it said aloud myself. I declared this because I wanted it to be true. But did I actually believe what I preached?

Tristan listened to my moaning, and he acknowledged how much it hurt. But he didn't have much time for the overwrought emotional examinations or even the theological contemplation. He didn't think the situation was that complicated at all.

"Of course you're going to have lunch with your parents," he said. "I'll see you after."

The day before graduation, we went out to the Farminary. Five students in the graduating class, including Wes and me, had taken enough classes at the farm to receive, along with our master's diplomas, a certificate in "theology, ecology, and faith formation." Nate had special cords for us to wear at the ceremony, three strands braided together—a red one to represent theology, a black one that symbolized death, and a green one that represented life.

Wes had brought Lincoln to the farm with him, and after Nate gave us our cords, while everyone was chatting, I walked out to the edge of the pond, the Jack Russell trailing a few steps behind me. Everyone else seemed so happy and upbeat, and I didn't want to be the rain cloud amid the sunshine.

Pastoral as ever, Lincoln sat with me. I looked down at him with envy. He always seemed so hopeful—in the kitchen, because of the possibility of a morsel of meat, and on the farm, because there was always another hole to dig or another deer to chase—and he always seemed to know when I needed to borrow some of his hope. Lincoln met my gaze for a moment, as if to say, *Have you got what you needed?* Then, whether because he was bored with my melancholy or had decided I'd be fine, he left me to rejoin the group.

I got a text from my mom saying she and my dad had arrived at their hotel. They were staying about twenty miles away, so I drove to see them.

My mom greeted me at their hotel room door with a quick hug. Then she quickly launched into an inventory of the things she'd brought me: Dried apples she'd made—and which she knew, but didn't say, Tristan liked. Dried scallops and shiitake mushrooms, which they'd brought back from their most recent trip to Hong Kong. Some Chinese ointment I always forgot how to use, even though she kept telling me. There was also a pair of cufflinks, which my dad had chosen for me. "Thank you," I said to him. He nodded.

I didn't stay long, because I didn't want to say the wrong thing. Self-control seemed like the least accessible fruit of the spirit at that moment, and I was more aware than ever of the cultural divide between me and my parents: They'd read any disagreement as disrespect, and self-advocacy as selfishness. As much as I wanted them to understand how I was feeling, I knew it was impossible. I felt a bit like Nugget on the wrong side of the chicken wire, constantly throwing myself against an unbreachable barrier that my parents didn't even seem to see.

The next morning, at the ceremony, my parents sat on one side of the chapel, Tristan with some friends on the other. Afterward, I spotted Tristan in the courtyard outside. As soon as I got to him, I burst into tears. Tristan held me as I cried. "It's okay," he said. "You know I love you? It's okay."

I was crying because I was confused. I'd just received a diploma declaring me a master of divinity, but what had I really mastered? I'd accumulated dozens of credits. I'd read (okay: skimmed) countless books. I'd waxed theological in class and on paper. I'd passed so many academic exams. But what had I really mastered?

I was crying because my spirit felt broken. I was crying because I was angry. I was crying because after all that studying, I still didn't know how to be both a good son and a good husband.

Jan had found Tristan and me in the courtyard, and she wrapped me in a hug as I kept on crying. "Oh, Jeff," she said. She didn't have to say anything more. There were more than a hundred other students whom she could have been congratulating at that moment. Just her presence was enough.

She handed me a tissue so I could wipe the evidence of the ugly crying off my face. We took a few pictures. Then Tristan gave me a tender look and a gentle push. "Go," he said. "Go find your parents. I'll see you after."

He headed to the farm, where some classmates and their families were gathering for a celebratory barbecue, and I found my parents in the courtyard on the north side of the chapel. We went to lunch, at a Chinese restaurant, of course. We talked about the food. I asked after my relatives in Hong Kong. Apart from our dress clothes, it could have been any other meal on any other day. They didn't ask me a single question, and I couldn't tell you why; perhaps it was that they didn't know what to ask, or maybe it was just that they, too, felt the unspeakable awkwardness of the day.

When we had finished eating, I said goodbye to my parents, told them I loved them, and drove to the farm. Tristan spotted me as soon as I got out of the car. He interrupted the conversation he was having, and he enfolded me in a hug. Then Lincoln trotted over to say hello. I crouched down to scratch his ears, and he buried his face in my crotch.

I told Tristan I needed just a minute. I picked Lincoln up and found a quiet spot away from everyone else. He sat on my lap, and the tears came flooding back.

Life never seems to get any easier, and death is omnipresent in so many ways. To not be seen or understood by those who say they love you is a little death. To be unable to celebrate on a day that is supposed to be celebratory is a little death. To have to choose between one's parents and one's spouse is a little death.

If life is a series of little deaths, when and how do we get to rise again?

There's a part of the story of Jesus's death and resurrection that doesn't make it to the page. I've always wondered, what did rising again feel like to Jesus? I find it hard to believe he was just lying there, bound up in his burial cloths and entombed, and then suddenly popped up as if he'd enjoyed a three-day nap. I want to believe his revival was somehow hard-won—that it was a fight, almost on a cellular level, to throw off death and make his claim on life. That would feel like solidarity, a feat worthy of celebration.

At so many points on my journey, I felt as if I had reached an end. Not *the* end, which for a seminarian inevitably conjures words like "telos" and "eschatological," but *an* end: that kind of utterly drained moment when it feels as if surely, now, there could not be yet another soul-sucking thing. I imagined standing on a beach, swept over by wave after debilitating wave, until all that remained was the sheer exhaustion of being a human.

Or another metaphor I mentioned to Nate one day while we were standing out by the barn. "I feel," I said, "as if I were hanging on by a thread."

"Is the implication that you'd be better off if you had a few more threads?" Nate replied. "Would you rather have a cord? A rope?"

I gave him a slightly annoyed look. He smiled, seemingly unable to resist the mini-sermon. To say I was hanging by a thread suggested I was relying largely on my own strength to hold me.

"What if you let go?" he said. "What if you just let go?"

"I'd die, Nate," I said.

He laughed, as I knew he would, and then he didn't say anything more.

Nate's question nagged at me and tumbled me into more questions as I drove away from the farm.

What if I just let go?

What if I allowed myself to feel all the feelings?

What if I opened myself fully to heartbreak and grief?

What if I knew there might be an argument at dinner but set a table for the feast anyway?

What if I lived as if I believed that this idea of hanging by a thread were just an illusion, and that, beneath me, love had been right there all along—the love of Tristan, the love of community, the love of God—waiting to catch me and enfold me in a healing embrace?

What if I decided to embody the theology of the compost, trusting death would never win and all things would be made new, with the help of forces I couldn't even see?

What if what seemed like an end was actually a necessary new beginning?

What if you just let go?

Late one night, less than a week after graduation, a text from Hana: If Tristan and I wanted to say goodbye to Lincoln, we had to drive down to Philadelphia now.

Lincoln had had a rough spring. His famed appetite had faded, and where he'd once sprinted for the door at the mere shake of his leash, he now sometimes barely lifted his head. His trots had become strolls, the bounce in his step dampened.

He'd rallied, though, for graduation week. The vet prescribed pain medication that seemed to rejuvenate him. By the time Wes's parents came to town for the festivities, it was as if he were young again—or at least just middle-aged.

After graduation, Wes, Hana, and Lincoln had gone on an overnight camping trip. That night at the campsite, Wes noticed that ticks had latched all over Lincoln, even in his mouth; the prophylactic Lincoln was taking, which normally should have killed the ticks quickly, wasn't working. While Wes and Hana prepared dinner, Lincoln dug a burrow in the sand and curled up for a nap. Wes went to go check on him, and noticed Lincoln bleeding.

Two days later, a friend came over to their house for a yoga session with Hana. The friend was grieving the end of her marriage. Usually, when Hana did yoga, Lincoln would be right with her, doing downward dog alongside her. On this morning, though, he settled himself at the end of Hana's friend's yoga mat and napped as they went through the poses. They figured Lincoln was just being Lincoln, reading the room as always, gravitating to the person who needed his company most.

When Hana and her friend finished, they noticed Lincoln's belly was distended. A gentle prod told them that fluid was somehow accumulating inside of him. Lincoln's usual vet directed them to take Lincoln to the emergency clinic at the University of Pennsylvania in Philadelphia. "We were hoping for a miracle," Wes said. But after hours and hours, they had a choice: dramatic measures that would cost at least $5,000, maybe even $10,000, which bought no guarantees, or a gentler goodbye.

"I think you should go," Tristan said. "I'll stay here."

Lincoln was lethargic, but he dipped his head in greeting when I said hello, requesting ear scratches. Wes asked if I wanted to hold him for a bit. I nodded, and he placed Lincoln gently on my lap.

"I love you, Lincoln Buddy," I said. "Thank you for being my Lincoln Buddy."

I handed him back to Hana.

The doctor came back into the room with a needle that seemed unnecessarily large.

Then it was over.

Why did I cry about the death of a dog that did not even belong to me?

That question tugged at me throughout the drive back to Princeton and then all night long, as I failed to sleep.

I suppose my tears had something to do with the fact that

Lincoln showed up for me. Again and again, he showed up. I don't doubt that he'd come to associate me with a steady supply of bacon and chorizo. But even when we were nowhere near a kitchen, he showed up—in moments when I couldn't even admit I wanted someone to sit with, at times when I was working alone at the farm but didn't want to be alone.

How did he know? What did he sense?

I've occasionally told friends that I'd make a terrible pastor because I don't like people much, and as much as I might talk about love, I'm often not very good at showing it.

Lincoln exposed the lie, and he taught me something about love. I tend to keep my heart's barriers to entry high, as if I only have so much love to give. But Lincoln trotted right through, tail wagging metronomically all the way. I'd allowed myself to fall under the spell of his affection. And in that magical vulnerability, I learned to see love as a renewable resource, which grows almost without limit in the one who has felt well loved. But that doesn't mean the object of one's love lives forever.

We love what passes away, right?

Early the next morning, Tristan and I met Wes and Hana at the farm. They had chosen a spot in an open area near the pond, in between two pawpaw seedlings that a group of students had recently planted. About twenty paces away, the bald cypress stood watch.

As the sun cleared the mist from the pond, Wes attacked the ground with a shovel. He dug and dug and dug, until sweat mixed with the tears trickling down his face. Then we buried Lincoln, and we all wept.

telos

Eis telos.

The phrase comes at the beginning of the Last Supper scene in John's Gospel, as Jesus is preparing for dinner with his disciples.

Jesus loved his friends *eis telos*, John tells us. The phrase can be translated "till the end." On one level, John is foreshadowing Jesus's death and emphasizing that Jesus loved his friends until the end of his life. Certainly, the context makes that possible, with its acknowledgment that "his time had come to leave this world."

But eis telos can also be translated "to perfection." In other words, perhaps John is describing not just the timeline of Jesus's care but also its shape and its texture: Jesus loved his friends as much as one human could love another. He washed their feet and broke bread with them. Surely they had inside jokes and pointless banter, heartfelt questions and soul-deep spells of conversation. They frustrated him with their haplessness, the Gospel writers tell us, and he confused them with his opaque stories.

He made himself vulnerable and shared his worries, even as he took on their vulnerabilities and their worries as his own. Isn't that the picture of friendship?

If John's story is to be believed, Jesus fully embodied love. He showed the rest of us how it was done, and he encouraged us to try, too.

The first interpretation of eis telos is moving, sure, but it also carries a note of somber finality. The second feels to me more invitational and also truer to Jesus's purpose. Who else could love anyone to perfection, much less the very people who would betray him?

I suppose that in the context of Jesus's love, we need not read it as either/or. It might be more faithfully understood as both/and.

This was not how I thought the story would end.

I always knew my time as a farmhand was term-limited. But I didn't think the culmination of this season, which I'd intended for spiritual growth, would bring grief upon grief upon grief. What kind of harvest is that?

My final weeks at the farm were remarkably unremarkable— the typical routine of transplanting and weeding, sowing and harvesting. The only real difference was that I went about my tasks a little more slowly, a little more pensively. Was this the last time I'd pull a tomato seedling from its first home and tuck it into this soil? Was it just two years ago that I couldn't even differentiate between a carrot top's feathery fronds and an ordinary weed? The edamame were flourishing, their bushy, deep-green leaves hiding fat pods that bulged with beans; what I wouldn't give to spot Lincoln's tongue popping out from their midst one more time. Now I was planting what I would not reap. Now I was feeding animals I would not be forced to slaughter.

Eis telos.

Jesus did not love his friends out of death but through it—through the sorrow and the grieving and the confusion and the pain.

Love doesn't protect us from grief. If anything, it makes grief all the more likely, because grief is love that has no place else to go. Grief is the love that remains after your friend has died. Grief is love that is still searching for home—and that home, for me, is in my memories.

Eis telos.

Even those who don't believe in an afterlife know love doesn't end with death. Even those who are steadfastly secular know death doesn't have the power to conquer love.

What does it mean to love someone not only till the end but also to perfection? I want to make the case that a perfect love does not mean a flawless relationship or friction-free understanding. I think perfect love transcends mistakes and misdeeds. I think perfect love can sit with an unhappy ending, knowing it isn't really the end.

Many of my classmates had packed up their apartments and moved on, but we didn't know where we were going next. We managed to wangle a couple more months in our campus housing. Early one morning in August, I drove out to the farm by myself.

I'd made this same journey so many times before that I didn't even need to think. I parked the car; crossed the gravel lot; ducked under the cherry trees, pretending I was tall enough to need to duck; went over the stone bridge; greeted the bald cypress; and went out as far as I could under the oaks, just to the water's edge.

The sun had begun creeping over the horizon. I cherished these moments when the first paths of light shot through the daybreak, so strong and clear amid the surrounding darkness that I imagined I could walk them straight into the sky. On the far side of the water, I glimpsed a heron. Mostly, it stood still and attentive. Every once in a while, its beak pierced the water, searching for breakfast; I could hear the soft *plink*.

I went to the chicken coop to say hello to Nugget, who was now a full-fledged chicken. She *cheep*-ed her greetings, and I pulled her out and set her in the open field to let her roam for a few minutes. In the tall grass, she looked like two giant balls of dark-gray lint—a small one atop a big. Only the little black beak gave her away as a bird.

I put Nugget back in the safety of her coop, and then I walked across the bridge. Normally I would have turned right, toward the pond. This time I went left, upstream, to a small pool of water just behind the pumphouse.

This pool was just six weeks old.

One of my last formal responsibilities at the farm had been to host a group of young people from Chicago, who were on a volunteer trip to New Jersey. They thought they were coming to help with farm chores. When they arrived early one morning, they slouched off their bus, pre-exhausted at the thought of the inevitable boringness that was to come.

We gathered the teens in a circle, purportedly to tell them what their tasks would be for the day. But first, we said, they would be surrendering their cellphones. Next, we told them that, for the next hour, they would do nothing but rest. We didn't define "rest." Each could figure out what that meant to them.

"The land is yours," I said. "Go."

A couple of them gravitated toward the pond. One girl wandered here and there, seeming nervous, as if she didn't know the right thing to do.

The quietest member of the group, a gangly guy named Ryan, followed the stream away from the bridge and tucked himself behind a tall tree, where nobody could see him unless they really tried. As far as I know, he spent his entire hour there.

Later, I went to see if I could find any evidence of what he'd been doing, and then I saw it: He'd built a dam.

Now, weeks later, his construction of rocks and branches remained. It hadn't stopped the stream's flow, but it slowed it enough to create a reservoir about the size of a kiddie pool.

I sat down to study the pool. Where the water now found some pause, the aquatic plants had begun to stand a little straighter. Fish had started to school. The relative stillness of the new pool had allowed them to settle; they were bigger than I'd ever seen in these waters. And were those tadpoles I spotted?

I stayed by that pool for a while. This was what the land had been for so many of us: respite, even amid the necessary activity. A place just a little gentler than the rest of the world beyond. Here, we had found some space to learn about ourselves and one another. Here, we had been taught to widen our lenses, to open our hearts a bit more, to ask what really matters. Here we had worked—and failed, and worked some more—to cultivate good soil. Here, we had tried to grow some love.

Eis telos.

Some days after the Last Supper, Jesus cooked breakfast for his friends on the beach. The Last Supper, it turns out, is a misnomer. It wasn't their last meal together, because, as the story goes, Jesus loved them through death and onward to resurrection—in that sweeping cosmic way, yes, but also in the small things that mark our lives. Fish grilled on the flames, bread baked in the hot coals, stories shared around a warming fire.

Eis telos.

I suppose "till the end" can sound ominous. But heard another way, it's also an invitation, pregnant with possibility. It invites us to listen in the midst of disagreement and to wrestle with our discomfort and to share laughter and to shed tears of solidarity. Love grows, but so often it takes its sweet time. This is not how I thought the story would end, but this is how it did.

Eis telos.

Where is the end, and what is the end? On the farm, I found belonging I never expected—but longing, too. I came to understand my own mattering better—but also others' mattering, and my entanglement with that, too. I began to send some things to my own personal compost pile, recognizing what I had to surrender to death so that something else might come to life. I'm not sure how good the soil is quite yet. Maybe the heirloom tomatoes will flourish next year? But it's a comfort, I guess, to know how the process works.

Eis telos.

I don't think you have to believe in Christian theology or hold any interest in the Christian faith to be inspired by John's testimony that his dear friend loved him and so many others so well. It makes me want to experience that kind of belonging. It also compels me to extend it to others—to still the waters, to create space, to offer refuge.

The wider world is not much different from the farm. It carries so many wounds and scars. It offers so much beauty. Its resilience is remarkable. Grief is inevitable and real. So is the

invitation to participate in healing and proclaim grace, to believe again in goodness and live a life of hope.

Eis telos.

That day, there were no ripe tomatoes, no peppers either. I
spotted spinach growing in the garden, so I picked some. I had
no plans, but now I had some spinach.

I started to do a mental inventory of what we might have in
our kitchen. Definitely there were some mushrooms and green
onions. Maybe we had some leftover rice. Maybe there was a
remnant of brisket in the freezer, too.

There was probably enough to make a batch of fried rice.

Yes, surely, there was enough.

appendix

GRANDMA'S FRIED RICE

Grace abounds: There are as many variations of fried rice as there are cooks. My version, which is modeled on my grandmother's, is not what you'll get in most Chinese restaurants. For instance, the restaurant variety typically has visible bits of egg; the egg is scrambled separately, diced up, and thrown back into the wok. I crack the egg straight into the pan so that it softens the rice and coats the meat and veg.

Also, this is not your typical recipe—no measuring cups, no tablespoons or teaspoons. Instead, I want you to trust your taste buds and your personal preferences. After a couple of attempts, you'll learn to make fried rice the way you like it.

First, pick a bowl that you'd eat your fried rice in. This will be your primary measuring tool. For four people, you'll also need:

*Four bowls of cooked rice (one per person). I use Thai jasmine rice. Long grain is better than short grain, but any rice works, except wild rice, which, while lovely in its own way, is a grass, not a

true rice, and lacks the correct consistency. Leftover rice is ideal;
since it has dried out a bit, it's less likely to turn mushy. In a pinch,
you could make a fresh batch of rice, pop it in the freezer for fifteen
to twenty minutes so that it rapidly cools, then use that.

*One scant bowl of cooked meat. Leftover roast chicken, ground
beef, meat pulled from a Thanksgiving turkey—I've used them all.
One time, I used remnants of short rib braised in red wine, and it
was delicious. Brisket is beautiful. If you like seafood, shrimp is a
classic. I wouldn't recommend fish; it's a texture thing.

*Two heaping bowls of vegetables. I typically do one bowl of finely
diced, non-leafy vegetables (onions, green onions, mushrooms, peppers) and one bowl of chopped-up greens (bok choy, spinach, kale,
chard). We never, ever use peas and carrots in our home, except
when my mom makes fried rice for non-Chinese people. When I
asked her why she did this, she replied, "Because they like it that
way."

*Four eggs (one per person)

*Vegetable oil (preferably canola or something neutral—so, not
olive)

*Soy sauce. Some super-traditional versions of fried rice don't even
use soy, because the chefs insist the meat and veg should be the primary flavor carriers. Keep in mind there are almost as many kinds
of soy sauce as there are people in China. Most supermarkets sell
Kikkoman, a Japanese brand and a safe bet; Kikkoman's gluten-free
version works well. (Tamari tastes different.) If you have access to
an Asian grocery store, look for "light soy sauce." Kimlan is my preferred brand; it has no preservatives.

*Sesame oil

*Salt

*Pepper

Heat a frying pan on high until a drop of water crackles as soon as it hits the surface. I prefer not to use a nonstick pan, so as to better develop a crispy, golden crust, but any pan is fine as long as it's large enough to stir things around without spilling rice everywhere.

Pour into your frying pan just enough oil to coat the bottom—maybe a tablespoon per bowl of rice. Let the oil heat up. The non-leafy vegetables go in first. Cook, stirring constantly, until the onions just turn translucent. Add the greens and allow them to wilt. Toss the meat in and mix well. Then add the rice, breaking up any clumps with your spatula. Give it a minute or two to warm up.

Lower the heat to medium. Crack the eggs over the top and stir to break the yolks and distribute the egg evenly. Next come the seasonings, soy sauce first. Here's the thing: I can't tell you exactly how much because I don't know what soy sauce you've got. I do a couple swirls around the wok—one Mississippi, two Mississippi. Once the soy sauce is stirred in, the rice might be slightly tinted, but it should never be dark brown; you can always add more soy later if you want more. Add a spoonful or two of sesame oil, some pepper (to taste—I like lots), and a couple of generous pinches of salt. Stir everything together, using your spatula to break up any remaining clumps of rice; you want every grain to get some love from the egg and the soy.

Once it's well mixed, leave it for two or three minutes, stirring only occasionally.

When the egg has turned from shiny and wet to opaque and dry, it's done. That's it. The rice should be slightly fluffy. If you like spice, finish with a squirt of sriracha.

Once you get the hang of this, and assuming you have leftover rice to begin with, you should be able to throw together fried rice in twenty minutes or less. And again, this is how *I* make mine. Use it as inspiration and guide, not rule and regulation.

Note: You might decide other proportions work better for you. If you're vegetarian, you might want three bowls of vegetables. If you want to make a meat-lover's fried rice, you might do two bowls of meat.

acknowledgments

On April 6, 2024, I was ordained as a minister of Word and sacrament in the Reformed Church in America. During the service, we sang the old hymn "Come, Thou Fount of Every Blessing," one of my all-time favorites. Even in those years when I refused to set foot in a church, church came to me when a verse from that hymn popped into my mind. Honestly, it was usually that bit about being "prone to wander." But every so often I'd remember the second verse, which begins, "Here I raise my Ebenezer / Here by Thy great help I've come."

Those lines allude to a story in the Book of I Samuel in which the prophet Samuel places a stone as a spiritual monument, a marker of gratitude to God, and an aid to memory. The Hebrew phrase "eben ezer" means "stone of help."

This book is my Ebenezer. My life has been enriched by the land I loved, my entire being transformed by the heaven-sent love I've received from so many.

Kenda and Nate, I blame you for this book's existence. Thank you for urging me to take on the extra work of writing, yes, but also of noticing and processing and thinking and praying and paying attention and not settling for easy answers, particularly during that last year of seminary. Nate, I'm especially grateful for your vision for the Farminary as well as for all your annoying questions, your care, and your friendship.

I wouldn't have survived seminary without my extended M7 crew: Annalise, Danny, Hana, Pearl, Werner, and Wes, but also Damian and Lincoln and Stoffels. Dear friends have sustained me in so many ways—you know who you are—but especially Beth, Noah, Ashley, Heather, Stacy, and Jan. I drew inspiration from my time at the Rural Writing Institute—James, your encouragement and example echo throughout this book—and from the trust of the people at Crosspointe Church in Cary, North Carolina, and the First Presbyterian Church of Berkeley in California.

Albert and Lily, you believed in this project, and in me, when other agents told me that nobody would care about some farm in New Jersey and no reader would see me as relatable. A hat tip to the entire Convergent team, with appreciation for their enthusiasm for this work. Derek, your editing is devastatingly awesome—and also sometimes just devastating; I'll never recover from your comment that some of my prose sounded too much like the words of a nondenominational youth pastor. Thank you.

I'm indebted to those who provided feedback on early chapter drafts: Jonathan, Laura T., Becky, Lyndsey, Lorraine, Brent, Nadia, Jude, and Yulan. Thanks also to those who read various versions of the full manuscript and responded with incisive notes, stirring pep talks, gentle correction, and probing questions: Sarah, Sharon, Farminary Nate, Indiana Nate, Sara, Mihee, and especially Laura S.

To my parents as well as my sister and her family: Thanks for loving me even when that love has been challenging. My gratitude, too, to the Ashbys and the Passmores.

As I was finishing the final draft of *Good Soil*, Tristan and I had to say goodbye to our beloved Fozzie. A dog unlike any other, the Fozz came to live with us when I was still struggling through the proposal for this book, and he napped at my feet for nearly all of its writing. His paw prints are all over this book. We miss you so much, little buddy, and will love you forever.

To my Tristan: We have built such a good life together. Thank you for creating space—such patient, hospitable space—for me to wrestle with all the hard things and for making me a far better, more compassionate human than I ever dreamed I could be. You are my heart and my home. Tristan is the one for me.

Finally, dear readers: A story can be told, but it's only complete when someone receives it. I'm so grateful that you have spent time with these words. May they bless you. May you plant your own seeds, and may your gardens flourish. May you draw hope from the picture of renewal that has been etched into creation. May you rest assured that you matter, and may you never doubt that you belong. May you never forget that you are so deeply loved.

about the author

JEFF CHU is an award-winning journalist and editor-at-large at *Travel + Leisure*. He is the author of *Does Jesus Really Love Me?* and the co-author, with the late Rachel Held Evans, of the *New York Times* bestseller *Wholehearted Faith*. Chu is a former *Time* staff writer and *Fast Company* editor whose work has also appeared in *The New York Times*, *The Wall Street Journal*, *The Washington Post*, and *Modern Farmer*. In his (mostly) weekly newsletter, "Notes of a Make-Believe Farmer," Chu writes about spirituality, gardening, food, travel, and culture. He lives with his husband, Tristan, in Grand Rapids, Michigan.

byjeffchu.com